BLOOD, SWEAT, AND FEAR

BLOOD, SWEAT, AND FEAR

VIOLENCE AT WORK IN THE NORTH AMERICAN AUTO INDUSTRY, 1960–80

Jeremy Milloy

UNIVERSITY OF ILLINOIS PRESS
Urbana, Chicago, and Springfield

Published in the United States by arrangement with UBC Press.

Manufactured in the United States of America
P 5 4 3 2 1
∞ This book is printed on acid-free paper.

Library and Archives Canada Cataloguing in Publication

Milloy, Jeremy, 1979-, author
Blood, sweat, and fear : violence at work in the North American auto industry, 1960-80 / Jeremy Milloy.

Includes bibliographical references and index.
Issued in print and electronic formats.
ISBN 978-0-7748-3453-7 (hardcover). – ISBN 978-0-7748-3455-1 (PDF). –
ISBN 978-0-7748-3456-8 (EPUB). – ISBN 978-0-7748-3457-5 (Kindle)

1. Violence in the workplace – Social aspects – United States – History – 20th century. 2. Violence in the workplace – Social aspects – Canada – History – 20th century. 3. Violence – Social aspects – United States – History – 20th century. 4. Violence – Social aspects – Canada – History – 20th century. 5. Automobile industry and trade – United States – History – 20th century. 6. Automobile industry and trade – Canada – History – 20th century. 7. Automobile industry workers – United States – Social conditions – 20th century. 8. Automobile industry workers – Canada – Social conditions – 20th century. I. Title.

HM1116.M556 2017 363.32 C2017-900050-0
C2017-900051-9

Library of Congress Control Number: 2017952872

Set in Segoe and Warnock by Artegraphica Design Co. Ltd.
Copy editor: Robert Lewis
Cover designer: Will Brown

University of Illinois Press
1325 South Oak Street
Champaign, IL 61820-6903
www.press.uillinois.edu

For Sarah, with love and devotion

Contents

Figures and Tables

Figures

Tables

Acknowledgments

I am enormously grateful to have been supported in this work by the care, attention, and labour of so many people, without whose efforts this would not have been possible. First, Mark Leier is an outstanding mentor. He has taught me a great deal about being a historian, a professional, a teacher, and a human being. Karen Ferguson constantly challenged me to sharpen my thinking, and she set an inspiring example with her own excellent work. Heather Ann Thompson's and Aaron Windel's challenging, insightful questions reinvigorated my thinking on this topic. I thank my colleagues for their support, collaboration, and inspiration, especially Maddie Knickerbocker, Eryk Martin, Sarah Nickel, and Ron Verzuh at Simon Fraser University (SFU), Josiah Rector at Wayne State University, and Ian Rocksborough-Smith at the University of Toronto. It has been wonderful to work with you.

I thank the many accomplished, generous scholars who shared with me their considerable gifts, knowledge, experience, and mentorship, especially Joan Sangster, Bryan Palmer, David Goldberg, Miriam Frank, Elizabeth Faue, Heather Ann Thompson, Dimitry Anastakis, Sam Gindin, Steve Jefferys, and the Labour History Working Group at the University of Toronto. Thank you for believing this work was worthwhile. I thank the dedicated, professional staff of the SFU Library, especially Rebecca Dowson, Catherine Louie, and David Chokroun; the SFU History Department, especially Ruth Anderson and Judi Fraser; the Walter P. Reuther Library in Detroit, especially William LeFevre; and the Windsor Public Library. Gord Gray graciously shared

Unifor Local 444's archives with me and helped to set up oral interviews. Brandi Lucier generously shared her outstanding research on race and Windsor auto plants with me. I thank everyone who took the time to be interviewed for this project. Thank you for giving me the benefit of your knowledge, wisdom, and experience.

Working with UBC Press as a first-time author was a rewarding experience that I would recommend to others without hesitation. Thank you very much to everyone at UBC Press who produced this book. I was extremely fortunate to work with Darcy Cullen, and I am grateful for her knowledge, support, and enthusiasm for this project. Thanks to David Carr at the University of Manitoba Press for his insight and encouragement regarding the publishing process. Every historian should be so lucky to work with Ann Macklem and Nadine Pedersen during the editing and publishing stages. Thanks also to the two peer reviewers and Robert Lewis who gave this work a close reading and provided many useful suggestions for its improvement. Thank you to Elizabeth Murray Clemens for locating images in the Reuther Library collection. Thank you to Don Hudson for sharing his striking photography for this book. Gary Gilson kindly shared a copy of his documentary about Detroit.

Currently, I am a Social Sciences and Humanities Research Council (SSHRC) Postdoctoral Fellow at the Frost Centre for Canadian and Indigenous Studies at Trent University. Thank you to all the staff, faculty, and students who make the Frost Centre and the School for the Study of Canada wonderful places to work. I thank the SSHRC not just for my current opportunity but also for its consistent funding of my research, writing, and travel, without which this book simply would not exist. I thank my students for their attention, challenge, and inspiration. I thank my wonderful family and friends in Bailieboro, Peterborough, Vancouver, Ottawa, Kingston, Brockville, Toronto, Hamilton, the United States, and Taiwan. Thank you for your love, laughter, encouragement, belief, and support. I am so grateful to know you. I thank Craig Burley, Laura Dunbar, Dylan DeMarsh, Eryk Martin, John Milloy, and M-J Milloy for being generous and perceptive readers of my work. Any errors, of course, are my own. I honour the memory of my mother, Catherine, with love and gratitude. Finally, I thank Sarah Hunter – a remarkable woman. I am very fortunate that she is my wife, partner, and best friend. Your love means everything to me. I am truly happy and thankful to share this milestone in our lives.

BLOOD, SWEAT, AND FEAR

1

Dripping with Blood and Dirt

Confronting the History of Workplace Violence under Capitalism

"We doe declare that we counte it a kind of Rebellion for a servant to threat, assault, or strike his master."

– ACTS AND ORDERS OF RHODE ISLAND, 1647

"Kill my boss? Do I dare live out the American dream?"

– HOMER SIMPSON, 1993

In 2013, Tennessee and Alabama joined twenty other US states that had passed legislation allowing workers to keep firearms in their cars while on the job. The debates over these "Bring Your Gun to Work" laws pit two of the most cherished tenets of American political culture against each other: the right to bear arms versus the right of employers to dictate what occurs on their premises. Opponents of the laws claim they encourage deadly acts of workplace violence. Supporters argue that giving workers access to their weapons enables self-defence at work and while commuting. Looming over this debate is the conviction that the disgruntled worker with a gun poses a compelling danger in today's workplace.

Mark Hogan, FedEx's vice-president of US security, testified before Tennessee's legislature in 2012 that banning all weapons at work, whether on the shop floor or in the parking lot, allows "an opportunity for the employee to cool off before they take an irrational action in response to something that happens at work."[1] A reader comment posted online in response to a *Wall Street Journal* article about these laws asks us to

> stop for a moment and think. How many of your current coworkers do you know well enough to know whether they have an explosive temper or not? How many of your current coworkers have given you personal access to their confidential medical records, so that you can determine whether they have ever been treated for mental health issues or not? How many of your coworkers do you know well enough to know whether they own a gun or not?[2]

We did not always think about violence at work this way. From the start of the Industrial Revolution well into the twentieth century, people discussed and debated the violence that resulted from work under capitalism. However, this violence was not viewed as an individual matter but as class struggle, a titanic clash between the employing class and the waged mob, which at times threatened the order of society itself. According to some, this struggle was rooted in the violent expropriation that had been necessary to enact industrial capitalism. In *Capital,* economist and socialist Karl Marx wrote of this expropriation of the means of production through the expulsion of peasants from land and into the wage-labour market, where surplus value was extracted from their labour by capitalists. He concluded, "if money, according to [French dramatist Émile] Augier, comes into the world with a congenital blood-stain on one cheek, capital comes dripping from head to foot, from every pore, with blood and dirt."[3]

To Marx, the working day of Victorian Britain was a battleground where the "vampire" of capital sought to suck every bit of labour from the worker, often at the cost of the worker's childhood, children, mind, spirit, health, or even her very existence.[4] Capital, he wrote, "extends the worker's production-time within a given period by shortening his life." Expanding the working day beyond twelve hours produced "violent and unmeasured encroachments" on every aspect of working people's lives.[5] Workers were thus compelled to organize and pressure the state to regulate capital and shorten the working day, in what Marx called a "civil war,"[6] lest they or their family were to be literally worked to death.[7]

Since then, many writers and workers have called attention to the violence of capitalist labour processes. To consider the meat industry alone, Upton Sinclair at the beginning of the twentieth century, in fiction, and Eric

Schlosser at the end, in journalism, both revealed vividly the decimating toll of wage work on working people. Until recently, however, *individual* workplace violence was not generally seen as an aspect of workplace health and safety concerns.[8]

In Canada and the United States, the establishment of capitalism was linked with imperial processes of expropriation and domination, most importantly settler colonialism and slavery. In the nineteenth century, when employers pioneered industrial capitalism, the violence of expropriation and accumulation was complemented by a different violence, one born of the struggles of industrial relations. The period from the mid-nineteenth century until the early twentieth was an age of mass violence. Names like Haymarket, Homestead, Pullman, and Ludlow evoke deadly clashes of workers with the forces of employers and the state. Early industrial relations in Canada were much less explicitly violent, but they did not lack for conflict either, as demonstrated by examples such as the Winnipeg General Strike of 1919 and the Ridgeway Riot of 1968.[9] Like the violence present at capitalism's birth, this later violence has been understood by observers then and now as a manifestation of class conflict, a systemic feature of a rapacious capitalist system. Many believed these conflicts would threaten the very survival of liberal capitalism itself if the inequality and exploitation that sparked them were not mollified. Some North American elites began thinking about managing conflict rather than simply repressing worker activism. After the 1910 *Los Angeles Times* bombing killed twenty people, Congress established the Commission on Industrial Relations.[10] After hearing from such partisans in class conflict as industrialists John D. Rockefeller and Henry Ford, labour organizer Mary Harris ("Mother") Jones, and labour leader William ("Big Bill") Haywood, the divided commission issued three separate reports, which respectively called for establishing labour boards, establishing industrial democracy, and strengthening trade unions.

William Lyon Mackenzie King, Canada's minister of labour in the early 1900s, was a significant transnational figure in the developing management of class conflict. King's Industrial Disputes Investigation Act of 1907 set up the Canadian state as arbiter of conflicts in utilities, railways, and coalmines. The Act was designed to promote labour peace and the uninterrupted working of the economy through boards of arbitration, compulsory mediation, and a cooling-off period before strikes or lockouts were permitted.[11] Transitioning to the US private sector in 1914 as a consultant in the emerging field of industrial relations, King advised the Rockefellers during and after the Colorado Coal Wars, before returning to Canada and becoming the nation's longest-serving prime minister. The reforms of King and US president Franklin D. Roosevelt during the 1930s and 1940s, notably the Wagner Act in the United States and Order-In-Council PC 1003 in Canada, blunted the sharpest points of open class conflict. Most scholars have agreed with historian Richard Hofstadter's judgment that "violence in labor disputes flared up in a last ugly climax in the 1930s and then abruptly died away."[12]

After the Second World War, capital, labour, and the state went forward on the basis of what is often called "industrial legality" in Canada and "workplace contractualism"[13] in the United States. This postwar settlement, epitomized in the auto industry by Canada's Rand Formula and by the United States' 1947 Treaty of Detroit, recognized and safeguarded nonradical unions. It created a framework for orderly, regulated union organizing and negotiations. It shifted the boundaries of industrial labour conflicts and eliminated their bloodiest excesses. The frontier of organizing and collective bargaining was enclosed in boardrooms and courtrooms. In the era of the postwar settlement, anti-union legislation, red-baiting, capital flight, and highly paid union-avoidance attorneys replaced the Pinkerton Detective Agency, police, and strikebreakers as the cornerstone of anti-union efforts.

Class conflict did not disappear, of course, and workplace struggles still exploded into public violence at times. Canadian examples include union buster Harold ("Hal") Banks's government-sponsored paramilitary campaign against the Canadian Seamen's Union; the violent struggles of *"les gars de Lapalme"* against the federal government and eventually against their own labour union in the Quebec United Aircraft strike, which was marked by physical altercations, bombings, and attacks on the homes of United Aircraft executives; and the 1978 killings of Robin Hood strikers in Montreal by a gang of paid strikebreakers in the employ of professional wrestler Paul Leduc.[14] In the United States, the National Guard was called out in several states during the 1970s to quell violence stemming from job actions by the International Brotherhood of Teamsters. United Farm Workers campaigns in California were marked by repeated incidents of violence. Struggles between the coalminers and the coal companies of Harlan County, Kentucky, continually featured violence. Martin Luther King Jr. was assassinated while in Memphis to support a bitter strike by sanitation workers.[15] We also know that the violence inherent to capitalism, the everyday, often unremarked violence of workplace injuries and death, certainly continued. Nonetheless, the overall trend is clear. Mass violence decreased. Capital, unions, and the state delegitimized and de-emphasized violence as an element in labour conflict in the postwar era. As the title of historian Robert Michael Smith's account of anti-unionism puts it, briefcases replaced blackjacks.[16]

Over the past forty years, however, the postwar settlement has been abandoned. Capitalism has discarded the limited security of Fordism and opted for the enhanced precarity and intensity of neoliberal production. Inequality has expanded as rights and safeguards won by working people have been destroyed or abandoned by employers and governments. Many observers have commented that today's economic arrangements look much more like the Gilded Age or the 1920s than they do the 1950s. Yet an age of mass class violence has not returned with them. Where did the mob go? What happened to these titanic battles? Whereas once the face of workplace violence was the mob, now it is the loner. Accounting for why we stopped fearing class war and began fearing the lone gunman "going postal" is the concern of this book.

To understand what happened, we must return to the postwar period with a new perspective. Historians have so far paid little attention to labour violence from the 1940s to the present. This makes sense, given the tendency in these years toward legalism and the regulation of conflict between employers, workers, and the state. But that is not the whole story. Violence at work did not disappear. It mutated. Between the Second World War and the 1980s, the prevailing mode of violence by workers gradually moved away from collective violence and toward individual violence.

Consider the automotive industry, which was not simply North America's most important economic sector of the postwar era but also the birthplace of the Fordism that underwrote the postwar settlement. Violence forged the very history of auto work, Fordism, and auto unionism. In the 1920s and 1930s, workers on both sides of the border had to defend their union organizing against the violence of the state and company thugs, which in Detroit, Michigan, culminated in the 1937 Battle of the Overpass, a brutal assault on organizers of the United Automobile Workers (UAW) by Ford Motor Company security guards. In Windsor, Ontario, Detroit's border neighbour, the fight to organize was often accompanied by physical confrontations.[17] Violence shaped the automotive workplace in other ways, from the hate strikes that white men and women conducted against the hiring or promotion of black men and women to the sexual harassment and assaults directed against female workers flooding into wartime auto plants.[18] Beyond the clashes and assaults, there was the simple fact that even after unionization the often dangerous conditions of auto plants – "a gold-plated sweatshop," as UAW leader Walter Reuther called General Motors in 1964 – posed a real threat of death and dismemberment to the people who made cars and trucks in North America.[19] As autoworker Charles Denby wrote of Ford in his classic memoir *Indignant Heart*, "they said it was the house of murder."[20]

After the 1940s, the massive battles over organizing ceased. But violence was still a significant aspect of the North American auto industry during the 1950s, 1960s, and 1970s. This violence was both structural and individual. It was primarily caused by conditions on the job, not by the psyches of individuals. Although it was shaped by the class relations of work at Chrysler Corporation, it was also mediated by relations of race and gender, as well as by factories' national and local contexts. This violence mattered. Depending on the context, violence was used to enforce prevailing norms or to contest relations of power in the workplace. It influenced how auto work was done, the culture and politics of the workplaces, the safety of workers, and the stability of the plants themselves. Occasionally, violence at work also made an impact beyond the factory or union hall, forcing a wider public to reckon with the effects of workplace violence in courtrooms and the media.

How much violence there was, what forms it took, what impact it had, and what people thought about it were not stable but historically contingent. These factors depended on time and place. In the 1950s individual violence erupted occasionally, but not frequently, at the Hamtramck Assembly Plant, known as Dodge Main, Chrysler's flagship Detroit plant. Workers rarely assaulted supervisors. Beginning in the late 1950s, however, well before the early 1970s crisis of profitability that historians have identified as a major turning point in postwar labour relations, Chrysler instituted several practices that are now considered fundamental to neoliberal workplace regimes. By the end of the decade, Chrysler had undermined worker traditions of job control and claimed dominance over the production process. Over the next ten years, the company sped up production, laid off workers, and refused to invest in plant safety. It hired a new crop of African American employees who had less seniority and stability than previous generations of workers. Chrysler used supervisory harassment, mandatory overtime, and frequent firings to ensure Dodge Main's workers met the new production quotas.

Black workers called this process "Niggermation."[21] It resulted in a working environment and industrial culture defined by fear, hostility, and danger. Workers responded with violence. After 1965 incidents of individual violence became more and more common at Dodge Main. Workers punched each other. They hit each other with crowbars. They stabbed each other. They tried to run each other over in the parking lot. Sometimes, they killed each other. And they attacked supervisors and plant guards with fists, knives, and guns. In 1970 *Newsweek* chose Dodge Main as the emblematic example of America's violent factories, calling it

> a grimy, 59-year-old pile of red brick and concrete harboring 9,000 of the most frightened, angry workers in America. The work force is a volatile mixture of Poles, blacks, and southern whites and, to hear some of them tell it, the man who doesn't pack a gun, a knife, or a length of pipe with his lunch break sandwich is either a fool or suicidal.[22]

Similar conditions prevailed at Chrysler plants throughout the city. In June 1970 James Johnson, a black worker at Chrysler's Eldon Avenue Gear and Axle Plant, responded to racist mistreatment and in-plant stress and violence by murdering two supervisors and a co-worker. In 1973 Regis Lantzy, general foreman of Chrysler's Jefferson Avenue Assembly Plant in Detroit, was murdered by autoworker Tilden Engle. Another Chrysler supervisor, this one working at the Huber Foundry, was murdered on the job by foundry worker Fred Simon. These were individual actions that occurred for a variety of reasons, some knowable but many not. Taken together, however, much of the individual violence that convulsed Chrysler plants in Detroit was a resistance by workers against the terms of their employment and against the violence and racism that often governed it. This violent rebellion in Detroit auto factories posed significant threats to those who worked there and was a major concern for the auto companies, the UAW, and outside observers. It interacted and overlapped with radical political organizing at the plants in complex, contradictory ways.

Chrysler plants in Windsor did not experience the same crisis of violence. Why not? Principally, Chrysler could not institute a policy of "Niggermation" at its Windsor plants. The national and local context compelled Chrysler to operate differently, while empowering Windsor Chrysler's UAW local to be more militant and effective than its Detroit counterparts. The result was a very different work environment. Well into the 1970s, workers continued to exercise some of the bottom-up control largely destroyed at Dodge Main in the late 1950s, so they maintained greater in-plant and union solidarity, albeit one weakened by racial and gender exclusion. Still, workers in Windsor did regularly employ violence as part of a masculinist work culture to enforce norms, settle disputes, regulate the behaviour of supervisors, and intimidate the women who began working at Windsor plants in the late 1970s. And as in Detroit, Windsor was rocked by an auto-industry murder during the 1970s. The killing of UAW Local 444 president Charlie Brooks by fired autoworker Clarence Talbot raised questions about violence and racism in the city's auto culture.

The example of Chrysler in Windsor and Detroit demonstrates that even in workplaces that were in the same industry, owned by the same company, and staffed by workers represented by the same union, there were significant differences in violence's prevalence, uses, expressions, and impacts. Therefore, looking at violence at work in a regional framework is essential. That is especially true for the 1960s and 1970s, the sunset of the postwar settlement and the dawn of a neoliberal order that would change the nature of work and thus the nature of workplace violence. A regional frame allows us to isolate the key causes of violence and to understand differing perceptions of violence. By comparing and contrasting violence in Chrysler plants in two contiguous cities, separated by a national border but joined in a continental production and export market, we gain clarity and perspective on fights, assaults, and murders. We see that workplace violence was not simply the product of individual conflicts and choices but was instead a phenomenon influenced by structural factors that were industrial, local, and national.

Analysts of the automotive industry have long recognized the need to place Detroit and Windsor in regional perspective as part of the Rust Belt, or Great Lakes, region, a link in what has become a global auto-production chain.[23] Historians of auto work or Detroit have generally not followed their lead until recently. This book joins work by Steven High, Tracy Neumann, and Jason Hackworth in considering Rust Belt experiences regionally and thus across the 49th parallel.[24] Doing so offers opportunities and presents challenges. It enables a comparison of plant-level, local, and national dynamics. It allows us to examine holistically the actions and perspectives of an employer (Chrysler) and a union (the UAW) that thought and acted regionally and transnationally. However, the differences between plant, city, and nation require careful discernment. A simple apples-to-apples comparison would flatten out the crucial differences in history, economics, culture, and politics that distinguish the American and Canadian contexts and the uneven development of capitalism in these two places. I have also taken care not to divert our understanding of these linked but distinct histories into a conceptual cul-de-sac by describing one city or state as more racist or more conservative. I seek to understand and explain, not to falsely valorize one or another national example of capitalism buttressed by racial and gender hierarchy.[25]

It is by reading the meaningful differences between Chrysler plants in Detroit and Windsor that we can learn important lessons about the causes of workplace violence. The varying levels of violence at work in the two cities were mostly determined by the greater in-plant impact of racial inequality in Detroit and by Chrysler's greater power to dictate working conditions in Detroit than in Windsor, where its conduct was regulated by the Canada–United States Automotive Products Agreement (or Auto Pact). This inequality was itself the outgrowth of the structural violence of American white supremacy. Canada also is and was a society of racial hierarchy, but its particular features have produced fewer incidents of physical violence. Other key differences proved relatively unimportant, such as between the two countries' national labour movements, labour law frameworks, national political histories, and treatment of violence as part of popular culture or national mythologies, as well as between the strategies of UAW Canada leadership and those of the UAW at Solidarity House in Detroit.

Is my argument, then, that Detroit's workplace violence was racial violence mediated by class and gender, whereas Windsor's class conflict was mediated by race and gender? No. As the actor with the greatest impact on the condition of those workplaces, Chrysler bears the greatest responsibility for the elevated risk of violent harm faced by workers. However, comparing these workplaces does demonstrate how the risk of workplace violence was mediated by relations of race and gender on the job and by Chrysler's relative position in Detroit compared with Windsor. The closely connected, mutually reinforcing power disparities of class, race, and gender, which are themselves forms of structural violence, were crucial in fostering violence at work.

Placing Detroit and Windsor in a regional frame also gives us a new view on urban and national histories. The fate of Detroit and Dodge Main shows how destructive capitalist transformation and racial inequalities can be in combination. In 1981 Dodge Main itself was demolished, and Detroit was enduring a post-Fordist annihilation from which it has yet to recover. Detroit's decline has become so iconic, its suffering so widely consumed, that we are in danger of adopting a complacent assumption that what happened to Detroit was inevitable, the product of vast, impersonal forces. Placing Detroit in its regional context reminds us that this was not the case. Detroit's fate was the outcome of choices made by governments, corporations, unions, and others during specific historical moments. Analyzing violence and class conflict at Windsor plants suggests that whiteness may have been a previously understudied reason for UAW Canada's nationalism in the late 1970s and early 1980s, which culminated in the 1985 split of the UAW's Canadian locals from UAW International and the creation of the Canadian Auto Workers (CAW). The importance of violence in regulating acceptable shop floor conduct and codes of workplace masculinity indicates that everyday violence has been a greater part of Canadian working-class history than generally appreciated. In terms of violence at work, borders mattered a great deal. The national border that divided this region may have been porous when it came to the exchange of people, ideas, and capital, but it was a crucial contextual factor that shaped very different workplace experiences.

Taking individual violence seriously and assessing it regionally not only enhances our understanding of place but also allows us to better understand time, specifically the historical shift from Fordist production to what we now think of as neoliberal production. That violence spiked in Detroit plants in the late 1960s and early 1970s is not solely a reflection of resistance to the degradation of work due to the exploitation of racial inequalities and union weakness. Nor is it indicative of some kind of violent pathology among the city's autoworkers. If we widen our gaze, we see that it also demonstrates how the death of Fordism and the birth of what we now consider neoliberal production was a violent process. Looking at auto work in the 1950s and 1960s shows that many of the features of the current labour market identified as hallmarks of neoliberal production go back a long way. Autoworkers, by reputation the aristocracy of the postwar industrial working class, endured frequent layoffs, probationary employment periods, and intensified production. This transition in production occurred unevenly in place and time. However, between 1950 and 1980, the general trend of labour-process changes in the North American auto industry was away from traditions of worker solidarity and shop floor control and toward managerial control and atomization. These changes and the intensification of work that they often facilitated were sometimes accompanied by violence. Journalist Mark Ames, whose path-breaking research on workplace shootings originally inspired this book, has demonstrated that when neoliberal work arrangements became widespread in the 1980s and 1990s, workplace massacres became common.[26] This study shows that the beginnings of these arrangements, and violent resistance to them, existed well before that time.

In doing so, it provides a historical dimension generally lacking in the literature on the topic. Ames's work contains many crucial insights but largely focuses on workplace massacres from the 1980s on. Similarly, lawyer and legal consultant Ronald D. Brown's *Dying on the Job* analyzes workplace murders only and again largely from the past few decades.[27] Much of the other literature on workplace violence that has appeared in the past twenty-five years approaches the subject without any historical perspective. Ames and Brown are correct that changing workplace cultures and more intense labour regimes contributed to an almost certain spike in workplace homicides starting in the 1980s. This study, by historicizing this spike in the context of a sustained analysis of violence in a single company over many years, significantly expands our understanding of violence at work – its causes, effects, and how these aspects changed over time. Therefore, it gives historical context for the emergence of the mass shooting as a recurring form of public violence.

It also allows us to see how workplace violence connected with, and contributed to, larger historical shifts. Historicizing workplace violence challenges received ideas about work and capitalism in postwar North America. Initial histories tended to emphasize a rapprochement between capital and argued that open conflict between workers and bosses was largely diverted into the bureaucratic arenas of grievances and arbitration. As this book shows, this argument obscures the ways that bureaucracy, workplace conflict, and violence intersect. The historian Stephen Norwood writes that after the Second World War, anti-union efforts "came to rely less heavily on brute force," and "men's labor militancy ... declined considerably."[28] However, although violence between groups of workers and the organized forces of capital or the state is almost unheard of today, individual violence has become a significant concern. What scholars have largely overlooked is that violence itself changed, first in ways that reflected resistance and control in an increasingly bureaucratized mass society and then in ways that reflected the dislocation and disconnection of those workers who experienced their work life as atomized individuals.[29]

A system of production in which management's will was checked to an extent by traditions of workers' control existed at Dodge Main until the early 1960s and in Windsor well into the 1970s. This system of production was characterized by insider violence. Insider violence was largely an expression of class conflict and the enforcement of norms – directed both upward at supervisors and downward at lower-status employees – by workers who had a stable union, some degree of power and autonomy, and a measure of shared identification, whether through class, ethnicity, religion, neighbourhood, or family links with management and union leaders.[30] Their class position rested on a shared commitment to the Fordist accord by capital and labour and on exclusions of race and gender. In Detroit in the 1960s, auto companies pioneered forms of work organization that anticipated the transformations of neoliberalism. Chrysler took control of the shop floor, brought the union to heel, and accomplished an intensification of work through the exploitation of racialized workers with less status, seniority, job power, and union support. The violence perpetrated during the late 1960s and early 1970s by these individualized, more excluded, mostly African American workers was outsider violence enacted by those without power or stability in the workplace, whose perspective and concerns were largely unknown and unappreciated by the mostly white members of Chrysler management and UAW leadership. Although individual violence often represented a contestation of power relations in the plant, it was not connected to a meaningful system of worker control, whether formal or informal. It was rebellion without foundation or program. In Detroit radical black workers' organizations that did have such a program, notably the Dodge Revolutionary Union Movement (DRUM), attempted to use these incidents of violence to build race and class consciousness, solidarity, and worker power. DRUM was trying to craft a moral economy among workers and to use the symptoms of their outsider status to make outsiders into insiders. In the context of Windsor and the Auto Pact, Canadian Chrysler workers were able to maintain their insider status, and the relative shop floor power on which it rested, for several years after it was destroyed in Detroit. Therefore, the type of violence that prevailed at Windsor plants throughout the 1960s and 1970s was largely insider violence.

The prevalence of outsider violence at Dodge Main in the late 1960s and early 1970s was a harbinger of the eruptions of outsider violence that have occurred in both American and Canadian workplaces, but especially in the United States, since the 1980s. In the 1980s and 1990s, as Ames has shown, capital established neoliberal modes of production across white-collar and blue-collar workplaces. Outsider violence, in the form of the one-man murderous rebellion, became much more common, prompting widespread alarm and speculation in the mass media. The media, along with a battalion of newly minted workplace violence experts, tended to define workplace violence as a new problem, without an appreciation of violence's long history in the North American workplace. Nor did media, experts, and later policy makers deeply consider political economy, structural violence, or the role of corporate policies and the labour process in producing violent reactions. They focused instead on a psychological analysis of a disgruntled worker likely to "snap" and target co-workers and bosses.[31] Looking at Chrysler plants in Detroit and Windsor demonstrates that this focus is misguided.

As this brief outline indicates, violence at auto plants in Detroit and Windsor was about much more than individual psychology. Nor was it solely a symptom of the labour process and class conflict. Violence was itself a key influence on the labour process, the work culture, and the consciousness of workers, supervisors, and management. As I researched and wrote this book, the impact of this violence became a major concern. At the beginning of the project, I was primarily interested in finding out how much violence had taken place, what caused it, and what had been done to stop it. Upon learning how much violence there was, I began to consider how much this violence, and the constant awareness of the risk of violence, affected the people who entered these plants every day and thus shaped the workplace as a whole. I realized that to assess violence's impact, I had to expand my consideration beyond any single fight or workplace fatality and consider violence's influence on social relations and workplace culture. In addition to investigating violence as a product of conflicts at work, I began to appreciate how violence itself was a productive force, informing the outlook and strategies of workers far beyond any single event. Finally, I had to wrestle with what exactly should be considered violence. In thinking through these issues, I found insightful the words of novelist Richard Wright in his recollection of the power of white violence to affect his fundamental view of himself in the American South prior to the Second World War:

> The hostility of the whites had become so deeply implanted in my mind and feelings that it had lost direct connection with the daily environment in which I lived ... It was as though I was continuously reacting to the threat of some natural force whose hostile behavior could not be predicted. I had never in my life been abused by whites, but I had already become conditioned to their existence as though I had been the victim of a thousand lynchings. The penalty of death awaited me if I made a false move and I wondered if it was worthwhile to make any move at all ... Indeed the white brutality that I had not seen was a more effective control of my behavior than that which I had seen.[32]

Wright's words testify powerfully to violence's ability to exert influence beyond the particulars of any single incident, conditioning identity, behaviour, and possibility while limiting the freedom and expression of those at risk. If, as Marx wrote, one makes one's own history but within circumstances not of one's own choosing, violence is a key way that those circumstances are circumscribed.[33] The American South of which Wright writes provides just one example of how people have used violence both to contest and to protect an oppressive social order.

How did violence exert its influence on the hearts and minds of the men and women who worked in North American auto plants? To understand the impact of violence at work, we must transcend a binary view of violence as simply a socially constructed product of various conflicts or as something stemming solely from individual psychology. The best way to do this is to treat violence as a variable worthy of sustained attention in itself. Reflecting the insights of contemporary scholars of violence, I investigate violence simultaneously as a material reality, which is experienced by North Americans and embedded in economic and social contexts, and as a discursive practice, which comprises a complex group of cultural discourses constructing the experience of these realities.[34]

Violence's discursive impact travels in two directions. As pioneering violence scholar Neil Whitehead noted, violent practices are "deeply infused with cultural meaning and are the moment for individual agency within historical embedded patterns of behavior."[35] From a public lynching to an exploded bank, from a labour riot to a war movie, from rocks thrown at a car speeding toward the town line to a joke about a murdered cheater, violence has always been a medium of communication – as tangible as a radio and as ephemeral and sinuous as the music the speakers pump into the air. It is time to turn up the volume and take a closer listen. But we must do so with an appreciation for the silences in the record. As anthropologist David Graeber and others have noted, violence often shuts down those with perspectives opposed to or dangerous to those with the power to wield violence.[36] Pat Cunningham was one of the first women to work in a Windsor Chrysler plant during the 1970s. Reflecting on the harassment and intimidation to which she was subjected by co-workers, she recalled, "It took me a long time to find my voice in the plant."[37] Violence silences as much as it amplifies.

Even when violence is used to communicate, it is often a brutalist form of communication deployed when the hierarchical gap between actors inhibits understanding or empathy. In Detroit Chrysler plants, for example, the structural violence of how auto work was organized created major disparities in everyday experiences and perspectives between management, union leaders, and autoworkers. The first two groups were insulated from the hardships and struggles of life on the line. They experienced the conflicts of the plant from bureaucratic standpoints. Bureaucracy, such as the grievance meetings and personnel reports that attempted to regulate conflict at Chrysler in the 1960s, obfuscates ongoing violent processes, enabling the operations of power, even if ultimately dependent on violence, to continue with the appearance of legitimacy and order.[38] Thus, as explored in Chapter 4, unionists and management were baffled by the often violent everyday rebellions of autoworkers, unable to see how structural violence was producing individual violence. They focused on fears of crime and black militants while ignoring how the labour process in the plants was encouraging drug use, violence, and radical political responses. The disparities between management, union leaders, and workers were less pronounced in Windsor, contributing to those plants' greater stability.

By now, it should be clear that defining violence at work is no simple task. Because violence is a culturally constructed phenomenon, the definition of violence is subject to historical change. Autoworkers in Detroit and Windsor attempted to disrupt the prevailing definitions of violence at work presented by Chrysler, the UAW, and society at large. They challenged what they saw as an artificial distinction between what was defined as "violence" and what was considered an "accident" or "just part of the job." They did so to draw attention to health and safety issues and in-plant racism as forms of structural violence faced by workers, as well as to argue for a connection between structural violence and individual violence. In his book *Violence,* cultural theorist Slavoj Žižek makes a similar argument. Žižek contends that in contemporary life, the focus on *subjective* violence, the interpersonal violence committed by individual actors, diverts our attention from systemic and symbolic violence, from the "often-catastrophic consequences of the smooth functioning of our economic and political systems," and from the relationships of domination embedded in our language.[39] Since systemic violence shapes the contours of everyday life and since everyday life is the "normal" against which the shocking transgressions of subjective violence are measured, systemic violence is often, Žižek claims, "invisible ... But it has to be taken into account if one is to make sense of what otherwise seem to be 'irrational' explosions of subjective violence."[40]

The radical Detroit factory newspaper *Eldon Wildcat* raised this critique four decades ago, under the headline "What Makes a Story 'NEWS'?" A worker was killed at the Mack Avenue Stamping Plant, his head crushed by an unsafe press, yet local newspapers and television stations did not cover the story. In contrast, when a fired worker lashed out by attacking his foreman and two others with a wrench, this story did make the newspapers, at least those that, argued the *Wildcat*, "present the bosses' view of life – a view that never examines WHY something happens – why a man is driven to kill another man or why workers are killed on the job."[41] Clearly, there is much at stake in what is and has been considered violence at work. Thus, rather than imposing a unitary definition of workplace violence on the automotive workplaces of the 1960s and 1970s, this book is more concerned with exploring how the very definition of violence at work has been a site of struggle. To this end, in the pages that follow we hear much from workers themselves. This approach highlights different views of what constituted workplace violence. It also centres workers' perspectives, which have traditionally been ignored in discussions of this issue.

Instead of adopting a singular definition of workplace violence, I pay particular attention to the manifestations and intersections of three forms of violence: physical, structural, and rhetorical. The primary form of violence discussed here is physical, such as fights, assaults, and homicides. I employ this focus not because this form of violence was the most common or even necessarily the most important. However, much as scholars of crime historically pay close attention to murders, the visibility and impact of incidents of physical violence allow us to apprehend the larger dynamics of violence at work. Structural violence, which included the disparities in how the work was organized, who did what work, the hazards and risks they faced, and the limits on their chances of improving their situation, was the essential context of individual violence. Finally, rhetorical violence was an everyday element of work culture and power relations in these plants. When autoworker James Netter invoked James Johnson's deadly example by threatening "an Eldon Axle incident" and when Windsor workers wrote that "if anyone does flip out he should know he'll be among other friends – autoworkers," they showed they knew structural and individual violence shaped their workplace, their work, and power relations in the plant.[42] By looking at these forms of violence in relation to each other, we can see the crucial links between the individual violence often thought of as emanating from an individual's psyche and the structures in which that individual worked. Although violence's impacts were complex and often contradictory, violence was undeniably constitutive of workplace processes and culture, not just something that resulted from them. It was a feature, not a bug; an integral part of 1960s and '70s autowork, not a strange aberration. Overall, despite the hopes of some radical workers that individual violence could be used to help unseat Chrysler's dominance of their working lives, violence was much more effective at maintaining existing power dynamics in the plants than it was in overturning them.

Violence is a complex force that is often used to silence people, ideas, and perspectives. This cirucumstance makes it challenging to study. In researching and writing this book, I was fortunate to have access to many voices from auto plants, especially those of workers and unionists. Beyond its historical significance, the automotive industry has likely been such a frequent site of investigation by historians because of the rich documentation available, particularly union records. I was always aware, however, of the countless silences and untold stories from these plants. This study has benefited significantly from that documentation, but it has also drawn on a variety of other sources to obtain the clearest possible view on a subject that is often obscured in the shadows.

The documentary records of UAW locals at Chrysler in Detroit and Windsor held in the archives of the Walter P. Reuther Library of Labor and Urban Affairs in Detroit were a major source of data, particularly union newspapers, material produced by and about radical groups like DRUM, interunion or UAW-Chrysler correspondence, meeting records, and grievance records. The Reuther Library holds the grievance records of UAW Local 3, the union representing workers at Dodge Main and its associated Huber Foundry, for the period 1950–75. These records were indispensable in crafting a picture of violent incidents as they were reported at the time. Using them allowed me to track the rise and fall in the levels of reported interpersonal violence in these workplaces over a twenty-five-year period, as well as violence's changing forms. However, these sources also contain challenges for the historian. I am certain that many, many incidents of violence at work were never reported or discovered and thus never made it anywhere near the grievance records. Grievance records are a discourse about workers that reflects a contested, adversarial process in which what actually happened, and why it happened, was sometimes in dispute. The records obscure or omit some important contextual information, especially the race or ethnicity of the parties involved in a violence grievance. Often, the grievance records leave out the ultimate outcome of the grievance, whether the worker was fired or returned to work, or what other disciplinary measures were employed. Therefore, I have combined my reading of these documents with oral interviews and contemporary writings on plant conditions, especially those collected in the Detroit Revolutionary Movements Collection and secondary sources. Although the Reuther Library does contain much of value about Windsor Chrysler plants and Local 444, which was the UAW Canada (later CAW and now Unifor) union for Windsor Chrysler workers, it does not hold a store of grievance records for these plants, making a paired empirical study of violence grievances between Local 444 and Local 3 impossible. However, this turned out to be a blessing, as the different tack of my research on violence in Windsor drew out valuable dimensions of the history of violence at work, dimensions not easily grasped through grievance records. Unifor Local 444 granted me access to a significant collection of local union files that are not currently available to historians. The rich store of union newspapers, in-plant bulletins, election materials, and leaflets produced by competing unions' political factions provided an illuminating perspective on the levels and understandings of violence in Windsor plants during the era. The oral interviews I was granted by former Windsor Chrysler workers were invaluable in revealing how workplace violence was understood and the role of violence in workplace culture. I also interviewed select Detroit activists, Canadian unionists, and legal professionals from both sides of the border to better understand crucial figures, events, and dynamics.

In the chapters that follow, I explore the ways that violence shaped every single day of auto work in Detroit and Windsor between 1960 and 1980. Chapter 2, "Fights and Knifings Are Becoming Quite Commonplace: Dodge Main, 1965–80," introduces us to Chrysler's flagship plant in Detroit. It shows how violence worked in the plant and discusses how Chrysler and the UAW undercut traditions of workers' control that had been the bedrock of workers' insider status. In Detroit plants, an intensified labour process, UAW-Chrysler conflict, racism, and national and local factors combined to produce the dangerous levels of violence in the late 1960s and early 1970s that attracted the attention of national observers, including *Newsweek* and the *New York Times*. This chapter also demonstrates that many workers understood individual violence as a legitimate response to brutal working conditions and racism.

Chapter 3, "The Way Boys and Men Took Care of Business: Windsor Chrysler Plants," investigates violence in Windsor plants. These plants experienced lower levels of individual and structural violence than their Detroit counterparts. However, they were also shaped by class conflict, violence, racism, and patriarchy. This chapter investigates how local and national contexts in Windsor created a somewhat safer workplace and thus demonstrates the important role of these contexts in influencing the relative levels of workplace violence in Detroit and Windsor Chrysler plants.

Nevertheless, violence played a significant role in workplace culture at Windsor Chrysler plants, especially as part of the hypermasculine tenor of the era's almost all-male plants. In Windsor insider violence was often used to enhance workers' masculine identity. Workers also used violence to regulate the conduct of co-workers and bosses.

The next chapter, "The Constant Companion of All That Earn Their Living Here: Workers, Unions, and Management Respond," outlines how Chrysler and the UAW responded to violent incidents in ways that failed to reduce or seriously challenge violence. Therefore, violence was a significant influence on the culture and politics of the plants. This chapter draws out the ongoing effects of workplace violence on the consciousness and strategies of workers, radicals, Chrysler management, and UAW leaders. What did these actors think about violence? Why did they think it was happening? What various definitions of workplace violence did they put forward? What remedies did they propose to reduce the risk of violence in their workplaces? Answering these questions reveals how crucial violence was in constructing how stakeholders understood their workplace, the challenges they faced, and the strategies they could pursue. Here, we see that violence, far from being an occasional eruption, was a constant element that shaped workplace dynamics on an ongoing basis.

Chapter 5, "Chrysler Pulled the Trigger: The Courts and the Press," shifts the focus to the world outside the factory by highlighting three shooting cases in the auto industry of the 1970s: James Johnson's murders at Detroit's Eldon Axle Plant in 1970; the 1974 shooting of UAW dissident Billy Harrell by UAW official David Mundy in Dearborn, Michigan; and the murder of beloved Windsor UAW Local 444 president Charlie Brooks by fired worker Clarence Talbot. These case studies historicize how wider understandings of workplace violence – what it meant, why it happened, and who was to blame – were contested in the public sphere. I analyze the competing visions of how to understand these events that were presented by the media, the public, prosecutors, and radical lawyers: were they brutal individual transgressions or the logical outgrowth of job stress, violence, union conflict, and racism in the plants?

Chapter 6, "Out of the Back Streets and into the Workplace: The Discovery of Workplace Violence in the 1980s and 1990s," extends this investigation of how understandings and definitions of workplace violence have been historically constructed. In this final chapter, I explore how the phenomenon of workplace violence as a discrete social problem was created and defined in the 1980s after several horrific workplace massacres, particularly at US post offices. What was included in the definition of "workplace violence" that emerged in this era? What was left out?

Thinking through the history of workplace violence is challenging. In 1970 Richard Hofstadter wrote,

> For historians violence is a difficult subject, diffuse and hard to cope with. It is committed by isolated individuals, by small groups, and by large mobs; it is directed against individuals and crowds alike; it is undertaken for a variety of purposes (and at times for no discernible rational purpose at all), and in a variety of ways ranging from assassinations and murders to lynchings, duels, brawls, feuds, and riots; it stems from criminal intent and from political idealism, from antagonisms that are entirely personal and from antagonisms of large social consequence. Hence it has been hard to conceive of violence as a subject at all.[43]

Beyond the conceptual challenges, thinking about violence means grappling with painful, traumatic events. It is a natural human response to trauma to try to forget, to dismiss it and move on, rather than examining it and bringing painful emotions to the surface again. Furthermore, as the women's studies and politics scholar Katalin Fabian notes in the case of domestic violence, confronting our history of violence, at work or elsewhere, is profoundly disruptive. Doing so interrogates power relations, questions social patterns, challenges our ideas of what is acceptable and tolerated in our workplaces, and raises questions about who bears ultimate responsibility for violence.[44] When we do investigate the history of violence at work, we learn us much about how power and social relations have operated in the workplace. As we will see, violent incidents can throw power relations at work, and contests over them, into sharp relief.

Violence, whether structural, individual, or rhetorical, suffused the postwar automotive workplace. Acts that were generally considered the unfortunate result of individual pathology were also heavily conditioned by the historical context and the dynamics of class, gender, and race. Chrysler structured the postwar automotive workplace in violent ways, creating a context in which individual workplace violence flourished. Violence was more effective in maintaining existing power relations than it was in contesting them. Bearing this in mind, we can better understand the role of capitalist social relations in conditioning who experienced violence in North American history, who used it, and how violence has affected identity and action. Doing so historicizes in the most fundamental sense, showing how economic, social, and cultural factors have shaped individual lives. In turn, we learn that incidents of violence often dismissed as the concerns of individuals have affected labour processes and influenced the consciousness of people at work. Much like the transitions to the eras of early industrial capitalism and postwar Fordism, the transition to the neoliberal era of production in the automotive industry was marked by violence.

I wrote this book in part because I was struck by how we have become more and more individualized and less connected yet bound as firmly as ever by inequities of class, race, and gender. These inequities are forms of violence that are maintained by violence and that produce the everyday violence that disfigures our lives. This book is an inquiry into how one current form of everyday violence came to exist. By understanding it, we may be able to address the conditions under which it flourishes so that we can live in a world that is more peaceful and just.

2

Fights and Knifings Are Becoming Quite Commonplace

Dodge Main, 1965–80

Between 1965 and 1975 the flagship plant of the Chrysler Corporation, one of America's ten largest enterprises, was the site of frequent, severe incidents of individual violence. In 1964 there were four such incidents mentioned in the grievance records of its union, United Automobile Workers (UAW) Local 3. There were fifteen in 1965, sixteen in 1966, twenty-eight in 1968, forty-one in 1972, and sixty-two in 1973. The incidents in 1973 numbered almost as many as the total for the fifteen years between 1950 and 1964, despite the plant employing about half the number of workers it did during the 1950s (see Table 1 on p. 61).

These incidents were not just fistfights between co-workers. Workers increasingly directed brutal attacks at their supervisors as well as at each other, and they used weapons to do so, posing a terrifying challenge to the shop floor order. Whereas there were just four grievances between 1950 and 1964 that mentioned attacks on supervisors or plant guards, there were fifteen in 1968 alone and nineteen in 1973.[1] Supervisors worked each day knowing that they risked being beaten, stabbed, or shot. Workers knew of their fear and leveraged it against them. In 1972 James Netter reportedly responded to a reprimand by invoking fellow Detroit autoworker James Johnson and his 1970 murders of two Chrysler supervisors and a co-worker at the Eldon Axle Plant, saying to the general foreman, "I'll wipe you all over Joy Road if I catch you outside ... This place is not above an Eldon Axle incident if enough pressure is applied to an individual."[2]

By 1969 the violent disorder in and around the plant was a major concern for Chrysler and the UAW. In February 1969, UAW staffer Frank Menendez informed UAW regional director George Merrelli,

> My understanding is that fights and knifings are becoming quite commonplace in the shop now. Six people have been discharged in the Paint Shop alone this week: the latest of whom stabbed each other with screwdrivers, Friday morning, February 14, 1969. Both suffered from multiple wounds that required hospital attention; fortunately no one was killed. A question naturally comes to mind as to the cause of the deep-rooted discontent that is prevalent in the Hamtramck Assembly Plant.[3]

By this time, the violence at Dodge Main, as the plant was generally called, had become a national news story. It was the plant featured in *Newsweek*'s 1970 article on workplace violence in America titled "Violence in the Factories."[4] A report issued by a Washington news agency the next spring read more like war reporting than labour analysis:

> Insiders report near chaotic labor conditions at Chrysler Hamtramck Assembly Plant. Like sitting on powder keg say executives who estimate one out of every five assembly workers is on narcotics. One in three carries a gun to work. Situation is almost out of hand, with management afraid to supervise workers for fear of physical attack. As result Hamtramck now has reputation of turning out poorest quality cars of any Chrysler plant. Whereas it was one of the best only few years ago. Closing at end of 71 model run of Chrysler's old Los Angeles Assembly Plant could stand as warning to Hamtramck.[5]

In 1981 Dodge Main itself would be destroyed by the wrecker's ball.

What happened at Dodge Main? In this chapter, I investigate the nature of workplace violence at the plant: what caused the violence, what forms violence took, and how violence was used. The United States was marked by violence and turbulence during this era. In Detroit growing frustration with police brutality, racism, and black poverty would explode in the 1967 uprising, during which forty-three people were killed and 2,000 buildings were destroyed, forever changing the course of the city's history.[6]

However, violence at Dodge Main cannot be explained as simply a symptom of the national mood. The primary causes of the skyrocketing violence were inside the plant. The increased violence of the labour process at Dodge

Main and the barriers that denied black workers better, safer jobs or meaningful power within Local 3 were major contributors to the increased risk of violence faced by workers and supervisors. The local context outside the plant – Detroit's urban crisis, crime, and the drug trade in and around the factory gates – also influenced the levels of violence at work, but working conditions, class conflict, and racism were the principal causes. As more and more workers at Dodge Main were treated like outsiders, harassed by supervisors to do dangerous work more quickly, and disconnected from their union, the plant was faced with a growing phenomenon of outsider violence.

Even before the 1960s, Dodge Main was no stranger to class conflict. In 1950 Detroit was a tinderbox, on edge from wartime wildcats and race riots.[7] Historian Kevin Boyle, who studied Dodge Main in his revelatory account of race, class, gender, and conflict in 1950s auto work, notes that the city was "crosscut with conflict" and that "tensions on the factory floor remained high,"[8] especially among the approximately 25,000 workers at Dodge Main. Although historians have often characterized the 1950s as a period of Fordist compromise, a study of Dodge Main lends further credence to those scholars who have stressed the continuance of conflict and struggle during this period.[9] Struggles at Dodge Main took place in the context of an automotive work culture suffused with a connection between masculinity and roughness, in which the male workers, who comprised the significant majority, participated in horseplay, bullying, violence against women, and fiery confrontations with supervisors.[10]

Nonetheless, the levels of violence faced by workers and supervisors were much lower than they would be after 1965. Why? Did workers just get more violent in the late '60s? Clearly, if we are to understand violence at Dodge Main, what we need is a way of seeing that can apprehend both individual violence and systemic violence, one that allows us to understand the structural factors that work to produce what can seem like individual, personal actions. In the 1980s and 1990s, public health scientists investigating drug addiction and the spread of infectious diseases, especially HIV/AIDS, increasingly emphasized "a new understanding which encompassed the social and environmental influences on health."[11] Previous approaches had emphasized drug use and drug-related harms as essentially matters of individual choice. They failed. A focus on individuals tends to write off, for example, the risk a drug user takes in sharing a needle as irrational, without considering the economic, social, and cultural factors that contribute to her choice. Similarly, in understanding violence at work as springing from individual

Workers leaving Dodge Main, 1972. During the 1960s and '70s, Chrysler's exploitative labour practices sparked a crisis of violence at the plant. Photo courtesy of Walter P. Reuther Library, Archives of Labor and Urban Affairs, Wayne State University.

choice alone, we miss the larger processes of violence at work, and also how violence and violent acts are socially constructed discourses.

In a landmark 1994 commentary, Tim Rhodes argued that "risk and response are *relative* phenomena, to varying extent[s] *situationally and structurally dependent* on the environments in which they occur."[12] He called for sustained attention to the environments in which drug users lived, worked, and used in order to better understand how drug-related harms were produced, and to better intervene to reduce those harms: "A focus on the risk environment encourages us to think about the social situations and places in which harm is produced and reduced. We can define the risk environment as the space – whether social or physical – in which a variety of factors interact to increase the chance of drug-related harm."[13]

This chapter considers the risk environment inhabited by workers at Dodge Main and the associated Huber Foundry. Assessing their world as a risk environment demonstrates how the risk of individual acts of violence was influenced by structural factors. It highlights the multiple sources that worked to produce violence at Dodge Main, and reveals the many different directions violence traveled. Most of all, it allows us to understand why violence got so much worse after 1965: new risk factors for violence were introduced at Dodge Main, existing risk factors were intensified, and individual violence became culturally legitimated as a response to structural violence. Amplifying these risks were company practices and union strategy that combined to make the environment more susceptible to violence and less able to effectively stem the rising tide of violence unleashed by the interaction of these risk factors.

During the 1950s, there were certainly real risks of violence, especially for female workers, but there was not yet a plant crisis of workplace violence because workers exercised significantly more day-to-day power on the job. After winning union recognition at the plant in the 1930s, union leadership and rank-and-file workers had enforced a significant measure of decentralized shop floor control over production and conflict, frequently enforced by spontaneous walkouts. Over the course of the 1950s, however, initiatives by Chrysler management and the UAW alike fatally undercut this tradition. Local 3's once-dissident leadership aligned with the ruling Reutherite faction and its policy of deferring to UAW International control of job action at the plant level. Chrysler management squeezed militant traditions from the other end by dropping its implacable opposition to the union presence at Dodge Main in favour of working with unionists – as long as they held the line on production and tamped down bottom-up working rules. Bureaucracy and a formalized grievance procedure began to replace informal, day-to-day job control. Indeed, the grievances considered here in investigating the risk environment at Dodge Main are themselves symptomatic of attempts to divert conflict resolution away from stewards and rank-and-file workers on the shop floor and into closed-door meetings between union representatives and Labor Relations personnel.[14]

The new emphasis on industrial legality, or workplace contractualism, coincided with Chrysler, after many years of struggle, seizing control of production and the right to manage. By 1958, according to historian Steve Jefferys, whose history of the plant remains the best available, management had removed most of the restraints workers had established on its supervisory power, although these restraints were still kept alive by some workers. Jefferys also identifies the return of "fear" with the new management control of work and the labour process after two decades of militancy and mutuality.[15]

Given these developments, it is not surprising that a more bureaucratic approach was never able to eliminate, or even rationalize, class conflict. As historian Joan Sangster has found in her study of grievances among female

Bell Telephone workers in Ontario during the same period, workplace tensions were often not translatable to the formal view of the grievance process; furthermore, "industrial legality never completely dampened all vestiges of worker resistance."[16] As shown later in this chapter, the grievance system at Dodge Main disastrously failed to regulate and resolve shop floor conflict, one reason why many workers turned to individual violence in the latter half of the 1960s. Management's assertion of unchecked control of production rates and the union's retreat into bureaucracy were two crucial factors that increased the Dodge Main environment's susceptibility to violence, precipitating the mid-1960s epidemic.

Conflict at Dodge Main in the 1950s was inextricably bound up with contests over race, gender, and status. Racial conflict and violence had spanned decades at the plant, ever since African Americans were first hired sometime in the 1910s. According to Boyle, white workers drove blacks out of semi-skilled work "time and again ... Black workers were intimidated or insulted until they quit, or whites laid down their tools until company officials removed the black workers."[17] By the 1930s African Americans at Dodge Main had been confined to menial positions as janitors or stock chasers, or they had been relegated to the plant's hottest jobs in the foundry. On their lunch breaks or after work, they encountered bars and lunchrooms in Hamtramck that were also segregated. Some taverns near the plant refused to serve black workers during the 1950s and continued to bar African Americans from working there into the 1960s.[18] Women were also restricted to a "handful of low-paying jobs," including in the wire room and the trim department, where occupations required dexterity, not brute strength, and thus were gendered as "women's work."[19]

Local 3 did not challenge these hierarchies but reflected and reinforced them. It "formalized Dodge Main's race and gender system,"[20] setting up seniority by department that restricted blacks and women to their segregated occupations, for to get a job in another area would mean losing one's seniority entirely. However, during the 1950s, African American and female workers effectively challenged some of the racial and gendered inequities they faced on the job. Like the traditional structures of workers' control, white male workers' place in the shop floor hierarchy was also under threat during the 1950s. The challenges of the Second World War paved the way for a "skyrocketing"[21] number of blacks at Dodge Main. Women also used solidarity and strategies developed during the war to expand the jobs open to them, notably positions on the trim line. Their challenge to factory norms exposed women at Dodge Main to intimidation, harassment, and greater risk of sexual assault. Increased automation also challenged traditional workplace structures.[22]

Obviously, if there was a détente in American workplaces in the 1950s, nobody told Dodge Main. The factory environment was shaped by conflict and posed real and ongoing risks of violence, especially to women workers. Struggle between union and management, foreman and worker, and workers themselves was an everyday feature. Incidents of physical violence were not an uncommon occurrence, including conflicts over bullying, ethnicity, gambling, and the labour process. The disproportionate concentration of African American workers in Dodge Main's worst jobs, a segregation accomplished through racial violence, was itself a structural violence endured by black workers. However, compared to the years that were to come, incidents of overt physical violence were rare in the 1950s, with fifty-three found among the grievance records for the entire decade. Despite the regularity of class, racial, and gender conflict, the problem was much less severe, and violence was nowhere near the legitimated cultural resource it would become in the latter half of the 1960s.

During the 1960s, Chrysler made two major changes to the labour process in the plant that contributed significantly to injury and violence. First, as Jefferys describes, Chrysler's wave of hiring in the 1960s divided workers into two groups: the older, higher-seniority, mostly white first shift; and the younger, lower-seniority, mostly black second shift. During the 1960s, job and pay security increased for the first group, whereas "parity of conditions was denied to the new labour."[23] Insiders were replaced by outsiders, and the systems of worker control that would have made them insiders were gone. By 1968 black workers made up approximately 50 percent of the Dodge Main workforce.[24] Whereas the possibility of losing enviable wages and benefits was a powerful threat that Chrysler held over the heads of the first group, there was much less reason for the second group to fall in line without these benefits and this security. Last hired and first fired, as well as alienated from a management and union they felt belonged to others, these workers more often saw their working lives in individualistic terms. Their jobs may have been less stable, but with the auto industry at a production peak in the late 1960s, they also knew they could get fired at one plant and be back to work there or at another auto factory almost immediately.[25]

Chrysler's second major change was to work its employees much harder. After the mid-1960s, foreign manufacturers captured a greater and greater proportion of the American automotive market, forcing the Big Three –

General Motors, Ford, and Chrysler – to scramble to defend their bottom line. Chrysler relied on increased production to outcompete foreign manufacturers on price. Because foreign automakers had a head-start in producing the smaller vehicles that were eating away Chrysler's market share – and because they were far more technologically advanced than Chrysler, which had never invested much in its plant infrastructure – the only way to do this was to squeeze as many cars as possible from the bodies of their workers. Labour writer and activist A.C. Jones characterizes this strategy as cutting costs "by way of an all-out assault on their workforce, especially through the reduction of employment and the radical speeding up of work."[26] The company not only ran its plants faster but also ran them longer, often instituting mandatory overtime. Workers were in the plant for unrelenting twelve-hour shifts six and seven days a week.[27] Chrysler used black workers to accelerate the pace of work at Dodge Main while doing nothing to address in-plant racism, improve conditions, or replace outdated, unsafe equipment and stock.

Faster work was more dangerous work. Chrysler workers were regularly injured and killed on the job by unsafe equipment running too fast.[28] Twenty-two-year-old Gary Thompson survived Vietnam but not Chrysler's Eldon Axle Plant, where he was crushed to death under an overturned forklift that had been pulled out of a repair bay and pushed back into service without being fixed.[29] In 1973 a group of workers cornered Local 3 president Ed Liska and protested that "two people died on Saturdays due to safety hazards in the skilled division."[30] Workers lost fingers and hands, being forced to forgo safety equipment at work because, as one worker pointed out, "you can't keep the speed up if you're going to use it."[31] Conditions at the plant were so unhealthy that in 1972 twenty-four workers in one area of the plant tested positive for tuberculosis.[32] Historian David Riddle wrote of a "steady stream of lost limbs and fatalities" because of Chrysler's refusal to ensure safe plants: "The company was running these plants into the ground and workers to the point of exhaustion as it pounded out the last pulses of production in the waning days of the great mid-century American automobile boom."[33]

As Riddle suggests, occupational injuries may have been called "accidents," but they were actually a facet of Chrysler's profit-making strategy. Unsafe plants that killed, maimed, and injured workers were better for business than upgrading to safe conditions, journalist Rachel Scott revealed in her 1974 book on occupational health and safety, *Muscle and Blood*. Scott quotes a Chrysler official who admitted to her that Chrysler had judged it was "more profitable to plan for disability and compensate sick and injured workers than it is to install safety measures to protect them."[34] Chrysler plants also cut the number of floaters, or relief workers, making it more difficult for sick or injured workers to go to First Aid.[35] Even if they did see a doctor and were declared unfit to work, foremen harassed workers at home to come back to the plant, a practice that had tragic consequences in the case of Mamie Williams. Ordered by doctors to stay home with a blood pressure condition, Williams was sent a telegram threatening her with firing and the loss of her benefits if she didn't return to work at the Eldon Axle Plant. One week after she went back, she collapsed on the job and died shortly afterward. She had worked for Chrysler for twenty-six years.[36]

Dan Georgakas and Marvin Surkin's enduring study of Detroit radicalism in this period is named for the deadly price extracted by the Big Three's labour practices. In *Detroit – I Do Mind Dying,* they cite the estimates of an industry-wide study commissioned by the UAW:

> [There were] 65 on the job deaths per day among auto workers, for a total of 16,000 annually, about half from heart attacks. There were also some 63,000 cases of disabling diseases and about 1,700,000 cases of lost or impaired hearing. These statistics did not include many long-term illnesses endemic to foundry workers and others exposed to poisonous chemicals and gases, nor did they include deaths or injuries by accident. Even these limited figures made it clear that more auto workers were killed and injured on the job each year than soldiers were killed and injured during any year of the war in Vietnam.[37]

To ensure that workers were meeting the new production standards despite the hazards that surrounded them, Chrysler added more supervisors in the 1960s, increasing "the numbers of foremen from a ratio of one to every seventy-five or eighty workers ... to one for every twenty or twenty-five workers," according to Jefferys.[38] Historian Heather Ann Thompson points out that these line foremen had less and less in common with the young black workers they supervised. Without the social lubricant of shared cultural identification or interests, conflict mushroomed.[39] Jefferys calls the new influx of supervisors "white-shirted strangers."[40] Black workers called the intersection of speedup and their concentration in auto work's toughest jobs "Niggermation."[41]

Thompson identifies "unmitigated foreman aggression" as the major cause of the era's increased shop floor conflict.[42] Although it must be kept in mind that these foremen were only symptoms of a larger regime of production at Chrysler, the bullying, racism, and even tyrannical behaviour of many supervisors were certainly frequent triggers for violent incidents. The dissident publication of the Eldon Axle Plant, the *Eldon Wildcat/Spark,* diagnosed how the role of supervisors in Chrysler's production process exposed them to a greater risk of violence:

> The only job protection a foreman has is to be riding our backs to get out as much work with as few people as possible. And if there's a chance that some foremen will be cut out, then that's more reason for them to be pushing us harder. The problem is that conditions are already pretty bad. And if foremen start pushing more, in an attempt to save their jobs, they will have to expect that more workers will be fighting back.[43]

At Dodge Main, the union claimed that workers were faced with "harassment, intimidation, and coercion" by foremen like one Reilly, who "may do bodily harm to a worker because of a lack of emotional control,"[44] or like Sally Brown, supervisor of the instrument panel line, who "shouts, threatens, swears, and picks on employees, causing extreme tension and impossible conditions of work."[45] The inspection department, which performed quality control on the vehicles built at Dodge Main, was a particularly contentious area. Under pressure to keep the cars rolling off the line, foremen and inspectors constantly clashed over whether cars were to be approved or not. In 1966 a new general foreman overseeing a new model allegedly harassed inspection workers, trying to browbeat them into approving defective cars by screaming.[46] Another time, the union charged that a foreman was erasing defects that inspectors had marked on cars and was attempting to rule through fear by writing up inspectors who left work one or two minutes early. In 1967 the union steward complained that foremen were refusing inspectors the right to drink coffee or sit down: "I guess you must work until you drop dead. It is like working in a concentration camp."[47] Given the levels of conflict and stress in the inspection department, it is unsurprising that physical violence occasionally resulted. In 1967 department employee Virginia Gagnon, a forty-eight year old with almost twenty years of seniority, was discharged for striking her supervisor. Another female inspector was allegedly told to "keep her mouth shut" and had a door slammed on her by her foreman before she slammed a car door on him.[48] James Netter, the worker fired for his dark allusions to "an Eldon Axle incident," also worked in this department.

Some foremen seem to have delighted in bullying their workers. Foreman N. Tessmar repeatedly told one worker that he was a lousy toolmaker who would never be as good as his father in front of the man's co-workers, including his father.[49] Chrysler management had to talk to supervisor McConnell about "goosing employees in the buttock" and using abusive language.[50] When Jean Kaminski reported for her night shift, her foreman returned her "hello" by calling her "a pig." When she asked him to repeat himself, he responded that she was "a dirty pig" and later bizarrely suggested that he had "no idea that the employee would feel anything derogatory was directed towards her ... Nothing wrong was intended."[51] A 1967 grievance complained that one foreman was driving Mrs. G. Bubenburr "to a point of exhaustion. Workers are giving Mr. Szeglia a fair day's work. What else does he want, blood?"[52]

Some foremen went beyond threats of firings or bullying to actual physical violence. Foremen placed workers in unsafe situations. The union charged that a worker named Manley was told by a foreman to use an unsafe machine that had cut his hand two months earlier, requiring several stitches. When Manley refused, as the machine had not been restored to a safe condition, the foreman allegedly threatened him with termination.[53] A 1968 grievance alleged that a foreman had repeatedly harassed an employee to the point that, enraged by the employee taking a break, he physically removed the worker from the plant with the aid of three Plant Protection staff. You "do not even see this many guards guarding a prisoner in prison," the union protested, calling it a "violent willful outburst of rage" and warning that "any employee injured by Mr. Templeton's unstable condition will be the sole responsibility of mgmt."[54] Grieving the firing of John Milledge in 1973 for striking supervisor James Range, the union claimed Range had first slapped Milledge, who "had to protect himself. Management was the aggressor."[55] In 1967 management spoke to foreman Larry Adler after he raised a hammer and threatened to bash a chief steward's head in.[56] It was widely known that many foremen, like many workers, carried guns. This knowledge must have worried workers, who were well aware foremen could act out violently under the pressure of constant job stress and conflict, as did foreman P. Auclair in 1969. Auclair allegedly pushed a steward after being crowded by four union members, while screaming incoherently, abusing one worker racially, and repeatedly threatening to take the three stewards "on the street one at a time."[57]

If physical assaults by supervisors were comparatively rare, harassment and intimidation by supervisors were everyday experiences for Dodge Main workers. As part of the violence of an intensified Chrysler labour process, this conduct was a significant contributor to the individual violence that ravaged Dodge Main after 1965. In 1969 a group of Dodge Main workers met with Local 3 president Ed Liska to protest the conduct of their supervisor, John Gerycz. Their complaints give an idea of the experience of Dodge Main workers under Chrysler's high-volume production regime. They accused Gerycz of harassing employees by telling workers they had five minutes to learn the job or be fired, threatening employees who filed grievances, refusing to show attendance and penalty records when the union requested them, calling for Plant Protection staff to remove a steward trying to discuss a problem with him, and refusing to call a steward when a worker asked for one. Liska noted, in the all-capitals style that was his habit, "IT IS REPORTED THAT IF THE SUPERVISOR CONTINIOUS [sic] TO HARASS THE EMPLOYEES, THERE WILL BE BODILY HARM TO HIM. THIS IS THE FEELING OF THE GROUP AND THE UNION IS MAKING A DIRECT REQUEST TO HAVE THIS SUPERVISOR TRANSFERRED OUT OF THE GROUP IN ORDER TO AVOID SERIOUS TROUBLES."[58]

However, the union was generally unable to curb the excesses of harassment and speedup or to make the plant a safe place to work. After the UAW abandoned claims to have a say in production standards and conditions after the Second World War, it placed itself partially in a management role, eventually opting to help the Big Three speed up production in order to encourage the industry's profitability. This situation created conflict between the UAW and its membership and hampered the union's ability to fight speedup and unsafe working conditions.[59]

By the 1960s, when Chrysler was running its decrepit plants faster than ever, the UAW was in a bind. According to Jones, UAW officials were "ever more reluctant to challenge the companies' 'right to manage,' dependent on the companies' profitability but needing to retain legitimacy with the rank and file."[60] By the late 1960s, the gap between the UAW leadership and its workers was probably larger than at any point in the union's history. One worker told Scott that union representatives were co-opted by the desire to stay in their comfortable, high-paid sinecures, especially because "in the process of these guys following orders and making it for themselves, they have climbed over the dead, injured, maimed, schizophrenic co-workers who they were supposed to represent."[61] Under pressure from company speedup and its own membership, UAW leadership relied on "coercion, ever less on consent," in Jones's words, to control the rank and file and to keep production moving.[62] Moreover, whereas the workforce, especially in

Detroit, was increasingly young and black, the leadership remained almost exclusively older and white. The result, as historian David Lewis-Colman points out in his study of race and the UAW, was that "many younger workers viewed the UAW and auto companies as indistinguishable."[63] Although this view overstated the situation somewhat, there was certainly an understandable feeling among workers, especially black workers, that their health and safety was often not a priority for their union.

On the floor at Dodge Main, the bureaucratic "work now, grieve later" system of dispute resolution, which had largely replaced more informal methods of job control, was hopelessly ill suited to the harassment, dangers, and risks that workers endured every day. In the 1950s workers and Local 3 possessed several accepted informal techniques that they could use to slow down their work or to have a safety concern addressed. By the 1960s these traditions were weaker, and the company enjoyed far more control over the labour process. As Jefferys points out, "there were no longer any fixed points of self-evidently 'fair' conduct or worker-influenced workplace rules by which management was constrained to operate."[64]

The grievance process became the primary means by which workers attempted to resolve problems. Autoworkers at other Detroit Chrysler plants argued that the draining grievance process actually fomented further resentment and conflict, while doing little to resolve the original issue. Workers seethed while waiting for a grievance to be processed. Hundreds of grievances were simply dropped every year, without resolution or explanation.[65] Therefore, as Jones notes, "UAW membership was left with little choice but to resist ever increasing company pressure on their own," which they did at Dodge Main by forming radical insurgent groups, leading wildcat strikes over working conditions or harassment, or choosing individual remedies, including absenteeism, drug use, and violence.[66]

Most notably, black radicals formed the Dodge Revolutionary Union Movement (DRUM). DRUM was the era's most potent manifestation of Black Power in the workplace. It presented a militant internal challenge to both Chrysler and the UAW. It also celebrated and advocated violence in response to the violence of racism and the labour process at Dodge Main. One DRUM leaflet threatened, "before we allow these racist guards to use teargas[,] roit [sic] sticks and MACE on us, we will not only destroy this motherfucking plantation but them too. JOIN DRUM, JOIN DRUM."[67] The revolutionary union movements quickly spread to several other Detroit plants. Later in this chapter, I explore DRUM's role in the levels of workplace violence at Dodge Main, and in Chapter 4, I discuss how violence profoundly shaped DRUM's outlook and strategies.

In this climate of danger, rage, and conflict, violence against supervisors proliferated. Writing about this era, Thompson identifies violence between co-workers as particularly revealing of in-plant tensions, but the grievance records indicate that these types of incidents occurred throughout the 1950s.[68] The greater frequency of violence between co-workers in the 1960s and 1970s is notable, but truly revealing is workers' new willingness to attack those above them in the plant hierarchy. The grievance records show just four such incidents in the fourteen years between 1950 and 1963, whereas there were five in 1963 alone, three in 1964, four in 1965, twelve in 1966, fifteen in 1968, and a peak of nineteen in 1973. Perhaps no data point demonstrates individual violence's bottom-up threat to order and hierarchy at Dodge Main better than the regularity and severity of violence directed at company personnel, which company officials identified as not only misconduct but also a clear danger to their orderly control of the plant and production. One common flashpoint was the very crux of the relationship between supervisor and supervised: discipline.

After 1965 threats of violence became a common response to discipline. M. Fischer, for example, given a five-day suspension for absenteeism, returned to the plant and "became extremely disorderly, threatening to kill the Superintendent and threatening the General Foreman with bodily harm."[69] He also tried to encourage his fellow workers to go out on a wildcat strike. R.G. Christianson was discharged in 1966 for drinking on the job. After his firing, he reportedly became belligerent, threatened a supervisor with physical harm, and waited for four hours at a plant gate, presumably to ambush the supervisor. H. Crumpler was reportedly instructed to drive a different forklift after arriving at work intoxicated. That he was allowed to drive heavy machinery while drunk testifies to the state of workplace health and safety at Dodge Main. Crumpler refused, and when the supervisor called for Crumpler's steward, Crumpler "threatened to cut out the supervisor's heart and put it in his mouth if the supervisor, L. B. Rose, caused him to lose his job."[70]

Some workers went beyond threats. The case of W. Cowan is a particularly brutal example of a worker responding to discipline with violence. While leaving his workstation to punch out one day in 1972, Cowan was told by his supervisor to go back and finish one operation he had left undone. Cowan refused. The next day, Cowan was told he had been given a thirty-day unpaid "disciplinary layoff," the Chrysler term for a suspension, with twenty-five of those days suspended provided Cowan stayed out of trouble after returning to work. Later that night, Cowan walked off his job, tracked down his supervisor, and "repeatedly struck the supervisor in the mouth with his fist and as the supervisor attempted to leave the area, Mr. Cowan struck him on the back of the head with a hammer."[71] Cowan then fled the plant, and the supervisor was later hospitalized. Another grievance record states that when foreman J. Elliott began discussing E. Snyder's performance as a repairman, "Mr. Snyder became enraged and struck Foreman J. Elliott with his fist. He was temporarily restrained by other employees working in the area, but broke loose from them. He then proceeded to pick up a flat steel bar and struck General Foreman Bill Blackwell across the back." Snyder's account differed. He alleged being harassed and assaulted by Elliott and Blackwell. Snyder was eventually reinstated.[72]

Violent crime was a major concern at Dodge Main and in Detroit during 1965–75; a period when, according to historian Heather Ann Thompson, the Johnson administration's commencement of the War on Crime in response to urban unrest, and the subsequent era of mass incarceration that resulted, *created* social harms and violent crime in Detroit, rather than responding to them. Thompson terms this a "criminalization of urban space."[73] Criminal activity was common at Dodge Main and other Detroit auto plants during this time. Drug dealing in the plant led to violence and was a major reason many workers began carrying guns.[74] Rip-offs and robberies in the plant were another source of violence, as in the case of L.J. Gray. Caught breaking into a vending machine with a crowbar by a Plant Protection officer, Gray assaulted the man with the weapon and fled.[75] Crime was also common in the streets around Dodge Main, which meant workers had to fear for their safety coming to and leaving work, as well as during work.[76] Workers leaving a night shift with a freshly cashed paycheque were targets for violent muggings. Many workers heading off shift discovered that their car had been stripped of its tires while they worked.

Although crime was not mentioned often in grievances of the time, likely because the Hamtramck police and Detroit courts handled criminal activity unrelated to the work process, it was a major concern for workers, unionists, and Chrysler management. Liska's daily diary regularly mentions crime in and around the plant. One particularly alarmed entry reads,

> GAMBLING, NARCOTICS, ROBBERIES, HARASSMENT, PROSTITUTION ARE GOING ON THROUGHOUT THE WEEK ...

> WORKERS FEAR GOING TO AND FROM WORK. POLICE PROTECTION IS NIL. COMPANY PLANT PROTECTION IS ROUTINE WITH LITTLE TO SCARE AWAY ANY CRIMINAL ELEMENTS.
>
> NARCOTICS ON THE LOTS AND IN THE PLANT IS ON THE RAMPANT. PILLS AND CIGARETTES OF NARCOTIC NATURE ARE COMMON AS CANDY BARS.
>
> NEED FULL PROTECTION ON PARKING LOTS ... MORE PLANT PROTECTION SECURITY ALSO POLICE PROTECTION ... THIS IS AN URGENT PROBLEM.[77]

The high level of crime at work was one issue that management, Local 3 leadership, and many dissident workers agreed was a priority. Unfortunately, as shown in Chapter 4, a conflation of crime, radicalism, and in-plant violence prevented Local 3 from fully grasping the major causes of in-plant violence: working conditions and racism. An issue of *Click*, a leaflet for skilled trades workers, complained, "There are shootings, theft and muggings in and around this plant constantly, which endangers Tradesmen."[78] Not all dissidents, however, condemned crime in the plant. DRUM responded to a robbery of workers maintaining the plant's vending machines by saying, "If a black brother reaches a point of frustration and is forced to rip in order to survive at least he remembered who his real enemy was ... Black brothers DRUM does not believe in apologizing for anything a black worker does." To DRUM, robbery was justified payback for how workers were robbed every day in ways both small, like ripping off vending machines, and large, like wage work under Chrysler. DRUM claimed that Chrysler owned the vending machine company, which in turn had a racist employment policy. Indeed, the vending machine was a powerful symbol of the everyday racism and rip-offs, the unending torrent of small, grinding indignities that characterized so much of a black worker's day at Dodge Main. DRUM's newsletter went on to complain that "when a brother goes to collect his money lost in the machines the white racist women handling the cash have the damn audicity [sic] to get an attitude."[79] DRUM's position – that violence in response to these slights was not only justified but also part of a revolutionary awakening to the real conditions of blackness and auto work that bound workers – is a telling example of how DRUM's critique legitimated violence as a valid response to the stresses of auto work at Dodge Main.

Another way that workers responded to those stresses was by numbing themselves with drugs and alcohol. Substance abuse and the illicit trade in drugs and alcohol created yet another set of conditions under which violence could erupt, both in and out of the plant. Scott interviewed one female Chrysler worker who told of "a lot of alcoholism" among her co-workers. Although she described herself as not much of a drinker, this woman told of one job where "my floorlady was such a bitch ... in order to keep from hitting the woman everybody had to have a drink at lunchtime."[80] Alcohol abuse was a common aspect of working culture at Dodge Main going back to at least 1950, but illicit drug use became a major issue in the late 1960s, reflecting the greater use and awareness of drugs in America generally at this time.[81]

A 1971 report relayed the Chrysler estimate that one out of every five Dodge Main assembly workers was on narcotics.[82] Heroin addiction was so rampant among Detroit autoworkers generally that Local 961 of Chrysler's Eldon Axle Plant received National Institute of Drug Addiction funding for Curb Heroin in Plants (CHIP), an innovative, union-run program that combined methadone therapy with job and family counselling for addicted workers. CHIP's board quickly expanded the program to serve all UAW members in the Detroit area, evidence of how common the problem was in all plants.[83] Chrysler's response to drug use among its autoworkers is harder to discern. Liska recalled that drug use was big business at Dodge Main, with both stewards and supervisors being part of a network of dealers inside the plant that was connected to larger criminal organizations in Detroit. According to him, the company generally turned a blind eye to drug use as long as production was maintained. Perhaps, as he hints, the company was afraid to tackle a large and dangerous criminal enterprise in its midst.[84] Perhaps Chrysler preferred narcotized workers to radicalized ones. Certainly, there are very few grievances at Dodge Main where workers were fired for drug use or possession, although again the Hamtramck police may have handled many of these matters.

Selling drugs was big business and resulted in the criminal violence that everywhere accompanies the illegal drug trade. Liska's diary mentions that "A FORMER STEWARD ... WAS FOUND DEAD IN A TRUNK OF A CAR JUST A FEW WEEKS AGO. HE WAS INVOLVED IN NARCOTICS AND DEALT WITH THE BIG PEOPLE DOWNTOWN ... DID THIS FORMER STEWARD SUPPLY THIS YOUNGSTER AND OTHERS WITH DOPE?"[85] Yet the violence of drug and alcohol abuse can also be seen in its less obvious, but no less damaging, manifestations. Workers turned the violence of monotonous assembly line work inward through chemical escapes that numbed their brains and ravaged their bodies and spirits. Substance abuse was one way the violence of this toxic workplace spread beyond the factory gates and into the bodies and minds of its workers, who then carried it into their neighbourhoods and homes. For example, Liska's diaries report,

> STEWARD LARRIE GARDULA'S WIFE CALLED SAYING SHE IS DISTURBED WITH HIS DRINKING AND HIS POOR HEALTH ... SHE SAID THAT HE SHOULD GIVE UP HIS STEWARD JOB BECAUSE IT IS NOT WORTH THE PROBLEMS OCCURRING WITH LARRIE ... SHE SAID HE IS OFTEN DRUNK, VOMITS AND EVEN PASSES OUT WHEN HE COMES HOME LATE ... HE SPENDS A LOT OF MONEY ON DRINKS, CLAIMING THAT IS HOW POLITICS ARE RUN AT OUR PLANT. HIS WIFE IS 48 YEARS OLD, LARRIE IS 57. SHE CRIED A LOT OVER THE PHONE.[86]

Clemens Fitzgerald, a psychiatrist and an expert witness in the James Johnson case who studied hundreds of autoworkers in his career, concluded that the aggression and frustration autoworkers battled at the plant often spilled over into family life. Fitzgerald told Scott that he was struck by the number of fights that took place in the homes of autoworkers, fights he diagnosed as workers' hostility toward the company or foremen being redirected at their wives and children.[87]

Stress at home was also carried into the plant. William L. Lynch, when approached about being drunk on the job, threatened his foreman with a rubber hose, pulled the foreman's tie off, and would not allow him to call for assistance. Local 3 objected to the company firing what it called a "sick man" who should have been sent to a rehabilitation facility "for another try at a cure."[88] For his part, Lynch claimed his drinking was caused by family problems. A note in the file claims he did not want to go back, although it is unclear whether he was rejecting a return to rehabilitation, home, or his job. Many Detroit-area autoworkers apparently never did make it home after work. A black worker at Detroit's Ford Rouge Plant said shift change at his plant

> made Indianapolis [500] look like a cake walk. And you say to yourself, what in the hell makes them drive like that and you realize – just trying to get away from that place ... And we've had guys killed half a mile from that plant before they got to the freeway, because they were driving sixty

> or seventy miles an hour when they should have been driving twenty-five or thirty, but they just had to get away from there. They drive like crazy. And they are crazy. They've been driven crazy by working conditions.[89]

These testimonies remind us that workplaces were permeable membranes. Racism and conflict over the labour process at Dodge Main were the primary reasons why working there became more violent, but they were not the only reasons. Dodge Main, like any other workplace, was not a hermetically sealed world unto itself but a place influenced by its surrounding environment. The violent crime in workers' neighbourhoods and around the plant did not wait outside the factory gates but influenced, and was influenced by, in-plant dynamics.

Management was well aware of the connection. In 1973 a Chrysler spokesman admitted that "crime is as much a problem in the inner-city plant as in the inner-city neighbourhood."[90] Violence entered as a material fact. For example, the crimes that were actually committed in the factories, such as drug dealing and robbery, increased the threat of related violence. Violent crime in the plant alarmed the union and management, who often seemed unable to distinguish between workplace unrest and crime, a dynamic explored in Chapter 4. But it also entered as part of the consciousness that workers brought to work, which was shaped by their traumatic scars from having lived in the shadow of violent crime and by the concomitant knowledge that violence might be necessary to survive at Dodge Main, just as it was in the neighbourhood or the prison.

The prison metaphor is appropriate, for incarceration became an increasingly common experience for Dodge Main workers after 1965, with the advent of what Thompson has termed "the carceral state."[91] In what would become an important dynamic in the American workplace in the late twentieth and early twenty-first centuries, workers frequently travelled between wage work and incarceration. Twenty-one-year-old William Enos, for example, fired in 1966 for threatening Plant Protection staff while intoxicated, had been incarcerated twice between his hiring in 1964 and his discharge in 1966.[92] In 1969 Liska wrote that a worker named Reid

> WAS DISCHARGED BECAUSE HE HIT A SUPERVISOR OVER THE HEAD WITH A METAL PIECE. HE WAS IN JAIL FOR A WHILE. HE HAD FOUR YEARS OF SENIORITY. HAD A REPUTATION OF BEING ABUSIVE IN THE PLANT AND THIS TIME HE GOT INTO REAL TROUBLE AND THERE IS NO DOUBT HE IS THROUGH WORKING.[93]

So common was incarceration that, after 1965, Dodge Main workers were frequently fired for falsifying criminal records when applying for employment. When Johnny Hatcher was discharged for striking a supervisor with a car door, the subsequent investigation revealed he had falsified his police record.[94] The issue became so widespread that it prompted a general union grievance complaining that employees caught falsifying their records, which generally meant hiding a criminal offence or exaggerating one's level of education, were being harshly treated. The grievance, titled "Criminal Treatment of Employees by Trim Management," alleged that two workers fired for the falsification of employment "experienced the humiliating practice of being escorted out of the plant by Plant Protection personnel. The Union alleges further that since there were no disorders of any nature, treatment of the employees in this manner was uncalled for, and the Union demands that those responsible for this procedure be properly educated."[95]

Local 3 demanded this practice be halted. Management called it "a general procedure implemented in this plant for the protection of the employees and facilities." The union responded that "management was out of order in treating well behaved employees in the above described manner. This action created ill will, bitterness, and resentment towards management among the other employees. The atmosphere in the department is tense and charged with bad feelings."[96]

The dispute shows that the criminalizing of discharged employees with what would become widely known during the 2000s as the "perp walk," the humiliating escort of dismissed workers out of the workplace by security personnel, had become part of Chrysler practice by the 1970s, an indication that the historical connections between the carceral state and the workplace need to be researched further. This practice was perhaps in response to the violence that was often directed at supervisors who disciplined workers. The growing presence of incarceration in the lives of Dodge Main workers is another aspect of the crisis of violence in Detroit and at Dodge Main after 1965. It was also another factor increasing the likelihood that Dodge Main workers would themselves commit violent acts. The experience of incarceration no doubt exposed many Dodge Main workers to violence not only as a traumatic experience but also as a legitimate means of preserving personal autonomy, dealing with authority or conflict, or policing the frontiers of one's identity.

The violent consciousness that workers carried into Dodge Main with their lunch pails can be seen in the increased number of grievances involving weapons, specifically guns, after 1965. In the period 1950–65, there were no grievances involving guns; after 1965 there were several. For example, probationary employee J.M. Peck was fired in 1968 after a Browning pistol was found in his locker, under his motorcycle helmet.[97] Later that year, twenty-two-year-old W. Etheridge was detained while trying to leave the plant. Slurring and unsteady, he tried to produce his pass, but a .25 calibre automatic pistol fell out instead.[98] Roy Ware Jr. was fired when, while engaged in an argument that in an earlier era might have been settled with fists, he pulled out a gun and shot at his co-worker.[99] Foremen at Dodge Main also carried firearms.[100] The 1971 report on the plant included estimates by Chrysler management that one in three assembly workers at Dodge Main carried a gun to work.[101]

This volatile mix of race and class conflict at Dodge Main, urban crisis, and the political struggle taking place in Detroit comprised the context for the emergence of the Dodge Revolutionary Union Movement. DRUM arose out of relationships between staff members at the radical black newspaper *Inner City Voice* and Dodge Main workers, most importantly the autoworker and organizer Gordon Baker, known as General Baker. Baker and the *Voice* shared a commitment to organizing workers at Dodge Main. In May 1968 Baker and other workers supported a wildcat strike of several white women frustrated with speedup and the treatment of women. Chrysler fired just two of the white women but also fired five black men who supported the strike. The company believed Baker was the real ringleader. Baker and a few other activists formed DRUM with the support of the *Inner City Voice*. To mark DRUM's genesis, Baker wrote an open letter to Chrysler. The letter touched on the history of structural racism at the plant, which included the barring of black workers from many areas of the plant until the 1950s and the hate strikes that many white workers launched to protest working beside blacks. It also noted that black workers "are brutally oppressed and overworked and harassed on the production lines."[102]

With the formation of DRUM, the Black Power struggle arrived on the American shop floor.[103] Between 1968 and 1971, DRUM would be a major political force at Dodge Main, consistently challenging Chrysler management and the UAW on racism, speedup, dignity, and health and safety. One example of how important DRUM was as a player in plant politics is a grievance that alleged management was allowing DRUM to hand out leaflets in order to undermine Local 3. The grievance shows how contested power relations had become at Dodge Main, with Chrysler, the UAW, and DRUM all attempting to win the allegiance of workers.[104] DRUM led several wildcat strikes, nearly ousted members of the ruling Liska slate during violently contested union elections, and exerted significant pressure on plant management through less formal means, notably by mobilizing the threat of violence.

What, then, was DRUM's contribution to the levels of individual violence at Dodge Main? Every aspect of DRUM's critique was informed by an understanding of Chrysler, the UAW, and America itself as violent toward African American workers. In response, DRUM articulated a vision of rugged, physical black manhood. DRUM leaflets reported and celebrated in-plant violence directed at supervisors. One DRUM leaflet congratulated the worker who dealt with the harassment and physical abuse of the aforementioned foreman Larry Adler "in a manner in which we can all be proud of, he stomped this drunken white sonofabitch into the floor."[105] More directly, DRUM members frequently used violence themselves. This ranged from spitting on members crossing a DRUM picket line, whom they called "UAW pigs," to assaulting plant guards and supervisors.[106] The most notorious example of the latter was the case of DRUM member Rushie Forge, who, while being escorted from the plant after being discharged, stabbed Labor Relations representative L. Young, an African American, three times before fleeing the plant and eventually the city of Detroit.[107]

DRUM's celebration of the Forge incident as a heroic act of resistance to Chrysler was tersely noted by management in its response to Forge's grievance: "there is no question of this incident ... for it was proclaimed in not one, but two issues of a paper named *DRUM;* also a front page article in Wayne State's collegiate paper, the *South End;* and on television, most recently, the program, "Haney's People."[108] The UAW, despite its antipathy to DRUM, nonetheless grieved Forge's firing, perhaps to deny DRUM a further rallying point among sympathetic workers.

There was also a considerable amount of violence directed against DRUM by the UAW and the Hamtramck police. DRUM leader General Baker claimed that, after a gunshot through a window paralyzed Detroit housing activist Fred Holsey, he was told by a Chrysler official that the shot was meant for him and that the assassination attempt had been organized by the UAW. Baker also recalled that after DRUM's first attempt to win a Local 3 elected position, running Ron March for a trustee slot, Hamtramck police went through the bars near Dodge Main where DRUM supporters congregated and beat the workers they found there with ax handles. Baker alleged the police were concerned that, as a trustee, March would learn that Local 3 had been secretly lending union funds to the police department, a revelation echoed in the title of the DRUM-produced documentary

Finally Got the News.[109] March won the initial election, prompting the police reprisals, but lost a run-off vote to the Liska-backed candidate in an election many workers believed was stolen.[110] DRUM charged that Chrysler, the UAW, and Hamtramck local leaders had colluded to ensure DRUM's defeat, claims that have appeared in the work of several historians. In Riddle's telling, "George Merrelli, UAW Region I Director, is reported to have led an assault on DRUM members during the Dodge Local 3 run-off election in March 1970. According to this story, along with fifty members of the UAW regional staff plus Hamtramck police officers, Merrelli expelled the election challengers from the DRUM slate before the ballot boxes were sealed."[111]

Liska himself wrote of the election that "IN PLANT RUMORS INDICATE VIOLENCE WAS GOING ON AND MANY FEARED TO VOTE."[112] Baker alleged that many times during union elections, police would pick up DRUM activists and hold them all day, preventing them from getting the vote out.[113] As historian Trevor Griffey has pointed out, because of the difficulty of obtaining records, the history of state and corporate repression of left groups is somewhat elusive, leading historians to overascribe strategic weaknesses and internal dissent in evaluating the failures of these groups.[114] Jefferys concludes that DRUM's progress was arrested in part by Chrysler's cost-cutting dismissal of many of the least secure workers at Dodge Main in 1969, as well as by internal divisions. Thompson identifies DRUM's own limitations and flaws, combined with disputes within the League of Revolutionary Black Workers, as major factors in its downfall. Jones points out Chrysler's hiring of black workers as supervisors, the UAW's stated refusal to protect workers involved in black radical strikes, and the union's "staffers physically [breaking] the pickets of DRUM-led strikes."[115] To what extent DRUM's downfall may have been caused by UAW violence and repression, backed by police power, remains an important question. The full extent of Chrysler's response to DRUM is also not entirely clear, as shown in Chapter 4.[116]

Obviously, DRUM's rhetoric and actions, as well as the corporate and union reactions to them, contributed to the violence at Dodge Main. Yet it is important to note that DRUM was by no means the only, or even primary, cause of the rise in in-plant violence. At Dodge Main, violence began escalating years before DRUM formed. As the grievance data show, violent incidents at Dodge Main were already increasing in 1965, three years before DRUM's formation, including violence directed at supervisors and plant security.

Moreover, violence, including violence against supervisory personnel, did not decrease after 1971, when DRUM ceased to be a meaningful presence at Dodge Main. In fact, it increased, peaking in 1973 at sixty-two total grievances involving violence, nineteen of which concerned violence against supervisors and Plant Protection staff. After DRUM disbanded, some workers still used violence, like T. Felder, who in 1972, when asked why he was failing to keep up with the line, told his supervisor to "stop f-----g with him," followed by a flurry of punches.[117] Another was Charles Williams, who was fired in 1975 for beating his supervisor with a board.[118] Although there is no doubt some DRUM members were quick to employ violence, both as a material force and as a cultural weapon, violence among workers at Dodge Main certainly did not begin and end with DRUM. Indeed, it is possible that DRUM's defeat, which marked the demise of the most effective collective response to racism and poor working conditions at Dodge Main, increased the likelihood of workers turning to individual violence instead.

Overall, DRUM's willingness to use violence and especially its celebration of violence as a legitimate response to on-the-job grievances had an impact in legitimizing and disseminating violence among workers. However, the increase in violence before DRUM's heyday and the even greater increase after its dissolution indicate there was a more complicated relationship between DRUM and workplace violence at Dodge Main. DRUM was *reacting* to the violence already present on the job in developing its critique of auto work and racism as violent and its promotion of violence as a useful form of resistance. As explored further in Chapter 4, it is just as important to consider how violence was partly responsible for DRUM as it is to recognize that DRUM was partly responsible for violence.

To fully understand the wave of individual violence in the years 1965–75, and how that violence operated to construct work, identity, and struggle at Dodge Main, we must go beyond solely structural explanations and also consider the other ways that violence manifested itself in the lives and consciousnesses of the people who worked there. Specifically, we must look at the role of violence in shaping workers' identities.

Exploring the connections between violence and the production and maintenance of identity at Dodge Main allows us a fuller understanding of the different sources and uses of violence at work. Closely reading incidents of violence at one workplace reveals that violence in auto work was not merely a reflexive outgrowth of class, gender, and racial conflict but also a resource drawn on by workers to express and defend their own identity. It gives us a glimpse of how important violence was to a crucial dynamic of labour history during the neoliberal period that began in the 1970s, namely the definition, and self-definition, of workers as atomized individuals, not as members of a collective class.[119]

For example, workers at Dodge Main were divided not just by race and status but also by age. The massive cohort of young workers entering the workforce at this time, with an attitude and consciousness that differed from the ethos of their parents' generation, was a key reason for the rank-and-file militancy and rebellion of the era. As Jones notes, autoworker rebellion was "no doubt enhanced by the rising number of young people within their ranks, workers under thirty constituting between 25 and 30 percent of the auto labor force in the late 60s."[120] At Dodge Main after the 1967 uprising, young workers, especially young black workers, had decided "not to take the shit they used to take," in General Baker's words.[121] Absenteeism became a chronic problem, as younger workers showed a weaker identification with work that they found harsh and unfulfilling. The number of young workers chafing against authority and factory discipline was likely another reason for the growth of violent incidents from the mid-1960s onward, as workers responded violently to challenges instead of suffering in silence or going through traditional channels.

Examining the post-1965 grievance records, one finds a large number of cases of violence involving young workers or workers with little seniority. For example, consider the case of twenty-three-year-old Clyde Coulter, who in 1966 got in an argument with a co-worker, stabbed him several times, and then fled the plant.[122] Another grievance concerned twenty-five-year-old C. Wilson, who became argumentative and abusive when twice told to clean up his work area and then pushed his supervisor off the platform upon which they stood.[123] In 1968 when L. Davenport was cautioned by his foreman about smoking while working with a flammable chemical, he spilled some of it, lit a piece of paper, and tossed the paper onto the fluid. Davenport had just a little more than two years seniority.[124] Nineteen-year-old S. Thomas was fired for threatening bodily harm to his foreman after being suspended for insubordination. The suspension came after Thomas had refused to accept being put on a fourth different job in one day.[125] O.L. Johnson had less than one year's seniority when he apparently exploded after his job performance was criticized. Johnson reportedly said, "If you want blood, I'll give you blood and you will have something to remember."[126]

Given that racial hierarchy, speedup, and harassment from supervisors were reinforced by the expectation that workers grit their teeth and adapt to the bureaucratic, conflict-ridden environment of the Chrysler workplace, it is not surprising that it was so often small, seemingly trivial slights that precipitated violence. When Jerry Haskins was questioned about parking his unauthorized vehicle in the salary workers' parking lot, he became enraged and hit the plant guard several times.[127] Willie Copland was told at his department office that his cheque would be ready at 3:30 p.m. It was not, and when he asked about his cheque, he "was given a very negative answer by Mr. Bob Coffee in harsh terms." Copland told the superintendent that he had better give him his cheque or Copland would "fill his fat belly full of hot lead." He further stated, "I never did anything here but if I don't get my check I'll get my gun and really - - - - this place up."[128] It turned out Copland needed the money to purchase clothes and equipment for his newborn baby, coming home from hospital that day with jaundice and in need of medical attention. The incident that prompted Charles Williams to hit his foreman with a board was being docked on his time card for leaving the plant early for lunch. Dennis Brown allegedly hit his general foreman in the head with a metal rod after a dispute over what day his paycheque was to be released. The following Friday, Brown returned to work brandishing a handgun and threatening co-workers. "Mr. Brown stated, while in his work area, that if he did see the General Foreman he was going to kill him."[129] When Joe Ross's supervisor told him he had to be at a meeting, Ross shot back, "Don't bother me while I'm eating lunch," even though the scheduled lunch break had ended thirty minutes earlier. Told again to attend the meeting, he pushed his supervisor several times. In support of firing Ross, management argued, "He has had ample opportunity to adjust to his working environment and he has demonstrated, clearly, that he doesn't intend to."[130] At a workplace not steeped in racism, speedup, harassment, and crime or at one with a union effectively addressing these workers' concerns, like Dodge Main in the 1950s, perhaps these small conflicts could have been resolved after a discussion or some harsh words. As the crisis at Dodge Main deepened, workers often responded to slights with force.

Some workers took advantage of the disorder, using violence, or the threat of violence, to bully their way into getting what they wanted. Ed Liska's diary relates that Steve Barry pointed a gun at his foreman and threatened him if he did not get picked to work overtime. The next day, "drunk with power of getting away with this latest incident, Barry ... threatened the foreman and reached for his pocket. The foreman grabbed him and held on," and Barry was fired.[131] Nonetheless, Barry apparently saw "no reason for being discharged" and said he "will be waiting for the foreman after work to seek his job back."[132] Despite his record of violence and two previous firings, Barry was allowed to return to work at the Huber Foundry within less than two months and was quickly back in trouble for threatening the captain of Plant Protection there.[133] Two months later, Barry was out of work again and making threatening calls to Liska's home at 11:00 at night, saying, "I am a black nationalist," "I hate all honkies," "Tired of all the bull shit," and "You better not be at the local in the morning, I am going to bring a machine gun and kill everyone in the Local Hall."[134] Liska, who had been trying to get Barry rehired again at the time of the call, also noted in his diary Barry's history of threats and threatening calls, his giving a gun to a girlfriend at the plant, and his attempt to run over a co-worker at the Huber Foundry. Barry repeatedly employed violence and the threat of violence to intimidate management, union personnel, and co-workers, with success and with virtual impunity.

This was the case partially because Barry was operating in a climate where many people justified acts of individual workplace violence. When Local 3 worker Fred ("Too Sweet") Simon shot and killed Huber Foundry guard John Elock after "receiving harsh disciplinary time off for a simple infraction of Chrysler's rules," some rushed to his defence. According to a radical leaflet that was circulated after the shooting, Simon was "driven to shoot the guard. Finding the union leadership incapable of helping him, 'Too Sweet,' like James Johnson and other fellow workers of the past resorted to the only means left to individuals: acts of terrorism and resistance to the exploiting and humiliating conditions we Chrysler workers are being force[d] to submit to by the owners of Chryslers."[135] The leaflet, excusing a man's murder because of management harassment and union failure, reveals just how legitimate violent reactions to the indignities of working for Chrysler had come to seem, all the way up to murder. As Liska recalled, "A lot of the guys didn't think hitting a foreman or stabbing him is doing anything wrong. So they say they're innocent."[136]

The performance of masculinity was also an important way that violence and worker identity intersected. In a plant that was comprised of a greater and greater number of black workers supervised almost exclusively by whites, masculine identity was inextricably tied to race. As previously shown, racism caused conflict that sparked violence. But race and violence also interacted in more complex ways. Although both white and black workers employed violence, it is worth investigating how many black male workers at Dodge Main articulated an aggressive, rugged black masculinity as a way to maintain dignity and self-respect in a plant that often denied them both.

Whereas an earlier conception of masculinity may have defined manliness as the ability to endure the capricious treatment by supervisors in order to earn the comparatively high wage of an autoworker, a new understanding of manliness took hold at Dodge Main in the late 1960s. Manliness at Dodge Main – influenced by high employment in the industry during an economic boom, the individualistic culture of both white and black young workers, the ideas of the Black Power movement, and conflict and violence on the job – emphasized personal autonomy and demanded that respect be paid.

The 1967 uprising in Detroit provoked a major change in the way that many workers carried themselves in the factory. Baker recognized several co-workers from Dodge Main among his fellow prisoners while locked up during the uprising. According to him, the experience of battling state authority altered their outlook. As Baker put it, "the same people that walked back into the factory after we got out of the penitentiary ... were not the same people that walked out." The Afro hairstyles that many black workers wore and the spent .50 calibre shell casings that many workers hung from their neck upon returning to the plants were militant symbols of a new determination to prevent authority figures from "fucking with" them. Supervisors noticed the necklaces and treated those workers wearing them differently.[137] Fear now ran in the other direction as well.

Violence often resulted from the clash between workers' assertiveness and Chrysler's treatment of its workers, a clash exemplified by the phrase "You better quit fucking with me." The expression appeared nowhere before 1965, but was common afterward, suggesting not only the link between identity and violence at Dodge Main but also workers' developing perception of their identity and experience on the job as essentially individual, not collective. T. Felder presaged his assault with the phrase. The term echoed the chilling explanation of Tilden Engle, a worker at Chrysler's Jefferson Avenue Assembly Plant, for why he had murdered his foreman, Regis Lantzy, after being laid off: "because he fucked over me." A security guard testified that Engle claimed to have shot Lantzy because "a man can only take so much, he's dead, he ain't going to bother nobody any more," and "I am a man; nobody wants to be walked over by nobody."[138] When violence against supervisors in the plant became far more frequent and sometimes deadly, even threats no doubt carried a chilling edge. A similar conception of masculinity appeared in many other incidents captured in the grievance records at Dodge Main. When F. Jenkins was disciplined for horseplay and poor-quality work, he threatened to shoot the general foreman: "Mr. Jenkins then approached even closer and repeated the threat ... If you don't stop f -- with me, I'll blow your head off."[139] E. Butler was suspended for insubordination after reportedly telling his foreman, "if you f- with my money, I am going to f- you up."[140] When R. Haley received a warning following his spectacular demonstration of manliness while performing his job of driving cars off the line, including speeding, squealing tires, and eating a sandwich with one hand while driving with the other, he approached foreman Zarko and said, "I am tired of your fucking over me, you were on my shit list but now you're on my death list and if you keep fucking with me, I'll kill you." Haley then got into another car and drove it at high speed before skidding to a stop on an exit ramp, at which point he remarked to Zarko, "I guess you'll want me in your office now."[141] Haley attempted to imprint a monotonous, repetitive job – driving cars off the line – with the risk-taking masculinity exemplified by reckless driving. When Haley was cautioned for doing so, he responded by threating violence.

Other forms of masculine identity were also articulated by means of violence in this period. Charlie Ranier was charged with being a day late returning from a five-day suspension for poor workmanship, a charge he disputed. Supervisor Luke anticipated problems because Ranier had been hostile in the past, so Luke asked stock foreman Dennis Stanton to be with him when he penalized Ranier. Luke called Ranier over and issued a ten-day suspension for poor attendance. In response, Ranier protested, drawing on his identity as a male breadwinner. According to the grievance, "At this point, Mr. Ranier then stated that he wasn't accepting any time off because he had a wife and several kids to support, and then he struck the supervisor Luke with his fist in his left eye, knocking him to the floor, and then jumping on him beating him about the head with a mirror."[142] This incident indicates that masculine family responsibility could be used to justify violence. In supervisor Luke's request that Stanton accompany him to confront Ranier, we also see a glimpse of how foremen attempted to protect themselves while performing a job that exposed them to a regular risk of serious retaliatory violence.

Masculinity was also an aspect of another role that violence played at Dodge Main: the celebratory expression of power. In the period 1965–75, workers drew on violence to cow the forces – the UAW and Chrysler management – that controlled their lives on the job, just as many may have defied Detroit police in the 1967 uprising. By displaying aggressiveness or by manipulating the currents of violence and fear that ran through the consciousness of company and union officials, workers had fun, relieved monotony, and asserted their own power to stick a wrench in the gears of control at Chrysler. This kind of attitude can be glimpsed in the grievance of W. Banks, who was disciplined because, when told to stop banging a jack handle against the floor and boxes in his work area, he replied, "If you are big enough, try to take it away."[143]

Workers also exploited the climate of fear in more playful ways. Although violence was sometimes open and overt, workers in other instances sowed fear with threats and tall tales. In 1970 foreman M.D. Blount informed his superiors of a conversation he had overheard in a restaurant near the plant. According to Blount, he was having a cup of coffee at Mattie's Restaurant when two men entered and sat beside him. The two men, young, black, and dressed in factory uniforms, began talking about "all the terrorism in Philadelphia and New York, the police station bombing and the Weathermen ... What really made me take notice was when they mentioned the Hamtramck plant." The two men discussed at length a planned firebombing of Dodge Main, speaking with firsthand knowledge of different areas of the plant, much to Blount's alarm. He noted that "they were sharp fellows. They talked like Detroiters. They had either been to college or were graduated from high school. It impressed me that they really meant business." The report went on to speculate about what part of the plant the men might have worked in and whether the waitress on duty might be able to help management identify these plotters.[144]

Why would two workers casually discuss a bomb plot in front of a foreman at a busy coffee shop near the plant they intended to blow up? The simplest explanation is that there was no plot: the workers were simply playing a prank on a foreman. Seeing Blount at the next table and recognizing the white shirt and tie that were standard apparel for Chrysler supervisors, they whiled away fifteen minutes before getting on the bus by exploiting the fear of terrorism to wind up a member of management. Perhaps they even hoped that a search for a bomb might win them a day off work; after all, bomb threats were regularly called into Dodge Main. Although no explosion ever occurred, Molotov cocktails were found at least once, and fires were periodically set in different areas of the plant.[145] If the two plotters had hoped to raise a false alarm and scare Chrysler managers, they certainly succeeded, given that the foreman's statement was typed up and distributed among management personnel. A copy also ended up in the union's possession, evidence that the union and corporation saw the violence in the plant as an area of shared concern. Whether serious or not, the two men leveraged the consciousness and fear of violence and exerted symbolic power over management. A similar dynamic can be seen in the union's 1970 request for Plant Protection staff to be stationed twenty-four hours a day in the main mixing room after the area received "numerous bomb threats and crank telephone calls."[146] Violence at Dodge Main was not just a response to harassment or a means to defend identity; it was also a celebration of power and vitality at a time when management and unionists alike often looked upon the rank and file, especially its black members, with fear.

Although the production of masculinity at Dodge Main was often achieved through violence, the evidence cautions historians against essentializing violence as an inevitable part of being a man at Dodge Main. Violence was also integral to the experience of being female there. This experience included not only the gendered violence directed at women but also the violence that women employed on the job. A particularly terrifying example of the former is detailed in the 1972 grievance of Donald Meade. After receiving a medical pass to go home, Meade entered the work area of a female employee and began harassing her. Shortly after, Meade grabbed her by the throat in a stairway and attempted to drag her off, striking her several blows on the head. A co-worker broke up the assault. The next day, Meade was observed removing the woman's car battery, presumably to facilitate another assault. When he returned to work, he was suspended. Incredibly, the union grieved: "The Union feels the discharge is too severe there were two people involved the Union demands – double standards be done away with. Man employee should also have been counselled and not discharged."[147]

This incident shows that, despite the resurgence of feminist activism throughout the 1960s and 1970s, very little had changed at Dodge Main concerning union consciousness of male-on-female violence. There is no evidence of any company or union initiative to mitigate the risk of violence to female employees. As in an earlier era, women walked the plant knowing that sexual predators roamed it too. One of Liska's reports details an attack in a way that betrays more concern for the transgression of racial boundaries than for the safety of female workers: "A GIRL WAS TRAPPED BETWEEN STOCK ON THE RECEIVING AREA BY TWO YOUNG BLACKS AND THEY ATTEMPTED TO RAPE HER. A BLACK JITNEY DRIVER DROVE BY AND THE TWO YOUNG BLACKS RAN AWAY. A SEARCH DID NOT ... FIND THEM. THE GIRL WAS SHOCKED, SHE COULD NOT SCREAM BECAUSE OF THE FEAR."[148]

Women workers were not simply targets. They employed violence themselves. Like every other measure of workplace violence at Dodge Main, violence by women rose after 1965. Female employees were disciplined for fighting with each other and striking supervisors. Violence involving women could also redraw boundaries jeopardized by socializing with co-workers off the job and then having to maintain respect in the factory, as was the case with Rosa Fox. The 1974 grievance discussing her discharge reads,

> Ms. Fox engaged in the art of horseplay with employee Robert Switzer, badge 3352-4971, which resulted in attempt on the part of Ms. Fox to do bodily harm to Mr. Robert Switzer by stabbing him with a knife. Further investigation reveals that prior to this act Mr. Switzer and Ms. Fox became involved in a conversation about Ms. Fox's conduct the previous night and her alleged being under the influence of intoxicants. Ms. Fox was angered by this conversation and proceeded to stab Mr. Switzer in the posterior with a knife.[149]

As the use of the knife suggests, although female employees appear less often in grievances as perpetrators of violence, women could perform violence that was as spectacular and dangerous as male violence in the plant. Georgia Turner had to be subdued by Plant Protection staff to stop her from using a vehicle to do bodily harm to another employee in Parking Lot 3. The grievance reads, "After attempting to run down another employee Mrs. Turner crashed her car into the parking lot fence she left her car and went after another employee with a brick and a piece of broken glass in her hands and at one point threw a quart pop bottle at him and the plant guard who was attempting to intercede."[150]

Despite the seriousness of this female violence, it was often considered cute or inferior by male observers. It was not taken seriously as an issue or problem but was laughed off as the antics of less emotionally controlled, physically inferior women attempting to access a display of power and dominance reserved for men. When Liska wrote of a fight between two women, one of them steward Edith Fox, his tone was one of amused interest: "The ten fingers on both gals were arched in cat's paws style and they went after each other. Annie got the best licks and got Fox's eyes and face ... They were really going after each other's eyes."[151] He sums up another fight between two female workers in a dispute over how much sewing work each was doing as "chicken fighting going on."[152] It is doubtful a fight between male workers of the same seniority (one women had thirty-five years and the other thirty-one) would have been described so dismissively. The condescension reflects what a female autoworker told Scott about the "paternalism, the degrading attitudes" faced by female hourly workers and female supervisors alike.[153]

On-the-job sexuality also intersected with violence and identity. Whereas men could deploy heterosexual power as part of a rugged masculinity, homosexuality presented risks. Heterosexual relationships were common at Dodge Main, but the discovery of a homosexual coupling was considered remarkable and scandalous. Liska's diary notes in 1970 that "TWO BLACK MEN WERE CAUGHT IN THE ACT IN THE BODY SHOP INSIDE OF A WELDING BOOTH. ONE HAD HIS PANTS DOWN AND THE OTHER MAN WAS INTERCOURSING HIM FROM BEHIND. ALEXANDER REPORTED THE INCIDENT WHICH IS WELL PUBLICIZED IN THE BODY SHOP AREAS."[154] A Dodge Main wife claimed that defending one's masculinity from unwanted same-sex advances was a justification for violence. According to Gina Braxton, her husband Eugene's discharge for hitting a co-worker "across the head and shoulder with a torsion bar"[155] was unfair because the incident was provoked by another man's sexual harassment. Braxton claimed that Eugene, who did have two previous incidents of violence on his record, was doing his job when he was approached by "a homosexual who tried to molest him." She wrote, "my husband defended himself as a man and as a human being due his respect. I don't feel that a man should have to endure with this kind of nonsense to keep his job. No one wants to be humiliated by having someone approach them sexually in public."[156]

David Johnson, during a night shift in March 1973, became "involved in a discussion with another employee over Mr. Johnson's being a homosexual. Mr. Johnson took offense to being heckled about being a homosexual and assaulted the other employee with a knife." The union further noted that the other worker hit Johnson with a motor yet was still working. Perhaps violence against an alleged homosexual was defined as justifiable.[157]

For David Johnson, Georgia Turner, Willie Copland and thousands of other workers at Dodge Main, violence was crucial in producing, defining, and circumscribing both their working day and their identity at work. Violence was central to producing identity, and this was the case not only with respect to the identities of rough masculinity or powerful blackness. Femininity, youth, sexuality, and of course, one's class identity as a production worker or foreman could all be produced and imperiled by the violence that shot through work on the line, contests with supervisors, and relationships with co-workers, be they friends, enemies, dealers, or lovers.

Because violence marked virtually every aspect of life in the plant, the experience of workers was often grim, marked by fear and desperation. The grievance of Donald Wesley, fired in 1973 for possession of a handgun, eloquently testifies to this anomie and illustrates how disputes in the community or neighbourhood could also enter the plant and trigger violence on the job.[158] In a statement that he wrote, Wesley describes how a fight between him and his wife's current boyfriend, Melvin Brown, led to Brown harassing him at work, calling him a "punk," and threatening him. Frightened of Brown's threats and cognizant of Brown's criminal past, Wesley claims he asked his general foreman whether there was any plant policy that would keep the two apart. There was not. When Brown threatened him with a knife, Wesley went to see his foreman again, but both the foreman and the Detroit police advised Wesley that they could do nothing until something actually happened. After hearing from his wife that Brown was threatening to kill him and had acquired a gun from his cousin for this purpose, Wesley went to his father's house and got a gun of his own, being "afraid for my life like I had never been before." On the way to work the next day, he stopped at a friend's office for advice. The friend recommended that he explain the situation to Labor Relations. On his way to work, "nervous as hell but still trying to compose myself," Wesley met another one of his foremen in the parking lot.

Wesley explained to the foreman that Melvin Brown was going to try to kill him, that Wesley himself had a gun "for the purpose of my protection," and that he wanted to go to Labor Relations. The foreman told Wesley he would send him to Labor Relations once he was in the plant. Wesley parked his car, got out, and started for the gate. When he reached the Bismarck Gate overpass, Brown confronted him. Wesley later wrote that "for him to reach the [traffic] light at the same time I did he had to be watching me." Brown had his hand in his jacket, and Wesley believed he had a gun, "but the question in my mind was whether or not he was going to use it." According to Wesley, he tried to ignore Brown, but Brown followed him and hit him on the head with the gun before vanishing into the crowd of workers. Wesley left to get his "badly" bleeding head wound treated at the plant hospital, where they put him to bed, and "people started asking me a lot of questions." When his gun was discovered and removed from his person is unclear, but that gun cost Wesley his job. As management stated in reply to Wesley's grievance, "The possession of a weapon whether carried for a real or imagined reason ... is a serious breach of the plant rules of good conduct and absolutely cannot or will not be tolerated ... The discharge of Mr. Wesley was justified and proper." No mention of any discipline of Brown appears in the files.

Wesley's account vividly depicts the fear felt by many workers who lived in dangerous circumstances and worked in a violent plant where there were few safeguards or protections against even known threats of harm. In such a dysfunctional environment, the propensity for workers and foremen to arm and protect themselves is understandable, even if it led to more individual violence, or as a worker described it in a *New York Times* article of 1973, the same year that Wesley was assaulted, "Jesse James stuff."[159] Fred Pierson worked at Dodge Main from 1945 until 1973, when he was shot dead by co-worker John Holston. A Hamtramck police officer called it "the old story of 'if he didn't have the gun with him he wouldn't [have] used it.' It appeared to be the kind of argument in which one guy might bust the other guy in the mouth, but unfortunately he had a gun with him when he shouldn't have."[160]

Dodge Main limped along for another four years after 1975, but the giant, rusting hulk had become an inefficient relic of an earlier era of car production, especially as Chrysler slid into economic crisis at the end of the 1970s. Violence continued to be a major factor in plant life, notably a 1977 incident between a foreman and an Arab American worker and steward that resulted in allegations of violence on both sides, and 2000 signatures on a petition in support of the worker. The incident reflected the increasing visibility of racial conflict involving Dodge Main's growing Arab American workforce.[161] The ongoing violence at the plant undoubtedly played a role in Dodge Main's closing, as the 1971 report had warned. Violence certainly shaped the manner of its closure. A 1979 letter from one UAW staffer to another discussing the transfer of Dodge Main workers to other plants notes, "Obviously, the corporation is pushing for something to tell these people before they go down January 4 to keep down violence and damage to the facilities. As you might recall, when the January 4 closing date was announced, there was coincidable [sic] sabotage."[162] The plant's closing was itself a traumatic blow to its community. The eminent environmental historian Samuel Hays said at a 1979 symposium on the future of Hamtramck, "It's almost as though you're seeing the death of the manufacturing city right here. And my point is: don't resurrect it. Why try to rebuild something that is gone?"[163] A *Detroit News* headline called December 7, 1979, which was the

Observers gather to watch Dodge Main's destruction, 1981. Photos by Don Hudson.

forty-eighth anniversary of the Pearl Harbor attack, "The Day the 'Bomb' Fell on Hamtramck."[164]

Before that bomb fell, working at Dodge Main had wounded countless workers, some fatally. In-plant racism and worker frustration with a brutalizing labour process were the key reasons for the explosion of violence at Dodge Main, the "deep-rooted discontent" that Menendez wrote of to Merrelli. By the late 1960s, Dodge Main was a dangerous environment that not only posed severe risks of violence to everyone who worked there, but also intensified the risk that a given worker would choose to commit a violent act. Violence played many important, if at times contradictory, roles in the processes and culture of the plant. Structural violence, especially related to on-the-job racism and a dangerous labour process, was essential to production at Dodge Main. It helped to shape how the cars were made, who did what job, how the work was gotten out, and how union politics were pursued.

Violence flowed not only from the practices of Chrysler and the UAW but also from workers themselves. Violence was both the glue that kept the industrial regime together and a solvent that threatened to make that structure collapse. Organizations like DRUM advocated violence to dismantle the relations of exploitation at Dodge Main. Individual workers resisted harassment and discipline with individual violence or the threat of it. Although violence unmade workers, they also used violence to produce and defend themselves and their identities.

However, violence was ultimately a profoundly destructive element. Violence at Dodge Main, and the inability or unwillingness of Chrysler and the UAW to address it, encouraged workers to pursue individual, not collective, solutions to the frustrations of work there. Individual workplace violence was a response to workplace dynamics at a dysfunctional, conflict-ridden plant, a reflection of the criminal violence that marked the lives of Detroiters, and a way for atomized workers – who felt less affective loyalty to either company or union than workers had in previous years – to develop and defend an individual identity. As traditional hierarchies and collective solidarities collapsed, violence became not just a material force but also a cultural resource upon which individual workers drew. This process legitimated violence, which in turn produced more of it. After the factory was demolished, deindustrialization, capital flight, crime, and mass incarceration continued to ravage Detroit and Detroiters for decades. Today, the Rage Against the Machine lyrics stencilled on the pavement outside where Dodge

Main used to stand express how the processes of deindustrialization contain their own violent logic: "Ain't it funny how the factory doors close / round the time the school doors close / round the time the doors of the jail cell open up to greet you."

TABLE 1
Violence-related grievances at Dodge Main

Year	Violent incidents recorded in grievances	Violent incidents involving management	Approximate Dodge Main workforce
1950	5	0	
1951	9	0	33,000[1]
1952	4	0	
1953	16	1	
1954–55	10	2	25,000[2]
1956	4	0	
1957–58	4	1	
1959	1	0	
1960	2	0	
1961	2	0	
1962	0	0	
1963	6	5	8,357[3]
1964	4	3	
1965	15	4	
1966	16	12	
1967	12	4	
1968	28	15	12,000[4]
1969	36	6	
1970	24	7	
1971	16	6	
1972	41	7	
1973	62	19	
1974	21	8	
1975	14	6	10,000[5]

1 Dodge Brothers Motor Car Company History, "The Chrysler Era, 1928–80," http://dodgemotorcar.com/factories/hamtramck/1928-1980.php.
2 Kevin Boyle, "The Kiss: Racial and Gender Conflict in a 1950s Automobile Factory," *Journal of American History* 84, 2 (1997): 501.
3 Dodge Brothers Motor Car Company History, "The Chrysler Era, 1928–80." Figure refers to production workers only.
4 Steve Jefferys, *Management and Managed: Fifty Years of Crisis at Chrysler* (Cambridge, UK: CUP Archive, 1986), 173.
5 Nabeel Abraham, "Detroit's Yemeni Workers," *MERIP Reports* 57 (1977): 7.

3

The Way Boys and Men Took Care of Business

Windsor Chrysler Plants

Across the border in the spring of 1975, while Canadians discussed a coming influx of Vietnamese refugees fleeing the victorious Communists and the Toronto Maple Leafs being swept from the National Hockey League playoffs by Philadelphia's Broad Street Bullies, workers at Windsor Chrysler plants were talking about a number of violent incidents in their factories. The *444 News,* their local United Automobile Workers (UAW) newspaper, called on workers to stop the violence:

> Several incidents of violence have broken out around the plant. One brother has died as a result of a violent situation. Two brothers have been seriously hurt and hospitalized. Horseplay has led to the incidents, and your local union takes this opportunity to remind all brothers: to hold a card in your union and a job in the plant carries with it a responsibility to respect each other ... Fun is fun and helps break the monotony but violence is out![1]

Some workers saw something taking place that was more serious than simply horseplay getting out of hand. They argued that the violence, especially a stabbing incident that had resulted in the hospitalization of two workers and the arrest of a third, was symptomatic of something deeply rotten within the plants. The *Rank and File Bulletin,* the pink-coloured leaflet that radical workers handed out at the plant gates, charged that "Chrysler was the direct instigator of this stabbing by its ruthless exploitation of the workforce which pushed workers to vent their frustration by turning on each other. The day before this incident, the line where these men worked was sped-up by over 10 cars an hour." The leaflet went on to tell Windsor workers about the James Johnson shootings at Chrysler's Eldon Axle Plant in Detroit: "The circumstances that drove Mr. Johnson to this action has many parallels with the recent stabbing. The terrible working conditions, the indifferent UAW, and racism were all similar ingredients to the Plant 3 incident. For those of you that feel this would not happen in Windsor, best consider this: DETROIT IS IN OUR PLANTS."[2]

This analysis was both revealing and misleading. Yes, injuries and even deaths on the floor did occur because of in-plant health and safety risks. Conflict between workers and management over conditions, speedup, and discipline was vociferous and continuous. Perhaps surprisingly for Canadians who traditionally view violence as central to American life but a rarity north of the border, individual violence at work, arising out of conflicts on the job and a high-production labour process, was a regular aspect of auto work and how working-class masculinity was defined in the city's Chrysler factories.

But was Detroit in their plants? This chapter investigates violence at work in Windsor Chrysler plants between the 1950s and the late 1970s, focusing on the latter part of that era, a time when violence skyrocketed in Detroit plants while remaining relatively stable in Windsor. Although the lack of grievance records makes it impossible to count discrete incidents of violence, a review of in-plant bulletins and leaflets, union newspapers, radical publications, and election material, supplemented by interviews with Chrysler workers and unionists, has produced a clear picture of violence at work in Windsor Chrysler plants. It both confirms and denies what the workers argued in the *Rank and File Bulletin*. Yes, violence was real and regular in Windsor Chrysler plants, where it was an ultimate resource employed by workers to settle interpersonal conflicts or to exert power over a supervisor. As in Detroit plants, violence was not an aberration or a freak occurrence but an understood part of the industrial culture and working-class manhood at Windsor Chrysler. However, different racial dynamics, the greater economic stability of Windsor Chrysler plants, a more effective union, and a safer city limited the atomization and brutalization of workers and thus limited the incidence of individual violence compared with the crisis of violence that exploded in Detroit Chrysler plants.

The varying experiences of Chrysler workers in the two cities demonstrate how important structural factors were to conditioning the risks of individual violence, as well as how important the national context was to constructing workers' lives and experiences on the job, even in two cities as tightly linked as Detroit and Windsor. Windsor's development has been inextricably entwined with Detroit's and with the auto industry that is so pivotal to both of their histories. In the 1910s and 1920s, thousands of workers from all over Canada, including scores of recent arrivals from Europe, migrated to Windsor in search of employment in the United States. They crossed the river on ferries to work in Detroit's auto shops by day and returned to their homes in Canada at night, until a 1931 law banned nonresident workers from employment in the United States as part of an effort to protect US jobs at the height of the Great Depression.[3] Although this ban eliminated most of the work available in the United States, the branch-plant automotive industry in Canada continued to grow, drawing on the armies of unemployed workers looking for jobs during Canada's Great Depression. Competition and conflict were fierce. Writing years later, UAW Local 444 president Charlie Brooks claimed that the vicious atmosphere of the era was the foundation of a combative class consciousness and his union's leftist orientation. This orientation, for Brooks, was the basis for shop floor action as much as for wider political struggle, deployed in part to defend working-class manhood:

> Each morning we came to work we had to push our way through the crowd of men and women standing at the gate. We were the lucky ones (so-called) who knew someone who could get you the chance to earn (really earn) 20 cents an hour. Across the street at the GM [General Motors] Plant supervisors were selling jobs, taking bribes, and propositioning husbands. Some of the supervisors were later exposed and fired.
>
> We were working 16 and 18 hours a day and the girls who took jobs had their reputation at stake. The employment manager had a free hand, a field day. One hundred and fifty hours would give us a pay check of [$]29.00 for two weeks. One became a part of [the] machine, who could not stop because of perpetual motion, little rest, no time for play, just work like hell, yet hundreds of willing hands stood at the gates.
>
> This was Motor Products of the 1933–35 era in Windsor, producing parts for Ford and Chrysler, and out of it came many of the UAW's good union men. Sure we had meetings, and those that did the talking were fired the next day. We wanted a union, but the bosses called us reds. As one

> brother put it ... "If fighting for decent working conditions is being a Red, than I am a damn good one."[4]

The battle to unionize auto factories was a physical battle. In Brooks's telling, "Our contracts were written in the blood of many of the brothers who bravely fought."[5]

Brooks's account of early auto work presents a violent world where women's bodies and reputations were at risk – where men asserted their rights with their fists as well as their politics. These conceptions of auto work and masculinity would remain an essential aspect of work and violence in Windsor plants in the decades to come.

By the 1950s Local 444 had established itself as the bargaining agent for workers at Windor's three Chrysler factories: Plant 1, the Assembly Plant; Plant 2, the Engine Plant; and Plant 3, the Truck Plant on Tecumseh Road. It also represented those who worked at a Chrysler foundry in Walkerville and at Young Spring and Wire, a parts supplier that Chrysler eventually bought outright. According to Gary Parent, the foundry closed in 1969, followed by the spring plant some years later. However, Chrysler did build a new truck factory on Pillette Road during the 1970s, in order to satisfy its domestic production obligations under the Auto Pact.[6]

The continuing growth of the auto industry provided for the continuing growth of Windsor itself. However, the 1950s and 1960s were not simply a time of placid prosperity in the city. Although Fordism was in its heyday, Fordism did not eliminate economic instability, even in the auto industry. The business cycles of the automotive industry caused frequent unemployment for many Windsorites, and fears of factories leaving town were ever present. Still, the thousands of jobs at Chrysler, Ford, and their many suppliers provided an economic base for a reasonably stable and solvent working-class city. Unlike in Detroit, there was no "urban crisis" in Windsor during the postwar decades.[7] The city's major automotive employers stayed rather than fleeing to the suburbs or to the southern United States. Although Windsor was sometimes hailed during the 1950s as a racially progressive city, the accolades were misleading. Windsor's black community struggled against racism and discrimination in employment, accommodations, and police harassment. However, since people of colour made up a far smaller proportion of the city's population, Windsor remained comparatively unaffected by the white flight and reckoning with racism that roiled Detroit.[8] During the 1967 uprising, while Detroit burned, Windsor watched.

Inside Windsor's plants as well, racial struggle was much less of a determining factor. Again, this difference did not mean that labour relations and plant culture were any less racist. Instead, it reflected demographics and exclusion. There were fewer black workers seeking jobs in Windsor's plants. During the 1950s there were approximately 2,050 black Windsorites.[9] Writing about the 1930s and 1940s, historian Pamela Sugiman has demonstrated that auto employers "exploited and reinforced the structural inequalities that working-class blacks faced."[10] Black men were restricted to the hottest, dirtiest jobs, reflecting stereotypes about their racial suitability for such work. Black women, meanwhile, were mostly excluded from any manufacturing jobs, even during wartime.[11] Historian Brandi Lucier's research on race and auto work during the 1940s and 1950s shows that "throughout the city in both unionized and non-unionized shops black workers were overwhelmingly segregated in the auto industry's foundries or turned down at the hiring gate." At Ford, black workers were restricted to less desirable departments and paid the lowest rates possible.[12] At Chrysler, black workers were not even hired. In 1953 UAW Region 7 education director William C. MacDonald alleged that Windsor Chrysler did not "have a single Negro in the plant as Chrysler in the US hires Negroes by the thousands." According to MacDonald, these segregation and hiring policies were no coincidence. They were "devised and enforced by the Canadian management."[13] Chrysler's response was to hire three black workers at its Windsor plants. Even afterward, Chrysler resisted placing a no-discrimination clause in its collective agreement with Region 7 and, two years later, refused to hire two production workers as Plant Protection staff because they were black.[14] Windsor Chrysler plants avoided most of the violence born of a racialized labour process that was such a persistent danger at Dodge Main, but it was thanks to exclusion and demographics, not justice or equality.

Sugiman's analysis of intersectional privilege and oppression in mid-century Canadian auto work skilfully traces how these factors produced a situation for black male workers of that era that differed from the one faced by their American counterparts. Because black men were rarely hired, they were not used by employers as a means to lower wages or as strikebreakers. This situation meant that black men achieved status as workingmen that was equal to that of their white or European counterparts, although blacks still faced everyday racism and harassment on the floor.[15] The UAW's union contract enabled black workers to combat some workplace racism, such as their restriction to the plant's worst jobs, on principles of equality, but it was not a platform for anti-racism. The black workers interviewed by

Sugiman believed that they needed to act individually in order to secure fair treatment and advancement; one of her informants stated he believed that the UAW would fail to follow up on black workers' grievances unless pushed.[16] Black workers, already too few and scattered to make group organizing straightforward, thus submerged their racial identity, which was somewhat depoliticized by these dynamics. Although many of the workers Sugiman interviewed were active in the UAW, most black activism of the era was directed at attacking racism in the community, not in the plant.[17] This focus on the community indicates how Windsor plants could be structured by racism and feature everyday racism yet not have a "race problem" in the same manner as American plants.

Because of the relative stability of its hierarchical structures, Windsor was also spared the twin crises of mass incarceration and rampant crime that plagued Detroit after white flight and disinvestment had eaten away at the city's economy and isolated its African American population, as well as many poor white Appalachian migrants, in crumbling ghettoes. Crime rates in Windsor rose during the 1960s and 1970s but remained well below rates in Detroit, reflecting a larger difference between crime rates in Canada and the United States. Therefore, one vector of violence in the lives of Detroit's autoworkers in the 1960s and 1970s, violent crime in their neighbourhoods and factories, was far less prevalent in Windsor. Whereas Detroit's yearly homicide count swelled from 188 in 1965 to 607 in 1975, the corresponding figures in Windsor were 2 and 16. In the five years from 1969 to 1973, there were 24 murders in Windsor and 2,784 in Detroit, a staggering disparity even considering Detroit's much larger population.[18]

In Windsor Chrysler plants, gambling and drug dealing certainly took place.[19] However, the type of drug-related violence that plagued some Detroit plants does not appear to have been a factor in Windsor Chrysler plants. The greater stability of the community was reflected in safer factories and perhaps vice versa.

Although a less violent community helped to produce a less violent factory, Windsor plants were no haven of industrial peace. Throughout the 1950s, 1960s, and 1970s, workers and management continually clashed. Windsor Chrysler workers and their union fought speedup, supervisory harassment, and plant conditions that sometimes killed workers either suddenly through violent accidents or slowly through years of toxic exposures. During the 1950s the practice of bringing in American managers to speed up lines was a constant source of conflict. Compared with their counterparts in the United States, Canadian autoworkers produced many more vehicle models on an individual production line. In 1965, for example, General Motors Oshawa produced 595 various models, over twice as many as any American plant.[20] Although this diversity meant slower-moving lines, it also led to job stress as workers scrambled to switch lines over to keep the production of different models going with the least possible downtime. Workers thus resented the attempts of head office to rationalize their work along American lines. In 1960 Brooks wrote, "Many of the Company Programs are brought over by the imported experts who are accustomed to plants where only one division of Chrysler runs down a line. Here the situation is different, where every division is on one line."[21] In 1957 Chrysler tried to get more production from its workforce. UAW Local 444, claiming that workers were maintaining production despite a reduction of 1,400 workers, charged a speedup was taking place. The fight over production standards went public and led to the union being accused of sabotaging production in the *Windsor Star*.[22]

Brooks and his union consistently blamed the company's work processes for the injuries and deaths suffered by members. Rallying workers for a 1960 strike vote, Brooks wrote of some prominent incidents:

> Matt Pavlic ... dead in a pool of blood, in spite of the many protests of the union to have no man work alone on a ladder. No man works alone now, but Matt is gone.
>
> Leo Schmidt, the faithful loading dock worker, after 24 years was crushed by a runaway truck in a boxcar. After being hospitalized for months, he is still suffering from internal trouble. The Company wanted to prove that fewer men could load more loads and they didn't care who got killed, the figures must be right. The foremen would still stand over the men, faster, faster. Leo, at his age, will never be right.
>
> Bro. Bugelli, a beautiful specimen of a man weighing 240 lbs., now walks the street a feeble cripple for life, because of the speed-up in the metal shop. He severed the arteries and muscles in his wrist on the razor-sharp panels he had to handle. Yes, he gets a small pension for life, but with tears in his eyes he would like to maim every stupid pusher in the Chrysler Corporation. How can I tell my wife and children back home in Malta that me, a big strong man, am a useless cripple unable to earn a living?[23]

Although work at Windsor Chrysler was difficult, dangerous, and sometimes deadly, local and national factors provided Windsor Chrysler workers with factories that were safer and cleaner than their Detroit counterparts.

The stability provided by the Auto Pact gave Charlie Brooks and Local 444 a foundation for militancy. Photo courtesy of Unifor Local 444.

The major event that altered the labour relations context in Windsor and revitalized Local 444 was the signing of the Auto Pact between Canada and the United States in January 1965. The agreement exempted the major US car manufacturers from duties on the cars they exported to Canada in exchange for a commitment to maintain certain levels of production and employment in Canada. For Windsor Chrysler workers, the Auto Pact brought immediate challenges. As political scientist Chris Roberts notes in his history of the postwar Canadian industry, "Canadians would now be faced with American management, faster assembly lines producing fewer models, tighter work standards transferred from faster US lines, and the rationalization of Canadian work practices."[24] The Auto Pact increased employment in Canada's auto industry while challenging Canadian workers to win wages and work standards that were as good as or better than those of their American counterparts. The nationalist orientation of the fight for parity would be a unifying force strengthening the union during a time of internal challenges and social upheaval.

In the short term, the Auto Pact sparked conflict. The late 1960s was a time of increased worker militancy and contestations of both corporate and union authority across Canada, and Windsor Chrysler was no exception.[25] Many of the younger workers streaming into the plants complained bitterly about the speedup on the lines and the concomitant disciplinary crackdown. Two days before Christmas 1966, tensions exploded. Cushion room workers refused to work overtime. Foremen responded by recruiting replacements from other departments. A brawl ensued between cushion room workers, foremen, and the replacement workers. A combination of worker-management hostility and Christmas drinking almost turned into a "wholesale riot." A union report noted that the company photographed twenty-eight empty whiskey bottles in one department.[26]

Younger workers chafed at the stern discipline and gruelling workday at Chrysler. A union-management conference held in 1965 described younger workers as "impatient – challenging – eager for action."[27] A union-election leaflet produced in support of John Horne, Local 444's most influential dissident of the time, identified the issues faced by the "vast majority" of membership who were under thirty as relief time, production standards, petty discipline, and the right to refuse direct orders not related to a worker's job assignment.[28] Another leaflet aimed at Windsor Chrysler workers charged "our shop paper printed an article which states people at the plant are abused by supervisors who constantly nag, refuse, or hold up first aid passes, speed up the line to steal jobs, and threatened [sic] the men." This type of management, the leaflet implied, presented a direct threat to the manhood of Windsor Chrysler workers: "Such supervisors must be proud to know they can whip a man who can't fight back."[29]

However, despite the intensification of work that resulted from the Auto Pact, the agreement helped to produce a better work environment for Windsor Chrysler workers and thus to mitigate some of the issues that sparked increased individual violence in Detroit. Most importantly, the Auto Pact safeguarded Windsor auto jobs, rescuing the auto industry in Windsor from a decade-long slump. The increased employment and prosperity in the city were in marked contrast to the growing deindustrialization and crime across the river. Unlike Detroit Chrysler unions, which were forced into the untenable position of trying to quell rebellion on the lines and to help Chrysler keep the plant going at all costs for fear of a plant closure, Local 444 knew that a certain amount of Windsor production was likely to be maintained.[30]

Roberts notes that pressure on workers "was directly connected to speedup and the deterioration of working conditions, as well as job insecurity."[31] This combination produced a crisis in Detroit Chrysler plants that encouraged insurgency and violence, a crisis averted in Windsor thanks in part to the Auto Pact and the leverage it gave Local 444. Whereas in Detroit union locals were undercut by the Big Three's movement of production out of the city, Canadian auto jobs stayed in Windsor. When the industry added jobs, it did so in Windsor, bolstering Local 444's material strength and credibility.[32]

The Auto Pact not only provided for Local 444's stability and growth but also encouraged militant union action on plant conditions. Unlike their counterparts in the United States, Windsor workers had no right to strike because of working conditions while their contract was in force. This situation paradoxically encouraged Canadian locals to be more effective on in-plant issues. Without the option to use brief in-contract strikes either as a means to gain temporary redress of a specific grievance or as a safety valve for frustrated workers, Canadian locals had to negotiate better contractual language on working conditions during bargaining periods. In the United States shop floor issues were not a primary concern at the bargaining table. In Canada the UAW was forced to be more effective in resolving the in-plant concerns of its members because bargaining periods were the only time that they could achieve lasting improvements in health and safety.[33]

As a result, by the early 1970s, when the crisis in Detroit Chrysler plants was at its peak, Canadian plants were cleaner, safer, and saner. In 1970 Brooks wrote,

> Absenteeism and huge numbers of quits indicate the auto industry is off track. The turnover of manpower in US plants due to poor work practices and other reasons makes their plants operate like a cheap paying car wash where a guy works just enough to get bus fare to travel on. Instead of green stamps, instead of discipline and overtime smorgasbord, they need to humanize the work place, they need to increase the pay to make up for shorter hours and more family time. They need more contracts like Canada.[34]

A plant handout titled "For a Canadian Contract" presented US plants as violent sweatshops:

> Working conditions in most US plants are intolerable. Compulsory 12-hour shifts are forced upon workers and there is no right to refuse any overtime. Steady night shifts are assigned to younger workers, there is inferior health and safety legislation, and some workers in Chrysler plants are still under

> discharge for heat walk-outs.[35] Job opportunity and transfer provisions of their contracts are virtually non-existent. Beatings, gangsterism and even murders are becoming commonplace events in U.S.A. factories.[36]

Windsor workers largely remained insiders at a time when Dodge Main's traditions of worker control were being severed. Windsor and its auto factories were not besieged by the crises and insurgencies that beset Detroit and its plants and thus were spared the high levels of violence they provoked. Nevertheless, insider violence was part of working life. Windsor Chrysler workers used violence to maintain order and status in a workplace where manhood and physical violence were closely correlated.

"It was a man's world,"[37] Gord Gray recalled of the Windsor Chrysler plants he entered as a teenager in the mid-1970s. Unlike Dodge Main, which had a significant cohort of female workers as far back as the Second World War, Windsor Chrysler plants remained almost exclusively male well into the 1970s and featured a male-dominated work culture similar to that present in the American auto plants analyzed by auto work historian Steve Meyer.[38] In the mid-1970s Local 444's membership was at its peak of approximately 13,000 active members, according to interviewees.[39] Almost none of them were female. According to interviewees, Chrysler did not hire women in any significant number until the latter half of the 1970s, when they were forced to do so by the federal government as a condition of receiving funding for the construction of the new truck factory on Pillette Road.[40] Gray remembered, "The gender of the factories was male."

The factories were a haven of rough working-class masculinity. Pornographic magazines were pasted up all over the assembly lines, where men worked long, arduous shifts with cigarettes clamped between their teeth. In some areas of the plant, the workers' hard physical labour produced impressive physiques. "Most of these guys were ripped," Gray recalled of the men who worked in machining.[41] On the job, workers faced the slow dangers of foul smoke and toxic chemicals, the challenge of boredom, and the risk of the occasional horrific injury or even sudden death. In his study of manly culture at the Ford Motor Company, economist Wayne Lewchuk argues that Henry Ford "created a fraternal system, a men's club, to help male workers adjust to a world of monotonous repetitive work." Ford believed that the benefits of a fraternal, single-sex workplace outweighed the advantages gained by hiring women into his plants at lower wage rates, and thus Ford plants became an almost exclusively male preserve until the 1940s.[42]

The near total absence of women at Windsor Chrysler plants and the boys' culture that dominated there suggest that a similar process was at work.

In their spare time on the line, workers indulged in manly recreation, according to interviewees. Drugs and gambling rings that provided action on horses or college sports were widespread. The Royal Canadian Mounted Police had at least one undercover officer working the lines. Despite the presence of the police, many workers were members of the region's motorcycle gangs and would display their colours in the plant. Another way workers broke the monotony was by playing pranks on new hires. They would hide rookie workers' lunches or pour grease in their boots. If a new worker could take abuse like a man, with a smile, he would be welcomed into the fraternity. If the new worker could not, he risked social ostracism and the loss of his job.[43]

Manly recreation included physically affectionate behaviour among male co-workers. An interview with Jim Monk, a Windsor Chrysler autoworker and political activist in the 1970s, reveals the "affectionate physicality" that was common on the floor in this era:

> Guys rubbed each other's backs, kissed – mainly on the cheek but sometimes on the lips – grabbed each other's balls, did dry runs at a bumfuck ... You know, when you're uptight and somebody grabs your balls some of it's gotta go ... If you suggested that it was homosexuality to these guys, they'd vehemently deny it and get really upset.[44]

When Monk came out as gay in the plant in 1978, he did experience some social ostracism for a time but never feared physical attack because of his reputation as a capable amateur wrestler. Monk's prowess at macho physical competition perhaps afforded him more space in the plant to express a nondominant and feared sexual identity.[45]

The men's club at Windsor Chrysler plants was a harsh and unwelcoming environment for the few female workers who began entering the workplace in the 1970s. Several of their male co-workers crossed the line from unfriendliness to intimidation and harassment. Pat Cunningham spent four years at the Spring and Wire Plant as a young woman in the latter half of the 1970s before moving to the assembly plant. When she started at Chrysler in 1975, there were only about five women in her plant. She recalled a "brutal" atmosphere, not because of the work but because of "the comments and the stares ... Some days you just wanted to go crawl under a rock ... A lot of days ... I went home crying." According to Cunningham, one male co-worker brandished a pornographic magazine at her, making obscene gestures. Another asked her, "Have you ever been gangbanged? Have you ever been raped?" On that occasion, she responded with direct action, throwing down her tools and sitting at a picnic table. When a supervisor asked her why she had stopped working, she told him, "I'm not working beside that pig any longer." According to Cunningham, the man was taken off his job immediately and eventually moved out of her section.[46]

Cunningham says she did not receive any assistance from her union until later, when another co-worker began following her home repeatedly, slowly driving by her front porch as she sat having a beer after work. She went to a union representative with the problem. Union reps spoke to the man, and the stalking stopped. Asked whether they had threatened him with violence, Cunningham said, "I don't know, that was the old guys ... It could have been a threat." She recalled, "It took me a long time to get my voice [in the plant] ... to say 'shut up,' not to walk away." Eventually, however, she became active in creating a women's committee at Local 444, as well as a key figure in making Windsor Chrysler plants a safer and more equitable place for women. Of the treatment she received as a young female worker, she reflected, "then I probably wouldn't have defined it as violence. Now, after the education I've had, I would define it as violence." This violence arose directly from the hypermasculine work culture at Windsor Chrysler plants and from the perceived threat to that culture presented by the arrival of women like Cunningham. Her ability to do the same tough work that men did "emasculated" macho co-workers, to use her word. She concluded, "That takes away some masculinity ... most guys define themselves by their job."[47]

The language and cartoons used in worker publications further illustrate how deeply workers saw their life on the job in terms of their masculinity and maintaining their manly status in the face of the company's threats to this masculinity. Workers mordantly invoked oral sex to describe negotiating with the company in order to get a fired worker back on the job, saying "only the knee pads got him back."[48] A cartoon in the *444 News* vividly illustrates the connection men made between working at Chrysler and their manhood, as well as the emasculation in store for any man who lost his job. The cartoon depicts a depressed-looking man on his hands and knees scrubbing his floor at home, while his wife looks on and says to a female friend, "Now that Chrysler's fired him, I've hired him!"[49] Monk recalled that cartoons of "a supervisor fucking a worker" were regularly drawn on bathroom walls.[50]

In this hypermasculine environment, workers widely accepted the use of violence among themselves to settle disputes and enforce acceptable standards of behaviour. In his study of masculine culture in mid-century Detroit auto plants, Meyer observes that fighting was a "prototypical form of masculine behavior ... a common and frequent means for the aggressive settlement of shop floor disputes between workers."[51] Windsor Chrysler workers had a similar understanding of masculinity, violence, and interpersonal conflict. Violence was, according to Gray, "just the way boys and men took care of business. You pay the punishment if you want to be an idiot."[52] At Chrysler, violence and masculinity informed each other. Masculinity justified using violence to resolve conflict, and the use of violence buttressed masculine status. Gary Parent and Rick Laporte, two long-time Chrysler workers who rose to executive offices in Local 444, recalled that when disagreements came to a head, "in those days workers went out [to] the parking lot and had a fistfight."[53] Gray concurred: "A good many times it was a fisticuff ... you get smacked in the head and hopefully the supervisor didn't see it."[54] According to interviewees, if a fight did not happen on the job, it might take place at one of the bars where many workers drank on their lunch hours and after their shifts ended. The Embassy, French Canadian Club, Fleming House, and others were places where "if people couldn't deal with [it] at work, they dealt with it outside the plant, and that meant [if] you're out with a couple buddies at a bar and you see the guy, there'd be a beating going on."[55]

As Gray suggested, violence was used to resolve interpersonal disputes without involving management. It was also employed instead of bringing a union representative into the situation. Gray contended, "We didn't wait for the rep to come down ... we had to deal with our own personal issues."[56] One prominent example of workers settling job conflict with violence involved Clarence Talbot, who would become infamous a few years later for murdering Local 444's president. Talbot was a relief man: his job was to fill in for workers who were away from the line on breaks or perhaps receiving medical attention. According to Parent, Talbot was a "bully in the plant" who pressured workers to cut their relief short and hurry back to work so that Talbot could have more "ass time," or breaks. "He intimidated workers as far as their relief time was concerned. He took time away. And if you didn't like it, he beat the crap out of you. Or threatened to beat the crap out of you."[57]

One co-worker took exception to Talbot's tactics, and the issue culminated in a "huge fight" in a storage shed. Despite being a professional heavyweight boxer, whose career had been chronicled in the Local 444 newsletter,

Talbot lost a brawl that became the stuff of Local 444 legend. According to Parent, Talbot's opponent always said he regretted not killing Talbot in that fight because it would have meant that Talbot could never have shot Brooks. No discipline resulted from the incident, simply because neither worker ever reported it. As Laporte insisted, "In the olden days it was really kept between the workers ... It was just two people working stuff out."[58] The story shows not only how workers used violence but also the mythic status a notable episode of violence could attain within workplace culture.

According to Parent and Laporte, it often fell to union representatives to deal with bullies at work. When representatives were regulating conduct on the job, they too drew on violence as a resource: "Representatives probably did more intervention than management did. Because management was as afraid of the individuals doing the bullying."[59] For union representatives, standing up to bullies and threatening to beat them up if they did not change their behaviour was "part of the life." "You cannot be a representative and have someone bully you. You will get run over." Parent and Laporte remembered that bullies would back down in almost every case, partly because the representative was backed by the solidarity of his co-workers. "Management wouldn't live up to the responsibility, but the rep always would because the workers were who he was protecting."[60] Violence, class consciousness, and ideas of masculinity and brotherhood were deployed in varying degrees to create and maintain the workers' shop floor order in the plants.

The code of violence at Windsor Chrysler was complex and sometimes contradictory. Although using violence was accepted and even valorized as part of shop floor masculinity, a reputation for violence could be a hindrance for workers who sought to rise from the shop floor to executive positions in the Local 444 hierarchy. Ken Gerard, a worker running against Charlie Brooks for the local presidency in 1968, complained of being smeared as "Wildman, Slugger, or Butch."[61] Gerard had not helped his reputation as a brawler with his own pamphlet, issued during the 1966 election, in which he boasted of saving Brooks from a member who "was about to clobber him over the head with a beer bottle when I was standing beside him. If it were not for me there is no question the Hero would have suffered a serious head injury." The pamphlet also accused Brooks of not intervening when another member was being beaten at the UAW's summer camp in Port Elgin. Although Gerard promised, "If I'm elected, my only fight will be to make management correct your problems, each and every one," workers were unconvinced, and they re-elected Brooks. Workers might have occasionally opted for violence on the line and in the bars, but they clearly expected a different approach from their local president.[62]

Although violence may have been part of their life on the line, Windsor Chrysler workers saw violence in their plants as much different from violence at plants in Detroit. Workers talked about the violence in Detroit plants, but according to Laporte, there was a "huge difference between the Detroit plants and us," a difference he connected to the levels of violence in the cities themselves: "You get 600 murders there, you might get one murder in Windsor."[63] This figure of 600 is an exaggeration, but homicide was certainly far more frequent in Detroit during this period. According to Parent, workers did not worry as much about the violence in Detroit plants spreading to Windsor as they did about Detroit plants getting production that they felt should be in Canada.[64] In 1965, after one year on the line, Jim O'Neil became a steward at age nineteen. He recalled dealing with very few incidents of violence in Windsor plants between 1965 and 1975, which supports the idea that what violence there was largely occurred outside the official channels of plant governance. He recalled that when he became a UAW International representative in 1976 and began servicing plants in Detroit, violence was much more of an issue. He was cautioned not to walk through Detroit Chrysler plants alone, for fear of being jumped by workers who were known to force their co-workers to sign over their paycheques at gunpoint. Union officials at the Detroit Forge Plant told O'Neil of a particularly unpopular supervisor who, they believed, had been thrown into a vat of boiling metal by workers one night after hours, never to be seen again. O'Neil did not recall violence being an issue at the Newcastle, Indiana, plant that he serviced, which further illustrates how crucial specific local dynamics were to violence in Detroit plants.[65]

In Windsor's more functional Chrysler plants, the role of violence in workplace culture is more elusive. To O'Neil, it was not a significant factor. Parent and Laporte remembered several incidents of violence but did not believe there was a resulting climate of fear in the plants. According to Gray, however, that fear was there all the time, and it contributed to the maintenance of order among the men of Windsor Chrysler. After seeing "some of the beatings that people had taken,"[66] he knew "people would clean your clock on the job, so you always kept to your own Ps and Qs and treated everybody with respect." Cunningham agreed that the awareness of violence was part of plant culture: "Everybody was aware that something was out there ... There was an understanding."[67] Perhaps workers' understanding of how crucial violence was to plant culture had a great deal to do with their position in the workplace's hierarchies of power, as well as how vulnerable to violence they felt they were. Younger workers or female workers may have sensed a greater risk of violence than did more established male workers. Workers who regularly employed violence or the threat of violence, like Clarence Talbot, may have seen violence as fundamental to their job. Union officials, who primarily dealt with conflict in offices and on grievance forms, may have been largely unaware of violence on the shop floor.

Whereas Parent and Laporte highlighted the way union representatives used violence in their own work, Gray recalled that the union largely left the men to regulate interpersonal issues themselves. The union was focused on the company, so the attitude among workers was, "You're a man? You get yourself into trouble, you take care of business at work."[68] As shown below, "taking care of business" sometimes meant using violence to control or influence supervisors.

Violence in Windsor Chrysler plants was largely self-contained. It never became a public issue like it did at Dodge Main, aside from Charlie Brooks's murder. Unlike in Hamtramck, violence involving knives and guns seems to have been extremely rare, and uniformed police rarely came into the plant. The level of violence directed at plant guards provides an instructive comparison between Detroit and Windsor Chrysler plants. In Hamtramck assaults on these representatives of Chrysler authority occurred regularly. In Windsor the suspension of several employees for using "abusive language" with the guards was itself worthy of a warning notice in the *444 News*.[69] However, just as workers occasionally committed acts of violence toward each other, workers also occasionally directed violence, or the threat of violence, at their supervisors. Windsor Chrysler plants may not have been "barrel[s] of dynamite" like Dodge Main, but they were workplaces where violence against management was a recognized element of class conflict and the shop floor order.

Historians have identified the racialization and intensification of the hardest, dirtiest jobs in Detroit auto plants, or what radical Chrysler workers succinctly dubbed "Niggermation,"[70] as a crucial factor in the breakdown of industrial order there. Since workers had less in common with their supervisors in terms of race, age, and employment security, and since supervisors employed racial abuse in managing employees, levels of conflict and violence spiralled. This dynamic did not exist at Chrysler plants in Windsor, where the workforce was almost exclusively white. But despite the fact that workers and supervisors in Windsor appeared to have more in common superficially, a real hostility and separation between the two groups existed. This division demonstrates that the labour process, class, and workplace conflict, not just race, were key causes of auto plant violence.

Gray recalled that Windsor Chrysler management during the 1960s and 1970s was "old school ... very militant." Supervisors drove their workers with intimidation, fear, and verbal abuse. "A lot of this [conflict] was put on by the company with their old-style management: 'You're a piece of shit ... Do the fucking job' ... A person can only take so much of that."[71] A union bulletin complained of a "little Siberia" in Plant 3 under supervisor Gagnon, charged with "arrogant, ignorant, foul language and mistreatment of his men."[72] The bulletin claimed that thirty men had quit in one week rather than endure Gagnon. The *444 News* alleged that foreman Wright forced injured workers back to work when they were still hurt. Wright was "known to insult and humiliate injured workers with his tirades – 'You're a nuisance around here, why don't you quit?' is a pet line."[73] As in Detroit, foremen often telephoned sick and injured workers at home to cajole them back to work. Often the worker's wife answered the phone to be confronted by a foreman accusing her husband of malingering.[74]

Many workers experienced this type of treatment as a direct threat to their manhood. Recall one in-plant leaflet's bitter connection of supervisors run amok with the emasculation of the line worker: "Such supervisors must be proud to know they can whip a man who can't fight back."[75] Although some workers, like Cunningham, appreciated the directness of the old-line supervisors, it is clear that the combination of old-line management and the younger workers flooding the plant in the 1960s and 1970s spurred significant conflict.[76] Despite the fact that Chrysler promoted from within, hostility and distrust between hourly workers and their managers was so high that social ostracism was the penalty for those who traded in their union card for a supervisor's shirt and tie. According to Gray, workers employed an "intimidation factor" to remind their peers not to fraternize with foremen: "Supervision's supervision. We're the union." Gray claims that supervisors feared going back on the line: "You'd be treated like a traitor."[77] One *444 News* article discussed a prospective union-conducted trial where a supervisor was to be held accountable for alleged crimes against workers while part of management. If the tribunal deemed these offences serious enough, the former supervisor would be denied union membership and thus denied benefits and the union's protection.[78] This is an example of the maintenance of informal means of worker control in Windsor long after management had eviscerated many of these controls in Detroit. They also show workers enacting a reversal of the power of economic violence, as the

Local 444 workers use gallows humour to make a point. Photo courtesy of Unifor Local 444.

deprivation of a worker of his livelihood was traditionally the exclusive province of management.

Despite this social separation, workers and supervisors often encountered each other in the taverns of the small city of Windsor. The combination of alcohol, masculinity, and an informal atmosphere meant that shop floor tensions often spilled over into barroom brawls. The worker publication *Workers' Unity* recounted one such incident in its October 1970 issue:

> Recently at the Coronation House, a former employee of the 6-line in Plant 2 who had a taste of harassment from Huggard, now a 9841 Foreman, got additional harassment at his table. Huggard told him how useless he was when he worked for him. So this guy decked [Huggard] and his buddy who attempted to intervene – The union on many occasions has appealed to management to stop this guy from harassing people and this is the result![79]

The *444 News* warned workers to mind their conduct when encountering supervisors in the tavern. In 1969 it published a report on Engine Plant supervisor Bill Doherty:

> [He] has tried to humiliate and harass them in every way possible. Other foremen who have to work with this guy are disgusted as well, though they'll not admit it.
>
> This particular foreman (now dept. 9841) boozes regularly at a local bistro 'til closing time and works off his resultant hangover next day by intimidating and aggravating his employees on the job.
>
> His antics don't stop in the shop but continue on after working hours against his employees who strongly object to his presence being forced on them outside the shop. This sometimes encourages disastrous actions from the employees – on one occasion this individual encountered employees who sooner than accept his presence and threats just upset his chair and upset his brew, and tore his shirt.
>
> While under the influence, he'll pretend to be an all around good guy by promising employees he'll clear their record cards and such. But, when confronted with reality the next day, he refuses and denies his promises.

The paper cautioned, "Don't drink with him; don't talk to him outside the plant; if he bothers you outside, call the police; don't buy his phoney good guy make-up; don't do him any favours because he's only using you; pity this mental hang-up."[80]

Despite this advice, union officials were not always above their own tavern altercations with management personnel. Parent recalled one election-night party when the arrival of four Chrysler Labor Relations officers at the festivities triggered a brawl. What started the incident? "Them being there." No discipline was issued for the brawl, which was consistent with how these off-hours incidents were customarily handled.[81]

Worker-supervisor violence was not restricted to the bars. Workers occasionally assaulted supervisors in the plant as well. Both publications of the time and the present-day recollections of Chrysler workers give the impression workers believed that this type of violence was usually provoked by management conduct and that this violence was often justified. As the *444 News* wrote in 1963, "When you hear of workers breaking down and crying on the job, or being carried out sick, or being restrained from punching the foreman in the nose, you can't help but wonder what gets into a guy. Work is heaped on the backs of workers to the extent that he will do it."[82] In 1966 the paper wrote about "Georgie in the cushion dept. who stuck his nose in once too often and wound up in a pile of cushion springs. Sure, the worker was fired for allegedly driving him there, but every man in the dept. knows just how this foreman asks for trouble."[83]

An incident the following year involving a sixteen-year-old employee named Kelly provides a window on what provoked on-the-job violence toward supervisors, how the company handled these situations, and how the union understood this type of violence. The reports that appear in the union newspaper are not clear as to what sparked the fight, but it seems the carnival-like atmosphere of the Christmas season, a time when alcohol flowed freely inside and outside the plant, may have played a role:

> Twas the night before Christmas and the Union had asked the Company to close the plant and let the night shift out. No dice, was the answer, and so the spirit of - Peace on Earth - Goodwill to Men prevailed and little George in his red suit gave 16 year old Kelly the gate, but not until Bradt's usual foul tongue got in a few licks.
>
> Kelly was in the plant underaged and after being told he was fired he proceed[ed] to do what many of the other people in this area have said they felt like doing. Kelly swung at Bradt several times but never landed a blow.[84]

After his firing, Kelly moved to Prince Edward Island. Although he apparently never actually struck Bradt, the incident still qualified as an assault under civil law. Chrysler took the incident seriously enough to pay for police to go after the boy and bring him back to Ontario handcuffed to a detective. According to the union, the fracas was the fault of both sides, and two employees had to intervene to "prevent the white shirts from clobbering the boy. Both Shelley and Dupuis were discharged for their part in trying to break it up."[85]

The union's defence of Kelly included vociferous attacks on Bradt's character and supervisory ability. In its words, "Numerous complaints have been made to top management about the attitude of Mr. Bradt ever since he quit the union plant chairmanship and went on Supervision. Prior to that the Company complained about his attitude towards the Company when he was a Union Rep."[86] The union also alleged that Bradt had been driving his car recklessly near the plant without penalty. The charges were eventually dropped by Chrysler but not until Kelly had spent twelve days behind bars.

The union argued that workers' violence against supervisors was an understandable reaction to poor management and that it was incumbent on management not to risk the wrath of Windsor Chrysler workers:

> The company claims that they charged Kelly because their foremen are afraid of their lives when they leave the plant at night. The Union replied

> that of the hundreds of foremen there may be a few afraid and that is because they know they are rotten beyond the call of duty and could expect people to lose their tempers. If a foreman acts halfway decent with his men, he has nothing to fear.
>
> Corporation foremen have hit lads in the plant and could have been convicted of assault. The better part of wisdom told the Union to keep the matter within the Chrysler family and that's where it stayed. The new policy of the Corporation's leaves us no choice but to support charges laid by the members against violent foremen and bring them to trial.[87]

The union closed its assessment of the incident by cautioning members not to argue with foremen and to report any threats or violence by supervisors.

The testimony of workers also indicates that assaults on foremen were seen as justified under certain circumstances. Of the reaction to such incidents, Parent said, "if it was an asshole ... there would be a celebration. If it was a supervisor generally seen as a 'good guy that got smacked,' then there was another reaction, a different ballgame."[88] As the Kelly incident suggests, workers saw violence as a resource, a last resort that reined in out-of-control overseers in a way management would not or could not. Gray told the story of a particularly difficult supervisor he worked under while on the trim line in 1981. The supervisor, a "confrontational" person who read the hypermacho, survivalist *Soldier of Fortune* magazine on his breaks, repeatedly threatened Gray, saying, "You're a piece of shit ... I'm gonna fuck you up ... I'm gonna punch you in the head."[89]

In Gray's telling, after about a year of this treatment, he was ready to "blow up," so he secured a transfer to another part of the plant. Unfortunately for him, the supervisor was soon transferred into his new area. Gray warned his union representative that "something's going to happen, someone's going to hurt him." If the retaliation was not a physical assault, Gray thought, perhaps a disgruntled worker would slash the supervisor's tires, which was another way that workers struck back at unpopular foremen. Eventually, one workday when Gray was not in the plant, a confrontation erupted between the supervisor and Gray's work partner. The work partner seriously assaulted the supervisor with "fists and boots," and the supervisor was taken out of the plant on a stretcher and missed an extended period of time.

According to Gray, because the supervisor was the brother-in-law of a plant superintendent, he had a privileged position within Chrysler's corporate structure that insulated him from the type of company discipline that may have forestalled the attack: "Management knew he was a total jerk and didn't deal with it." Gray also said there was "no training for supervisors like there is now." Gray's work partner faced assault charges after the beating but won the case when the court considered the supervisor's provocations a mitigating factor. Although the incident was violent, Gray recalls that it was not surprising and was seen by many in the plant as the reaction that the supervisor's actions deserved. Gray concluded, "everybody saw it coming ... A lot of people felt good about what happened, about taking a beating as bad as he did."[90]

Sometimes, Gray recalled, workers struck back at supervisors in more creative ways. He recalled a story about three brothers who, in Gray's telling, were among Chrysler's most notorious supervisors, famed for tormenting workers verbally and plotting to have them fired or suspended. One worker painted murals throughout the Engine Plant, a project for which the company paid him in an effort to beautify the dirty conditions. He painted the glass doors of the brothers' office in a Western-style O.K. Corral motif, an image that emphasized masculinity and confrontation. The brothers would congregate in front of this backdrop. One day, they left their coffees unattended, and word went out up and down the lines to keep an eye on the brothers. Their coffee had been drugged, and "whether it was THC, windowpane, mescaline ... about twenty minutes later, they were flying high." The brothers were hospitalized. Police were called in to search workers' lockers, but no one was ever caught. One of the brothers stayed off work for an extended period of time, and another went to work at the General Motors Transmission Plant. According to Gray, even fellow supervisors, who believed that hardliners like the brothers made their own jobs more difficult, commented that the incident "looks good on those idiots."[91]

The union publications of the time show workers drawing on awareness that supervisory overreach could be met with retributive violence. Writers leveraged violence's rhetorical force, raising the spectre of physical assault to warn foremen to change their conduct. In 1970 an Engine Plant bulletin mentioned "one young supervisor on midnites, who is going into the bathrooms [at] the plant, trying to find someone sleeping or away from their work station. Perhaps Mr. Lebouefe should be on guard for barrels rolling down stairs when he makes his rounds of the washrooms."[92] In 1978 a Plant 3 bulletin warned,

> [There is] a particular general foreman who likes to go around bragging about the discipline he gives out and refers to the workers as F...Ups. My advice to this particular arrogant and ignorant parasite is that if you think

> that the metal shop brothers are going to continue to put up with your attitude then you are going to find yourself "TITS UP" [i.e., seriously injured or dead].[93]

One reason workers may have believed violence was justified in certain cases was that they saw violence as an effective tool that modified supervisory conduct in real and noticeable ways. Gray recalled a "remarkable" supervisor who treated him nicely. When he asked his co-workers why his supervisor was so nice, he was told that the man had been beaten up a few years earlier and had spent significant time outside the plant recuperating. When he came back from this trauma, his attitude toward his workers had changed.[94] Although rare, violence was the ultimate resource that workers in Windsor plants employed to retaliate or intervene against supervisors whom they felt had crossed a line.

This violence was not intended to overthrow the workplace power structure but was one of a variety of tactics that workers used to enforce accepted norms of behaviour, or what historian E.P. Thompson has called a "moral economy" of violence. In Windsor Chrysler plants, where, according to Monk, there was a "war being waged" over production rates, the length of the workday, and working conditions, workers employed several strategies to control supervisors, temporarily upset the hierarchy of the plant, gain an advantage, or simply blow off steam.[95] These tactics included direct action, such as sit-downs, walkouts, sabotage, and vandalism. These incidents were so common that Chrysler senior management sent letters to UAW Canada officials every few weeks detailing them. In 1971 alone, for example, sixty-eight incidents of sabotage, thirty-seven walkouts, and eighteen sit-downs at Chrysler Canada plants appeared in these reports, almost all of which caused work stoppages and the loss of production.[96]

At times, the distinction between workers employing direct on-the-job action and workers using violence and harassment against supervisors was blurred. For example, consider one slowdown in which Monk participated while working a job that involved inflating tires and then loading them onto an assembly line. The time-study men had set a target for the work that the workers found intolerable, so they employed slowdowns and harassment to maintain three workers on the job, not two, and to improve working conditions: "We used every considerable form of slowdown we could think of to prevent them making production with six men, let alone three. We tormented our foreman so much that he had a nervous breakdown and was removed from our department, and put on the night shift to recuperate."[97]

The dispute came to a head when Monk and his coworkers initiated a sit-down, which was supported by workers from other parts of the plant. Chrysler made the improvements that the group had demanded.[98]

Monk and his co-workers were not the only ones employing psychological warfare. During one campaign of harassment in the chassis division, workers broke into a foreman's office, removed his record cards, poured glue on his files, and removed his schedule sheets "for the third time in one shift." Less than one month later, the power-tools locker was found jammed with a piece of wood. The door had to be forced and the lock replaced. Eight days afterward, the wires of the area's public address system were cut, something that had been done several times already: "To this date this calendar year the cost of repairs to the system has been $5,000."[99] Some workers went a step further and attacked their supervisor's personal property. During a midnight shift at the Windsor Assembly Plant in March 1973, the general foreman of the maintenance division learned that his leased car "had been sprayed with a white spray bomb on the right side (fenders, doors, quarter panels, tires, and both rear tail lights). Also, there were derogatory statements on the door."[100]

Violence among co-workers and toward supervisors, then, was one tool among many that these workers employed to defend their prerogatives as workingmen. As was the case at Dodge Main, violence at work in Windsor Chrysler plants was not aberrant, bizarre, or senseless. It was just the opposite: in both Detroit and Windsor plants, violence was built into labour processes, workplace practices, and the shop floor culture. There were two major differences between Dodge Main and Windsor Chrysler plants with respect to violence: first, individual violence occurred more sparingly in Windsor, being an extreme resource that workers occasionally used either rhetorically or actually, whereas violence at Dodge Main rose to endemic levels; and second, the severity of individual violence was greater in Detroit plants, with stabbings and shootings occurring far more often. Violence in Windsor occurred in a confrontational but functional plant, whereas violence at Dodge Main occurred in the context of a plant plagued by Chrysler's economic pressures, racism, the collapse of the UAW's racial liberalism, and Detroit's urban crisis. This distinction underlines just how crucial racism and the national context were to the situation in the two cities and in their plants – and thus to the corresponding levels of violence at work that occurred in each.

At work, Windsor workers faced less violence from the labour process. Although workers were injured and killed on the job in Windsor, working conditions were safer than in Detroit's decrepit, dysfunctional Chrysler plants. Different labour relations and industry dynamics, especially after the Auto Pact came into effect, headed off the worst management excesses that were seen in Detroit during the same period, enabled the union to take a stronger, more confrontational approach with Chrysler Canada management, and provided a measure of plant-level job security unknown in Detroit. The Auto Pact kept capital, jobs, and production in Windsor and revitalized Local 444, a more militant and democratic organization than Local 3. The provisions of Canadian contracts and the drive for parity with the United States encouraged the union to be aggressive in improving plant conditions, and thus Windsor workers had a union better able to maintain standards on the floor and to act as a vehicle for collective struggle. Unlike Local 3, Local 444 managed to incorporate, not crush, dissident challenges and was much more effective at resolving on-the-job conflict. The widespread disillusionment with an ineffective union that legitimated individual violence in Detroit was thus muted in Windsor. Meanwhile, the city thrived on the continued presence of the automakers and on the well-paid working-class jobs of autoworkers.

Although the national context bolstered the position of the mostly white Windsor Chrysler workers and their union, they were also largely insulated from the coruscating racialized struggles that drove the crisis ravaging the black and white workers of Detroit, its Chrysler plants, and the UAW during the same era. Racism and inequality produced the white flight that took place in Detroit in the 1950s and 1960s, which was exacerbated by the uprising of African American Detroiters in 1967 against decades of racialized underdevelopment, overcrowding, and police brutality. Structural racism and the struggles against it were other key reasons why levels of violence were higher in Detroit plants. Although there was certainly racism inside Windsor plants, race was far less of a dividing issue, and the labour process was not heavily racialized, which in part reflected the racial exclusion practised in hiring.[101] Nationalism, conversely, acted as a unifying factor for workers in their struggles with the company, government, and UAW International.

All of these factors combined to make the lives of Windsor Chrysler workers, spared the crises of a city in revolt and a collapsing industrial order, generally much safer and saner than the lives of their counterparts across the river. Windsor Chrysler factories boiled with rough masculinity and class conflict but were functional and responsive to worker action in a way that Detroit Chrysler factories were not. Violence in Windsor was part of a system of understood roles and practices, a system that endured largely intact until the late 1970s. Workers remained insiders much longer at Windsor, thanks to whiteness, nationalism, and economics, which forestalled the outsider violence that sprang from the brutalization and disenfranchisement of workers at Dodge Main. Comparing the Chrysler plants of Windsor and Detroit underlines that violence at work was not simply the product of individual conflicts and choices but also a phenomenon influenced by structural factors that were industrial, local, and national.

4

The Constant Companion of All That Earn Their Living Here

Workers, Unions, and Management Respond

Willie Brookins was hungry. On the night of September 7, 1967, Brookins, a stock checker with seventeen years seniority at Dodge Main, walked up to the plant gate at the end of his lunch break. He carried a paper bag. He showed the bag's contents to the plant guard stationed at the gate – two hot sausages, purchased at a nearby deli – and passed through.

As Brookins continued walking to his spot on the assembly line, a second guard demanded Brookins show him the bag, hinting that perhaps it contained a bomb. Brookins ignored the guard and got on an elevator. The second guard followed Brookins onto the elevator. When Brookins got off on the third floor, so did the second guard. He watched Brookins work for a while and then phoned for the captain of the plant guards.

When the captain arrived, an altercation broke out between Brookins and the two guards. One guard allegedly dumped Brookins's meal and stomped it into the factory floor. According to another source, Brookins hit the captain in the arm with a pair of wire cutters and punched him in the face with his fist. The plant guards retreated and called the Hamtramck police to arrest Brookins.

When the officers arrived, "they were greeted by a hail of washers, bolts and nuts and catcalls thrown at them by the workers on the line." Instead of being arrested, Brookins was taken to the Labor Relations office before being sent home.[1]

Four days later, Brookins was called back into the plant and fired. In addition to the industrial discipline, Brookins was charged with felonious assault and arrested. He paid a $500 bond to secure his release. If convicted, the married father of four faced up to five years in prison. The assault charge also made Brookins ineligible to collect state unemployment insurance.[2]

The Dodge Revolutionary Union Movement (DRUM) alleged, in a feature story of the very first issue of its newsletter, that Local 3 had abandoned Brookins, claiming that his steward now chided him for "making it hard for all of us" and that Local 3's black vice-president, Andy Hardy, had told Brookins, "you should not have gotten a black lawyer to handle your case." DRUM's implied message was that the union was punishing Brookins for having challenged the racial hierarchy of the plant. "Damn the grievance procedure," spat a *DRUM* article on the Brookins case. The headline atop the story asked black workers, "Will You Be Next?" A year later, after two criminal trials, Brookins had been found not guilty of assault but had not been reinstated to his job.[3]

High-ranking officials of the United Automobile Workers (UAW) had not forgotten Brookins's case either. UAW staffer Tony Conole wrote to Chrysler's UAW department head Doug Fraser in October 1968, noting Brookins's acquittal and discussing whether the UAW should pursue his grievance again. Conole warned that the Brookins incident "was one of the sensitive areas utilized by DRUM for propaganda purposes" and that reopening it "might give them another opportunity to propagandize on the matter."[4] The UAW declined to file a second grievance on Brookins's behalf.

Willie Brookins's case indicates that some incidents of workplace violence echoed long after the particular fight or attack was quelled, prompting responses and critiques from workers, unionists, and management. When Brookins clashed with the plant guards, rank-and-file workers employed direct action and anti-authoritarian violence in support of a co-worker. Radical workers seized on the incident to excoriate Chrysler and the UAW. Local 3 and the UAW, caught between grieving on behalf of a fired worker and combatting radicals, sought to maintain their legitimacy as the only vehicle for autoworkers' struggles. Chrysler used the police and courts to subdue a violent worker and send an example to others, while also making changes that it hoped would prevent similar incidents, such as adding more black foremen and stepping up its hiring of the so-called "hard-core unemployed" of Detroit's inner-city neighbourhoods. Workplace violence did not fizzle up and fade away. It was not simply the culmination of a conflict. It had an influence on the culture and politics of the plant.

Here, I explore this influence by looking at the responses to individual violence at work. There are two important points to note when considering what was done about violence. First, as the opening section of this chapter shows, plant-level responses – the practices of security, discipline, grievance, and returning offenders to work – failed to seriously reduce levels of in-plant violence. Second, because of this failure, violence remained a significant part of workplace culture. Therefore, violence on the job, whose very definition was contested, shaped the outlook of those struggling to control these workplaces, as examining the diary of a union president, the leaflets of radical autoworkers, and the initiatives of automakers demonstrates. Workplace violence was more than just a product of tensions on the job or crime in the plant. It was also a productive force in its own right, a dynamic affecting the consciousness of individuals and groups that influenced their strategies and actions.

I begin by looking at primary responses. How did the company and the union deal with incidents of violence and with workers accused of committing a violent act? These acts were expressly banned by Chrysler policy. The 1960 company-issued "Guide to Good Conduct for Chrysler Employees" states, "Certain ... acts of misconduct are considered sufficiently serious to warrant no less than an immediate suspension and disciplinary layoff (Example: Fighting)." The "Acts of Misconduct" include several different forms of violence: "inflicting grievous bodily injury upon any other employee or any person," "assaulting any member of supervision," "fighting," and "threatening, intimidating, or coercing supervision or employee," in addition to proscriptions against abusive conduct toward supervisors and horseplay.[5] In both Detroit and Windsor, Chrysler employed a range of frontline responses to violent incidents, including suspensions, discharges, and police involvement. These situations were often resolved with company discipline and the union's defence of a disciplined worker, both of which are detailed in grievance records.[6]

At Dodge Main, Chrysler's Plant Protection staff, sometimes reinforced by Hamtramck police, was the primary third-party respondent to workplace violence. Guards snuffed out violent incidents and escorted workers to the Labor Relations office or off of plant property entirely, sometimes into the custody of the police. However, this system often created conflict and violence rather than preventing it. For example, at Dodge Main most guards were white, and the workforce they oversaw was largely black. This was a sore point with radical workers, who saw it as evidence of the "plantation" system in which they worked.[7] Among DRUM's formal demands, for instance, were that 50 percent of all guards be black and that "every time a black worker is removed from plant premises ... he be led by a black brother."[8] Mainstream unionists echoed this point. Alonzo Newkirk, Willie Brookins's shop steward, protested to Local 3 president Ed Liska in 1969 that "white plant protection men should not be called when black workers are in trouble because it provokes an incident. Officers should talk to management about having black men come to take a black man out."[9]

After a violent situation was suppressed, Chrysler discipline would follow, usually taking the form of a suspension or a firing. The union would grieve virtually any discipline meted out to a worker accused of a violent incident, no matter how severe. The outcome of grievances filed by workers accused of violent incidents varied.[10] The success of a grievance depended on the strength of management's case, the level of provocation of the violent incident, and the griever's work record and character, as perceived by management and the union. Political horse trading between Local 3 and Chrysler management was also a factor in the resolution of grievances. As discussed in Chapter 2, during the 1960s, a formal grievance system superseded older, informal methods of conflict resolution that were rooted in workers' power to slow or halt production. With that power greatly diminished, union representatives had less authority with management. They now resorted to "pleading a case" instead of "bargaining by threat," according to Liska. To resolve one matter in a worker's favour, then, a union representative would often have to acquiesce to the company's wishes in another matter.[11] All of this meant that a worker might be reinstated or permanently dismissed after being accused of a horrific incident of violence.

Although the final outcomes of grievances could vary greatly, Chrysler's policy was to fire the aggressor in a fight; this is similar to the practice observed by Joan Sangster in the Ontario arbitration cases she examined.[12] There is also evidence that incidents involving a weapon were treated more seriously. Clyde Coulter, for example, was fired after allegedly stabbing a co-worker several times during an argument and then fleeing the plant. The union concluded that the facts did not warrant pursuing his grievance beyond the initial stage. When workers Burns and Shelton came to blows, both were discharged. Burns was returned to work, but Shelton, who threatened Burns with a knife, was not.[13]

Although the handling of violent incidents varied, the overall effect was that many workers accused of serious violence were returned to work, and thus the company and the union made no real progress in making the workplace safer. In 1972, as mentioned in the previous chapter, a supervisor asked Dodge Main worker T. Felder why he kept falling behind on the line. Felder allegedly "told the supervisor to stop f-----g with him and struck the supervisor with his fist on the back of the head and the middle of the back. After again telling the supervisor not to f--- with him employee Felder struck the supervisor a third time."[14] Despite the severity of the incident, Felder was returned, with the loss of his seniority being the only penalty.

Often, grievances arising from discipline for violent incidents were resolved through less formal channels. "Will talk to him" or "will interview" are common handwritten notes on grievance records. Rome Kinderick's discharge grievance was resolved with a combination of these informal methods, Alcoholics Anonymous, and counselling. In 1971 Kinderick, a man with over twenty-five years seniority at the plant, allegedly approached a female co-worker "and became abusive and directed derogatory remarks toward this female employee and threatened to kill her." Kinderick's record featured many previous discharges, but the grievance file was marked "this man should be talked to" by Local 3 staff, along with the recommendation of "COUNSEL AND AA."[15] Other workers were also occasionally referred to Alcoholics Anonymous or the Greater Detroit Council on Alcoholism. However, most employees who were returned to work after being disciplined for violence were simply put back on to the job with no more than a warning to improve their behaviour.

Workers accused of serious incidents often ended up in court, as Willie Brookins did. In 1963 E. Mattson was discharged "because of a drinking problem and a fracas with the Chief of Plant Protection. Mattson threatened the Plant Protection man with a knife. He was taken to a civil court and charged with assault and battery and was found guilty."[16] George Dowd was fired and returned to work several times, but he was finally discharged permanently after being found guilty in court for threatening a Labor Relations director. Even after the conviction, Liska tried to get him back to work at Dodge Main, but the the director, William Prokopy, was "not budging" because there had been "too many threats in the past. Prokopy said that he had his home guarded all night by police who circled the house all the time after George Dowd threatened over the phone to kill him."[17] The incident shows just how far Local 3 would go in some cases to return workers to the plant. It also provides evidence of the impact of workplace violence on the lives of Chrysler managers and how seriously they, and the police, viewed it.

Many workers accused of violence, however, were simply returned to work in the same plant. Liska's diary discusses Tiny, a worker at Dodge Main who "LAST WEEK BEAT UP A GOOD MAN AND IT TOOK 5 MEN TO TAKE TINY OFF THE GUY, HE WOULD HAVE KILLED HIM. YET NOTHING WAS DONE, EVERYONE COVERED FOR TINY."[18] Instead of being fired, Tiny was moved into a different area, an action that co-workers and DRUM still protested. No further discipline appears to have been imposed.

Foremen accused of violence toward workers were also regularly returned to work, a practice that radicals repeatedly condemned. *Dodge Workers Speak* ran an article titled, "Is It Chrysler Policy to Have Mad-Dog Foremen?" The article explained, "Another foreman pulled a knife on a worker. The foreman and the worker were both suspended. But the foreman wasn't really suspended, he was just transferred. He went to 9190. Then he turned up working in the employment office. Now he's crawling around somewhere else."[19] A subsequent issue of this newsletter discussed the case of another foreman:

> [He] was sent to Dodge Main because he was in a fight at another Chrysler plant. He was then sent to Dodge Main on day shift. He was involved in a fight on days and pulled a knife on a man.
>
> When he became a foreman at Dodge on night shift (he was transferred to nights for fighting), his first group walked out on him for his mad-dog tactics, causing line one to shut down that day.
>
> In his next group, he got into a fight with a woman employee. In Feb. this year, he got into a fight with a repairman. He tried to hit him in the head with a couple of seat belt motors. Then he tried to hit the repairman in the head with a 2 by 4 plank, which Labor Relations took from him.
>
> The repairman was fired but the foreman never missed a day. He was shipped to 9190 the next day and was sent home because his presence was causing agitation. He was then sent back to Foreman Training for the second time. Then he was put in the employment office at Dodge on days. No one wanted him around there. Now he is back on second shift, fourth floor, 9150, where he is bound to start more trouble.[20]

In 1968 the radical black newspaper *Inner City Voice* reported that a white foreman at Dodge Main threw a welding gun at a black worker, who then assaulted the foreman. Both were suspended five days, but the foreman was back at work the next day, prompting workers to walk out in protest.[21]

Many workers and foremen returned to work after being accused of serious violence, but the underlying factors that sparked the violence remained unaddressed. This situation contributed to the prevalence of violence and dysfunction in Detroit plants. For example, a *Time* magazine article about violence at Dodge Main claimed, "union officers insist that the fear spread by such incidents has damaged plant discipline because foremen shut their eyes to infractions rather than risk personal attack."[22] Many foremen carried guns on the floor, either for protection or to intimidate their workers. Some Chrysler personnel even insisted that a foreman had a right to pre-emptively assault employees. Discussing a foreman who threatened a worker with an iron bar, Labor Relations representative Carl Paulsgrove asserted, "Any Foreman or Supervisor has a right to defend himself against any employee, and even attack the employee if necessary if in the supervisor's judgment the employee is a threat to him."[23] For frontline managers, like workers, the absence of effective collective solutions to day-to-day violence encouraged more individual violence.

In Windsor's more functional plants, violence was a less urgent concern. However, it was certainly an acknowledged part of shop floor power relations and workplace culture, as shown in Chapter 3. In Windsor, workers fired for fighting usually got their jobs back, albeit often after an extended period off work. Even when workers hit foremen, Local 444 could usually return them to the plant, although it took six months to a year on average. Whereas workers fired for violence sometimes got their jobs back, Parent stated workers fired for theft were never rehired. This variance suggests that theft was beyond the pale of shop floor morality but violence was not. Perhaps theft, a furtive activity that directly injured company profits, was viewed as irredeemable, whereas the culture of the plants rendered violence an understandable, "boys will be boys" offence.[24]

In both Windsor and Detroit, frontline responses to workplace violence reinforced existing dynamics. In both cases, workers accused of violent incidents were often returned to work. There was no larger plan to resolve conflicts and reduce violence beyond the grinding, adversarial mechanism of the grievance process. In Windsor responses to violence underlined violence's understood place in work culture as an occasional "part of the job," if not one to be officially encouraged. In Detroit the effectiveness of the union at reinstating workers accused of violence, combined with the lack of meaningful action from all parties in creating a safer, saner work environment, made Detroit Chrysler factories iron cages that locked violence in instead of keeping it out.

UAW dissident Jordon Sims, later a UAW leader at Local 961, eloquently described the miasma created by the ongoing violence in Detroit Chrysler plants: "On all shifts and in all the departments and among all of our people, this same feeling of apprehension, uncertainty, distrust, and fear are the constant companion of all that earn their living here."[25] Sims was writing about work at Chrysler's Eldon Axle Plant, but he could just as easily have been describing Dodge Main. Liska's diary chronicling his workdays during the critical years 1968–70 is suffused with stories of violence in the plant, at the union hall, and on the streets. It shows the serious challenges that in-plant violence posed for him as the president of Local 3 and how this violence influenced his outlook. It also shows that violence was simultaneously immediate and distant for Liska, who dealt with threats of violence both in his office and at hotel conventions but was shielded from the day-to-day violence of the plant by his position as a union leader and by the bureaucratic procedures that Chrysler and the UAW had put in place to manage class conflict. Thus Liska was affected by violence but poorly situated to see what was causing it, namely an exploitative labour process and conflict born of company and union racism. Liska's response, guided by his conflation of militancy, race, crime, and violence, was a reactionary administration that prioritized order over addressing the issues responsible for Dodge Main's discontent.

Liska was elected president in 1968, as the white leader of a unity slate that included black unionists on the Local 3 executive in exchange for their delivery of the votes of black workers. As president, Liska spent much of his time responding to violent incidents. In June 1969, for example, he had to deal with the case of Steve Barry, a worker fired after he threatened foremen and flashed a knife. There was also a report that a group of workers were going to physically attack an abusive supervisor unless he was transferred out of the department. The next month, Liska was confronted by the cases of a woman threatening a man's life over an alleged theft, Barry pointing a gun at a foreman, a foundry employee shooting five policemen one weekend, and an incident of racial abuse that could have led to a shooting. In his diary, Liska concluded, "Explosive situations going on."[26]

One of the most combustible elements in the Dodge Main mix was in-plant racism. Racial tension was rampant at the plant when Liska took office, and DRUM became a force at the plant just as Liska became president. In August 1969 he was called upon to respond to an incident in which general foreman Ed Sowa allegedly called worker William Lewis a "black motherfucker." This same month was marked by assaults on management members by DRUM activists Rushie Forge and Chuck Wooten. As previously discussed, neither racism nor DRUM was the sole factor producing violence in the plant. But as a white unionist leading a mostly black membership and challenged both by in-plant violence and by radical Black Power insurgents, Liska saw the situation in simplistically racial terms.[27]

Thus DRUM and black violence became inseparable in Liska's thinking. Among his first diary entries was a report on key DRUM leaders that was particularly concerned with their possible connections to violence. Whereas Liska recorded almost nothing about DRUM's program or its critiques of Chrysler and the UAW, he repeatedly noted links between DRUM and violence. The month after the Forge and Wooten incidents, Liska wrote about DRUM member Sidney Lewis beating up a supervisor and putting him in the hospital. When confronted by DRUM's radical challenge, Liska was primarily concerned with repressing its violent potential. Therefore, he focused on maintaining order rather than responding to DRUM's critique by implementing needed reforms.

Incidents of racialized violence at Dodge Main that escalated into major disturbances fuelled Liska's fears. In September 1969 an argument between a black worker and a plant nurse turned into a violent brawl in which workers threw heavy automobile wheels at Plant Protection men, and Hamtramck police were called in. From this "Near Racial Riot," as he called it in his diary, Liska concluded that "MANAGEMENT MUST HIRE NEGRO PLANT PROTECTION MEN. AT PRESENT THEY ONLY HAVE A FEW ON THE STAFF."[28] When a similar incident occurred just two months later, Liska feared that this was no spontaneous eruption but a coordinated action by the plant's black workers. Liska recorded a report he received about the incident, from someone named Jerry Selke:

> A YOUNG BLACK MAN HAD A PROBLEM WITH A WHITE SKILL MAN. ABOUT 2 AM, HE WENT INTO THE WASHROOM AND HIT THE SKILL MAN IN THE FACE. THE BLACK MAN WAS TAKEN TO THE OFFICE AND DISCHARGED. HE WAS TAKEN TO THE PLANT PROTECTION OFFICE AND HE WAS QUITE [sic] BUT PLAYED A DELAYING GAME. HE WANTED TO TALK AND KEPT LOOKING AT HIS WATCH. NEAR 3 AM THE POLICE WERE CALLED AND WHEN IT WAS 3 AM HE WENT WITH THE POLICE. THIS IS THE TIME THE PLANT SECOND SHIFT END THEIR WORK AND WERE COMING OUT, THIS BLACK MAN WITH THE TWO POLICEMEN ON HIS SIDE THEN BEGAN TO SCREAM "POLICE BRUTALITY ETC." WITHIN SECONDS OTHERS [sic] BLACKS JONED [sic] IN AND HIT THE POLICEMEN AND DAMAGED THE CAR. OTHER BLACKS

IN THE PLANT ON UPPER FLOOR THREW OBJECTS AT THE CAR, DAMAGING IT SO [sic] MORE. MORE POLICE WERE CALLED AND THEY HAD TO USE MAIZE [sic] IN ORDER TO BRING THINGS UNDER CONTROL. THE MAN WAS TAKEN TO THE POLICE STATION.[29]

Liska feared Dodge Main was about to be consumed by a race war. He quoted a fellow unionist's account of the riot: "200 young blacks at the urging of about six blacks converged on the Police and had intents of killing them. They acted like madmen."[30] He soon wrote that "MANAGEMENT OUGHT TO MAKE UP THEIR MINDS TO TAKE THEM [BLACK MILITANTS] ON NOW AND SHOW THEY WILL NOT BUCKLE UNDER PRESSURE. BUCKLING UNDER MILITANT THINKING WILL HURT OR BRING DOWN THE SYSTEM IN WHICH OUR COUNTRY PROSPERS."[31] Even the moderate black unionists in Liska's coalition were viewed in a new light. Liska groused, "THE UNITED MEMBERSHIP BLACKS HAVE SHOWN THEIR TRUE FEELINGS AFTER YEARS OF APPEARING LOYAL."[32] These unionists were being pushed by DRUM and black workers to demonstrate more forceful initiative in solving plant problems, especially racism. The challenge Liska faced was put to him bluntly in February 1970: "BLACKS STATED WE HAVE BEEN ALLOTTED WHAT THE WHITES GAVE US IN THE PAST, NOW WE ARE TELLING YOU WHAT WE WANT."[33]

Race and violence were consistently paired in Liska's thinking. When discussing violent incidents, he invariably considered the race of the people involved. In September 1969 he noted,

TWO SKILL PEOPLE IN THE ASSEMBLY PLANT HAD A VICIOUS FIGHT NEAR THE TUNNEL ON SATURDAY NIGHT. IT IS SAID THAT ONE SKILL MAN CUT UP THE TIRES OF THE OTHER MAN AND HE FOUND OUT AND SEEKED [sic] HIM OUT AND SOME CHAINS WERE USED IN THE VICIOUS FIGHT (BOTH WHITE MEN). THE MAN WHO DID THE BEATING JUST CAME OFF SUPERVISION.[34]

When discussing a worker arming himself, Liska again considered the situation in terms of race:

A FELLOW FROM TRIM SHOP CAME BY SAYING HE WAS INVOLVED IN A FIGHT WITH A YOUNG BLACK MAN AND THAT IT WAS A

> BLOODY MESS. HE WAS HIT IN THE EYE AND HE HIT BACK. IRONS WERE TOSSED AROUND BEFORE THINGS COOLED DOWN. BOTH MEN ARE FIRED. THIS WHITE MAN HAS 18 YEARS OF SENIORITY. IN THE LOCAL HALL WHILE TALKING TO THE PRESIDENT, A LARGE PISTOL WAS OBSERVED ALONGISDE [sic] HIS RIGHT BELT LINE. HE SAID THE GUN IS FOR HIS OWN PROTECTION. "I AIN'T GOING TO TAKE NUTHIN FROM ANYBODY ETC."[35]

Incidents like this one were understood by Liska as evidence that white workers were under siege by black aggression. In August 1970 he wrote about talking to a suspended young white worker: "AFTER TALKING TO HIM AND CHECKING OUT THE STORY, IT HAS A THEME [ABOUT] WHAT IS GOING ON IN THE PLANT." According to the worker, he and a black co-worker had been arguing constantly on the shop floor. One day, "THE BLACK MAN ASKED HIM TO COME TO HIS CAR, AFTER WORK, HE HAD A PISTOL AND AIMED IT AT THE WHITE MAN, WHO SOMEHOW DIDN'T SHOW ANY FEAR TO THE BLACK MAN EVEN WHEN HE DISPLAYED THE GUN." The white man began carrying a gun of his own. Liska continued,

> LAST WEEK, WHILE ARGUING IN A PLAYFUL MOOD ACCORDING TO HIM, AT THE TIME CARD AT QUITTING TIME, BOTH MEN WRESTLED AND THE WHITE MAN ACCORDING TO WITNESSES PULLED OUT A GUN AND FIRED THREE TIMES AT THE BLACK MAN, MISSING HIM. WHEN THINGS COOLED DOWN, AND THE MAN [WAS] BROUGHT TO THE OFFICE, HE WAS SEARCHED BUT THE GUN WAS NOT FOUND.

Management suspended the white worker, and according to the plant committee, he risked losing his job, as it was believed that black workers would refuse to work with him. To Liska, this was another case of white workers being unfairly penalized for defending themselves in the face of black aggression: "THIS IS AN ODD CASE BECAUSE THE MAN ACTUALLY SEEMS TO BE A QUIET TYPE OF PERSON WHO BROUGHT THE GUN FOR PROTECTION AND LOST HIS JOB. WHILE THE OTHER MAN WHO SEEMS TO BE THE CULPRIT OF PICKING ON HIM AND OTHER WHITES ALSO HAVING A GUN ON PERSON GOES SCOTT [sic] FREE."[36]

Liska's opinion of the situation may have changed after the fired white worker violently confronted him at the union office. The man claimed he had no gun, despite ten witnesses saying he passed his gun to an accomplice after the shooting and three shells being found at the scene. He became "BELLIGERENT," complaining that blacks got away with everything and boasting that there was no way he had fired at the man, for he would have killed him if he had. Before he left, he "KEPT RAVING ABOUT KILLING" and made threats to the union, warning "THIS IS THE LAST TIME I AM COMING TO SEE YOU TWO ABOUT MY JOB."[37]

Liska was right, of course, to see racial tensions as a crucial part of the violence at Dodge Main. But he was unable or unwilling to understand the reasons why black workers were so frustrated with their workplace and their union. Without this understanding, Liska assumed that black pathology and criminality were primarily to blame, failing to distinguish meaningfully between parking-lot robberies, worker frustrations, and radical organizing. He ignored the principal factors causing violence, such as speedups and structural racism. He saw crime but did not comprehend the reasons and, worse, conflated crime with workplace unrest. He devoted little energy to improving working conditions, tackling racism in the plant, or creating unity among black and white workers. To Liska, black workers were a group that Andy Hardy, Local 3's black vice-president, was supposed to deliver to his coalition. Beyond that, he had little sympathy or understanding for their situation at Dodge Main. Steve Jefferys assesses Liska, a man who idolized union leader Walter Reuther and former US president Franklin Roosevelt, as someone whose "self-congratulation" and "complacency" about the UAW's race problem were "unacceptable to many hundreds of black workers whose outside political experiences were teaching them to stop requesting civil rights and to start fighting." When they did begin fighting back, Liska responded with suspicion and fear.[38] Rather than alerting him to the underlying problems of speedup, racism, and poor working conditions, in-plant violence fostered a siege mentality in Liska.

It is understandable that Liska saw crime as a major issue. Reading his diaries provides a visceral sense of how the concerns about crime that gripped the city in the late 1960s and beyond instilled fear and despair in Detroiters. Liska often wrote of people he knew from Local 3 falling victim to crime:

> ONE FELLOW FROM THE BODY SHOP CAME OVER REQUESTING SOME BLOOD FOR HIS BROTHER WHO ALSO WORKS IN THE BODY

> SHOP. WATSON A GRINDER WAS SHOT LAST WEEK WHILE GETTING HIS AUTO READY TO GO TO WORK EARLY IN THE MORNING. THE WHO WHO [sic] HIM USED A LARGE CALIBER GUN AND THE BULLET WENT INSIDE OF HIS CHEST HIS [sic]SOME VITAL ORGANS. HE IS FIGHTING FOR HIS LIFE AND NEEDS A LOT OF BLOOD.[39]

Another worker named Bernice "WON A RAFFLE GOT HER PAYCHECK AND WENT HOME EARLY. SHE WAS ATTACKED ON THE STREET AND BEATEN UP BADLY AND THE MONEY TAKEN AWAY FROM HER."[40] The murder of A. Busch must have been particularly disturbing for Liska. Just before his death, Busch visited the local and had a pleasant chat with the president:

> HE WAS IN FINE HEALTH AND JOVAL [sic] MOOD. HE TALKED ABOUT HIS BOAT AND WAS AWAITING TO GO FISHING AS SOON AS THE ICE MELTED. HE WAS AN AVID FISHERMAN.
>
> ON WEDNESDAY TUESDAY EVENING HE WAS SLAIN IN AN ATTEMPTED HOLDUP OF A TAVERN. SHOCKING THE WAY THINGS ARE GOING.[41]

In September 1970 Liska wrote of a worker at the nearby Huber Foundry who went out for lunch and, while standing by the parking lot, was shot twice. The man, a worker with over twenty years seniority, died the next day. The incident prompted Liska to recall another murdered worker:

> ABOUT A YEAR AGO, A PAINT SHOP WORKER WAS THE FIRST TO LEAVE THE PLANT AND RAN TO HIS AUTO WHICH WAS PARKED ON THE COMPANY LOT. INVESTIGATIONS REVEAL, HE WAS STOPPED BY A COUPLE OF MEN WHO ROBBED HIM OF HIS MONEY AND HIS THROAT WAS CUT. HIS BODY WAS FOUND SUNDAY AFTER INQUIRIES FROM HIS WIFE WHO CALLED POLICE THAT HER HUSBAND DID NOT RETURN FROM WORK ON FRIDAY. HIS BODY WAS FOUND IN THE CAR LYING ACROSS THE FRONT SEAT AND HIS THROAT CUT.[42]

The frequent robberies and homicides that took place in the plant parking lot led Liska to think of it as a "BATTLE GROUND."[43]

Workplace violence did not happen only to friends or fellow members. Liska was also affected by his own direct experience of danger. In the course of his workday at the Local 3 hall, workers upset over a firing or suspension often threatened Liska, either in person or over the phone. Some of these workers were carrying guns. One day in 1971, Liska pretended to have a gun in his pocket to disperse a group of "TEN ANGRY YOUNG BLACKS" who had gathered in his office to seek retroactive pay. He wrote, "OFFICERS FELT LIKE SITTING DUCKS. WE MUST DO SOMETHING TO PROTECT THE LOCAL OFFICERS AND STAFF IN THE FUTURE."[44] Guns were so prevalent that at a membership meeting the year before, Liska scanned the group to see who was packing heat: "GUNS AT THE MEETING WERE IDENTIFIED BY THE FOLLOWING MEN WHO TOTED THEM POSITIVELY: ANDY HARDY, VP. JOHN SMITH PLT COMM, WILLIS MARSHALL ANTI ADMINISTRATION, ALBERT DAWKINS ANTI EVERYTHING."[45] Even at a UAW convention in Atlantic City, Liska found himself at gunpoint, the gun held by a Dodge Main skilled trades delegate looking for money. When Liska related this story to another delegate, the man reached into his suitcase and offered Liska a gun of his own.[46]

Indeed, violence and militancy were major concerns for Liska and other UAW officials. At a fractious 1970 meeting where UAW officials discussed these issues, Liska stated, "IF BEATING THE HELL OUT OF SDS [STUDENTS FOR A DEMOCRATIC SOCIETY] IS WHAT MUST BE DONE, WE MAY HAVE TO DO IT." It is unclear why Liska referred to this group, as there is no indication that they were organizing at the plant, so perhaps Liska simply misidentified where dissent was coming from. UAW Region 1 head George Merrelli stated his concern about "Local Officers Being threatened so much." Another attendee, Gordie Buchanan, asked, "What do we do if someone gets violent and before the cops come one of us gets killed, it's too late to wait for the cops."[47] Buchanan then asked a UAW lawyer about carrying a gun. As Liska concluded about the work of his stewards, "IT IS A TOUGH DANGEROUS JOB TO REPRESENT PEOPLE TODAY IN THIS PLANT."[48] Basic safety became a serious issue, diverting time and energy from representing workers and pressing the company.

Instead of considering the larger causes of these dangers, Liska's leadership was reactive. Maintaining order dominated his agenda. There were few new initiatives, nor was there sustained pressure on Chrysler, to address safety, speedup, racism, or harassment. Summing up his first term in office, Liska wrote, "THE PAST TWO YEARS WERE PROBABLY THE MOST TURBULENT IN OUR LOCAL #3 HISTORY. PROBLEMS OF A NEW

NATURE DEVELOPED DURING THE PAST TWO YEARS WHICH THREATENED THE EXISTENCE OF THE ASSEMBLY PLANT."[49] His listed record of accomplishments consisted of little more than restoring financial security to the local and winning a few more grievances. No progress was made on working conditions, speedup, job security, racism, or sexism; violence and racial militancy occupied and preoccupied Local 3's president.

Even his claim to have restored financial health to Local 3 was strongly contested: the title of the DRUM documentary *Finally Got the News,* produced in association with the League of Revolutionary Black Workers, is a reference to DRUM's accusation that Local 3 dues money was being surreptitiously funnelled to the Hamtramck Police Department to cover its payroll shortfall. This department was the same one that had harassed and assaulted DRUM members during their election campaigns against the incumbent Local 3 administration headed by Liska. In his diary notes, Liska called the Hamtramck police "SAVIORS OF LOCAL #3. THEY ARE CLOSE AND ALWAYS GAVE THE DRUM GUYS TROUBLE. THEY CAN BE COUNTED UPON TO DO A JOB IF NEEDED."[50] Workplace violence, in-plant radicalism, and crime prompted Liska to view safety, security, and order as his highest priorities. His solution was to seek a closer working relationship with those he thought could help to enforce order – Chrysler management, Plant Protection staff, and local and state police – regardless of whether they were allies of his Local 3 membership.

As the above indicates, Liska did not draw any distinctions between the workplace issues, conflicts born of anti-racist organizing in the plant, and criminality. Protests were invalid, being regarded as little more than a threat to order that needed to be quashed. In September 1970, two years after Liska assumed office, about two dozen paint shop workers, joined by some workers from other departments, walked off a night shift in a wildcat, or illegal, strike. The paint shop workers expected their action would be part of a plant-wide walkout, but most other workers stayed on the job. After drinking across the street from the plant for about an hour, they returned to the plant parking lot and began causing havoc. According to Liska's account, they slashed the tires of a hundred cars on the company lot, blocked a road outside the plant with a concrete bench, trash cans, and other debris, and chained the main plant gate closed. They then began hurling projectiles at the cars on the blocked street. Many workers were "IRATE SEEING THEIR AUTOMOBILES DAMAGED." Some came out of the plant at 3:00 a.m. with bolts and hurled them at the wildcatters, who fled. Afterward, several

Molotov cocktails were found inside the plant. Liska blamed DRUM for the violence, as he believed that outsiders were involved in fomenting the situation, a theory that he felt was confirmed by his observation that influential radical organizer "GENERAL GORDON BAKER WAS OUT IN THE MORNING PASSING OUT LEAFLETS."[51]

In the wake of the incident, Liska and Hardy met with Chrysler's Labor Relations head, William Prokopy, and Dodge Main's personnel manager, Dick Clancy. At the meeting, they also discussed the bomb prank outlined in Chapter 2. Management placed all supervisors and Plant Protection staff on twelve-hour shifts to police the plant, with vital areas being watched twenty-four hours a day. Liska and Hardy were asked to keep the bomb threat from their workers, likely because workers would not enter the plant if they knew. The request put the two unionists in a bind. As Liska put it, "IF SOMETHING DID DEVELOP IN THE PLANT AND PEOPLE WERE HURT OR KILLED, HOW COULD WE EXPLAIN OUR SILENCE?" Nor did Liska fully trust Chrysler management. He noted, "ACTUALLY, NO PROOF OF ANY BOMBS HAVE BEEN SHOWN TO ANY UNION REPRESENTATIVES." Nevertheless, Liska kept his silence and later called Clancy to suggest that the union stewards on the night shift be informed of the situation so that they could help with the surveillance of the plant, a revealing example of management-union collaboration against the threat of radical violence.[52]

Just over a week later, the union and management met again to discuss, in Liska's words, "THE VIOLENCE AND BOMB THREATS AT THE ASSEMBLY PLANT ... THE INCIDENT ON MONDAY SEPTEMBER 14TH, MOLOTOV COCKTAILS LOCATED IN THE PLANT, PARKING LOT VIOLENCE, MURDERES [sic] ON THE LOOSE, WORKERS AFRAID TO GO TO PARKING LOTS, NARCOTICS, DRINKING, PROSTITUTION, THEFTS, BEATINGS ETC. AT REAR OF BARS BY PARKING LOTS ... THE ENTIRE SITUATION WAS DISCUSSED AT LENGTH."[53] Notice how politically motivated incidents and street crime were lumped together. Notice also that discussing "the entire situation" did not include a consideration of violence arising from job stress, racism at the plant, supervisory harassment, or the health and safety violations that were injuring and killing workers. The company and the union framed the problem of violence at Dodge Main in a way that reflected their shared interests in suppressing DRUM and cleaning up the crime around the plant. The other sources of violence, issues that the UAW and Chrysler may have had very different opinions about, were placed outside this frame. The meeting ended with a commitment to schedule a meeting with city leaders including the mayor and senior law enforcement officials, as well as to "CLEAN UP THE REAR OF THE BARS, POLICE THE LOTS MORE FREQUENTLY, CHECK IN PLANT AREAS FOR BOMB THREATS ETC. ON THE DRUM REPRESENTATION, MARCH AND JOHNSON [DRUM ACTIVISTS] WILL BE STRAIGHTENED OUT AND THEY AND OTHERS WILL ABIDE BY THE RULES."[54] It is unclear whether "straightened out" meant conversations, threats, firings, physical violence, or something else.

In October the union and management met representatives of the Michigan police, Detroit police, Hamtramck police, and county sheriff's department at a Howard Johnson hotel, far from where they might be observed by Dodge Main workers, to discuss "CRIMES NEAR AND ON THE COMPANY PARKING LOTS ACROSS FROM THE ASSEMBLY PLANT." Although all parties expressed their concern about the situation, with Liska mentioning that "THE FEAR IS GAINING AMONG WORKERS" and that "WE COULD LOSE THE PLANT IF WE CANNOT SOLVE THIS PROBLEM," few specific plans were put forward.[55] At the same time that Liska was working with Chrysler and law enforcement on the violence issue, the *Inner City Voice* accused Liska of doing nothing in local bargaining to combat racism, improve safety and working conditions for rank-and-file workers, or settle grievances. The *Voice* noted that whereas having guards in parking lots was an item relegated to the negotiating list, Chrysler had provided union officials with greater safety and comfort, such as locks, telephones, and fans for steward rooms.[56] This disparity reinforced the notion that the union and company looked after each other while ignoring the needs of workers.

The article also charged that corruption was a key reason why Liska was unwilling or unable to press for better conditions:

> All stewards are given the right to leave and enter the plant at will. If you disbelieve call for one now. The plant committeemen are receiving double pay for their threats. Most carry their time cards in their pockets. Some let their stewards punch them in and out, giving them 11 and 12 hours a day when they are on Official Union business (which pays for loss time). Plant Protection complains daily about the gate activities but to no avail. Management, Labor Relations and Personal [sic] just call Liska to remind him that they know.[57]

Enabling corruption of union officers had been a management strategy for many years, according to Jefferys.[58]

By 1972 Liska was out of power, defeated by Andy Hardy, Local 3's first black president. Despite the change in leadership, violence inside and outside the plant continued to be an issue for Local 3 until the plant closed in 1979. Executive member Joe Elliott wrote to UAW staff, requesting "a complete buzzer system be installed and that I be given a permit to carry a gun to protect my person"[59]; and to Michigan senator Donald Riegle, about dangerous situations at the union hall. In 1979 Local 3's then president, John Smith, put forth a resolution to a UAW convention that an impartial committee be formed to investigate "disputes involving physical contact between members of management and our union."[60]

Throughout the late 1960s and the 1970s, violence was the crucial issue for Liska. It shaped his outlook on UAW members and their issues, and it shaped his actions. But instead of seeing this violence as deeply connected to the labour process and racism, which would have required pressing for change, he saw it as caused by pathology and searched for order. He was alienated from rank-and-file workers, especially black workers, and perhaps felt closer to management, which he saw as a partner in maintaining order. One moment from 1969 poignantly conveys his alienation from the workers he represented. After gazing at the workers streaming in and out of Dodge Main, Liska wrote,

> THE WORKERS WHO CAME TO WORK OR LEFT THE PLANT WERE KEENLY OBSERVED BY THE LOCAL PRESIDET [sic]. IT IS HIS FEELING THAT 98% OF THEM ARE OK. THEY ARE HARD WORKING AND RESPONSIBLE WORKERS WHO WANT TO WORK AND MAKE MONEY AND EXPECT THEIR UNION LEADERSHIP TO [PROTECT] THEIR JOBS AND HELP THEM IN TIMES OF TROUBLES. SOMETIMES WE SPEND TOO MUCH TIME ON RADICALS AND PLAIN NUTS WHO ONLY TALK IN GENERAL TERMS AND DESTROYING EVERYTHING IN SIGHT. THEY MUST BE HEARD AND ROLLED OVER WHEN DESCIONS [sic] ARE MADE FOR THE GOOD AND WELFARE OF THE ENTIRE MEMBERSHIP.[61]

To Liska, violence was fundamentally the product of dangerous individuals. The solution to violence, then, was to work with management and the police to root out the bad apples, repress radicals, and restore order. Liska's radical critics contended that violence went much deeper than he perceived and that any solution would therefore have to do likewise. As with Liska, violence played a crucial role in their understanding of the situation. According to DRUM and other dissidents, violence was a product of the dangerous, degrading work environment at Dodge Main and the larger structures of capitalism and white supremacy. Plant violence resulted from the violence embedded in those systems, not in the minds of a handful of "plain nuts."

In an article titled "Bonus vs. an Ass Kicking," DRUM's newsletter made plain this link between structural and individual violence:

> We all know that the less equipment a foreman uses such as gloves and drill etc., the bigger his bonus. When profit becomes more important than workers safety, then it is time to take a stand. Since the work force is 70% black, this means that more black people are affected by this policy. In the Body Shop, this situation is more acute, due to the fact that most of the stock is razor sharp. The Brothers in the body shop are told, by the white foreman's [sic], that they have to wear their gloves a week, whether they last or not. DRUM feels that since our safety is in danger, than [sic] it's only fair that somebody else's be in danger also. So it's a bonus vs. an ass kicking, and you can have both.[62]

To radical workers, individual workplace violence was inseparable from the violence done to workers by their jobs.

Although less celebrated than their critiques of racism and the UAW, a perceptive analysis of workplace violence was one of the most important contributions made by radical autoworkers. In the 1980s and 1990s, when the phenomenon called "workplace violence" was first named and defined, experts and policy makers quickly restricted their field of vision to the violence of individuals. But according to voices emerging from Detroit and Windsor auto plants in the 1970s, individual violence was a symptom of the wider violence essential to the functioning of the dominant systems of production, distribution, and governance.

The *Eldon Wildcat,* a regular publication produced by a secretive group that white autoworker and radical John Taylor described as "Old Left," observed of a 1971 union election campaign,

> Some of the candidates have included a "law and order" plank in their platforms. They want to "Take a tough stand on Violence in the plant." But it isn't clear which violence they are talking about. If they are talking about

> the year-round violence that Chrysler uses against us, most of us would agree. Eldon workers haven't forgotten the brutal disregard of our health and safety that last year led to the deaths of Mamie Williams, Rose Logan, and Gary Thompson.[63]

An article in the *Eldon Spark* titled "Murders for Profit" drew a comparison between gas explosions that killed miners and the death of a driver at Dodge Main who was crushed by a forklift: "Both Chrysler and the coal companies say these were accidents. But really these workers were murdered. The bosses set things up so that many workers are killed or seriously injured every year." The article alleged that since there were no safe places to take a break at Dodge Main, the slain worker had rested near his station and been crushed by a forklift whose driver was shoving stock against a wall. The article concluded, "This policy of speed-up led to a worker's death. The mine owners and factory workers commit murder every day. Some workers are killed outright. Others die the slow deaths of black lung, cancer, and other diseases. Other workers are killed by the alcohol, heroin, and many other drugs which they use to put up with the horrible conditions."[64]

According to radical workers, the violence of capitalism went beyond health and safety violations and was intrinsic to the very system of wage labour. Commenting on automation, the *Spark* charged, "In a world where it takes money to eat and get along, it is criminal to take away peoples' [sic] jobs – and their life. The companies that do this are criminal!"[65] As an article in *Dodge Workers Speak* put it, "THIS IS TERRORISM. The company uses the terror of poverty against the workers." The article went on to link economic violence and physical violence as mutually reinforcing facets of corporate power: "Then a foreman pulls a knife on a worker, or swings a motor, or uses a hammer. These mad-dog foremen are using terror also – physical terror. Destruction is quicker under physical terror, but poverty also destroys."[66]

After twenty-four workers tested positive for tuberculosis at Dodge Main, the *Eldon Wildcat* attacked management for keeping the plant running and identified the fundamental issue as systemic: "Under any humane system we would be warned of all these dangers. But this system isn't humane. Chrysler isn't about to shut down its plants just to save lives. All they care about is profits."[67]

Radical autoworkers in Canada drew on events in Detroit to conceptualize the situation in their factories. As shown in Chapter 3, when a stabbing

"Shorty claims this is Step Three of the grievance procedure under the new contract."

Radical publications like the *Eldon Wildcat* often discussed in-plant violence, occasionally in light-hearted fashion. Image courtesy of Walter P. Reuther Library, Archives of Labor and Urban Affairs, Wayne State University.

occurred in a Windsor plant, the *Rank and File Bulletin* compared it to the James Johnson shootings, blaming Chrysler, the UAW, and in-plant racism for provoking both incidents. Their admonition "DETROIT IS IN OUR PLANTS" was an attempt to convince their Canadian co-workers that the border was not a defence against speedup, racism, and violence.[68] Canadian workers also insisted that workplace violence arose directly from the labour process. As one man interviewed in the publication *Workers' Unity* succinctly argued, auto work was "violent work that breeds violence."[69]

Supporters of the Eldon Avenue Revolutionary Union Movement (ELRUM), the radical Black Power insurgency at the Eldon Axle Plant, made an explicit connection between industrial capitalism, the US war machine, and the violence that American blacks faced at home. Lambasting a Chrysler campaign that exhorted workers to spend their Chrysler wages buying Chrysler products, the *Eldon Ave. Liberator* pointed to Chrysler's government contracts building tanks and military-transport vehicles: "There sure as hell ain't no highways in Viet-Nam and you better believe that you'll see these monsters rolling down Grand River, Twelfth St., Linwood, Mack, and anywhere else where 'hot niggers need cooling off!!'" The paper exhorted,

"JOIN ELRUM!"[70] During the 1967 uprising, of course, Eldon Avenue workers had direct experience of the United States Army violently putting down an insurrection in their neighbourhoods, and this occurrence informed the *Liberator*'s conception of the logic of American capitalism and racial hierarchy, in which black workers were not only alienated from the product they built but were also helping to build the very equipment that would be used to crush them.

Radical responses to violence, however, were much more complicated than a simple redefinition and condemnation. Although violence was fundamental to radicals' understanding of the predicament of workers in the automotive industry, it was also a tantalizing, if potentially double-edged, weapon for radical change. Many radical workers viewed violence against foremen as understandable and sometimes even laudable, considering foremen's role as the sharp end of the dangerous, fast-paced Chrysler labour process. As the *Eldon Wildcat* saw it,

> The only job protection a foreman has is to be riding our backs to get out as much work with as few people as possible. And if there's a chance that some foremen will be cut out, then that's more reason for them to be pushing us harder. The problem is that conditions are already pretty bad. And if foremen start pushing more, in an attempt to save their jobs, they will have to expect that more workers will be fighting back.[71]

At the same time, they warned workers of "mad-dog foremen." As they complained in 1973, "There are foremen in here that believe in packing pistols. That's not helping the situation any. The worst of it is that one of them drinks a lot. A drunk foreman armed with a gun is surely going to get somebody annihilated, possibly more than himself."[72]

Radicals believed that foremen's aggression toward workers made them logical targets for violence. A 1974 *Eldon Wildcat* piece discussing a new Chrysler policy of issuing foremen yellow badges instead of ties mocked, "Now they don't have to sneak into the plant and then put on their ties, or worry about taking them off before they go out into the dark parking lot, to face 'their' employees." Chrysler "sure picked the right color for those badges!"[73]

The newsletters of DRUM and ELRUM as well as the organs of the various other revolutionary union movements (RUMs) were even more openly confrontational than the *Wildcat* and the *Spark*. DRUM regularly justified and celebrated violence against company personnel, including robbery and assault. As Chapter 2 detailed, DRUM was not the cause of violence at Dodge Main; rather, violence was rising before DRUM's inception and continued to rise after DRUM's influence waned. However, the violence of both auto work and American racism was central to DRUM's analysis of the dilemma facing the black autoworker. DRUM cultivated a fearsome, violent image that its members believed was crucial to fostering a revolutionary outlook among black workers. General Gordon Baker, one of the leaders of both DRUM and the League of Revolutionary Black Workers, recalled, "we advocated violence and fighting back. We thought we had to break with the passivity. We took too much stuff from supervision and union people too." Any time violence broke out, "we ended up backing it and supporting it."[74]

A good example of DRUM's celebration of violence as revolutionary and heroic is a 1969 article titled "Rebellion inside the Gates." A black worker named Harris was fired for an altercation with a white millwright, the same incident that Liska discussed above. Harris physically resisted being handed over to the Hamtramck police, and as black workers left the gates at the 3:00 a.m. whistle, they found Harris struggling with four officers, who cuffed him and threw him into the back of a police car. According to DRUM, "our black brothers rose up as one and rescued him from the car." An officer responded by macing several workers. The article continued,

> At this point some black workers retreated inside the plant and began bombarding the police cars with auto parts and 50 gallon drums, bolts, washers and scrap steel. A long steel shaft thrown through the windshield of one of the police cars barely missed the driver. All of the plant guards fled to safety. The police were barely able to get Bro. Harris back in the car as it was being rocked by black workers. After the 2nd surge by gallant black workers, the police fled for their lives.[75]

DRUM celebrated the clash as a heroic victory, no doubt seeking to rally more workers to its side. The writer of the article proclaimed triumphantly, "The day is long gone when black workers can be brutally assaulted with impunity."[76] The RUM papers were also far more likely than the *Wildcat* or the *Spark* to celebrate violent workers. James Johnson was repeatedly hailed as a hero, with one article claiming that the largely apolitical Johnson "has moved Black Workers' struggle at the point of Production to a new and higher level." The same article praised Rushie Forge, Sidney Lewis, and

Chuck Wooten, all DRUM members fired for violence against supervisors. It also mentioned Ike Jernigan, not a DRUM or UAW member but a California aerospace worker who killed his foreman, union president, and another union official after being harassed and fired for Black Power organizing.[77]

DRUM argued that employing violence was a crucial part of black workers reclaiming their manhood and overcoming their oppression. Violence, masculinity, and revolution were inextricably linked in their writing and practice. As one letter to the editor put it, their enemies "only understand violence. We must get on their ass like black on white and let them know that we are black men and not boys and proud of it."[78] To DRUM, the auto plants were simultaneously a place that emasculated black workingmen and an arena where those workers could reclaim their manhood and wrest power from white capitalists.

This arena was imagined as a man's world, one with little role for women as part of the revolution. One DRUM article even described the introduction of female workers into the traditionally male grease pits at Dodge Main as "a form of castration." The article concluded with the exhortation "BROTHERS AWAKE!!/ FIGHT FOR MASCULINITY/ JOIN DRUM!!"[79]

The aggressive masculinity that DRUM believed crucial to reclaiming the manhood of black workers was a double-edged sword. In the short term, it certainly posed a ferocious challenge to the UAW and the auto companies alike that could not be ignored. In an article titled "What Has DRUM Done?" the organization claimed that its aggressive posture "ended brutal and physical abuse of Black Workers by the racist thugs in supervision" and that "DRUM has instilled a new measure of pride in the Black workers to the point where they won't tolerate any harassment in or out of the plant."[80] However, the RUMs elevation of rough masculinity alienated many older and female autoworkers.[81] The RUMs largely ignored the difficulties that a hypermasculine culture presented for women workers or for men who did not fit the mould. Taylor noted that older female workers at the Eldon Axle Plant were terrified of ELRUM activists, who carried guns and who, they thought, were going to "go berserk."[82] The veneration of violence and machismo cost the RUMs potential allies and votes in union elections. However, radicals did occasionally consider some of the specific violence that female workers faced in the plants. DRUM called out foreman Robert Brooks for firing a female worker who had rejected his sexual advances.[83] Indeed, female workers often faced harassment and sexual abuse at work, and the *Spark* called on men to play their part in redressing these wrongs. Writing about a foreman sexually harassing a female worker, the paper noted,

> [There are] many other cases of foremen or supervisors using their job to try to force a woman worker to have sex with them. Women workers have hard jobs and lousy working conditions. Often they also have to deal with this kind of pressure from a foreman to put out. There is the threat that if they don't, the foreman will have her fired [or] put her on a harder job. The other side of this pressure is the promise that if she is nice to him, maybe he will make ... life easier for her. Sometimes a foreman plays this game really openly. Union reps know about it but say nothing. No wonder that sometimes women get caught in the trap and go with [foremen]. On the other hand you see women that won't go along with this game. Some will let the foreman know they will take a harder job if necessary. Some fight as militants in the plant and in the union.
>
> But women should not have to fight this crap alone. It is not just a problem for women workers. They suffer from this – but so do men workers. Because this is one of the ways that the capitalist system tries to divide workers. As long as men workers think of women as fair game and go along with foremen trying to pressure women like this, or stay quiet, it will be harder to stick together and fight against the company.[84]

Since there was less violence in Windsor plants, violence did not play as significant a role in plant culture and politics. However, violence was also a part of the critiques of Canadian unionists and workers, in ways that reflected their distinct situation. Because of demographics, a much smaller local civil rights movement, and the legacy of racial exclusion, Local 444 did not have to confront the type of racial divisions with which Local 3 struggled. In fact, it could appeal to a hegemonic nationalism to bind the membership. Thanks to these factors, and the big-tent style of leadership practised by its president, Charlie Brooks, Local 444 was better able to accommodate dissident perspectives and channel them. Unlike the precariously placed, racially divided Local 3, Local 444 had a springboard for militancy.

This militancy can be seen in the willingness of Windsor union officials to condemn unsafe conditions in terms not very different from those used by Detroit radicals. After the deaths of two men and crippling injuries to others, Local 444 official Gary Parent called the Windsor Truck Plant a "slaughter house."[85] When a foreman drove a truck marked "Do Not Drive" on the assembly line at the Truck Plant and killed worker Jim Medwick, Brooks charged that what the company called an accident was actually criminal. The local pressed for charges of criminal negligence to be filed against the foreman. Brooks argued that the prosecution "would serve notice on all supervision that the workers' safety comes ahead of production."[86] Windsor union officials also pointed out the less immediately visible toll that car production was taking on some workers. In 1979 Local 444's second vice-president, Gerry Bastien, contended, "I feel very strongly that the incidences of suicide by some of our members may be directly related to their inability to cope with all the harassment."[87]

As a result of Local 444's militancy and its willingness to absorb dissident members into its power structure, the critiques of Windsor radicals often sounded similar to those directed at Local 444's leaders. For example, in the publication *Workers' Unity,* a male worker observed, "We do a lot of hard work – 8 hours – it takes a lot out of you. It's violent work that breeds violence. Sometimes you only feel like going out for a beer or hollering at your wife and kids."[88] This worker would likely have had sympathy with Brooks's repeated calls for shorter workdays and workweeks in industry.

During the 1970s, the major radical faction in Windsor Chrysler plants was the Rank and File Caucus. Jim Brophy, a black autoworker from Detroit who had left the United States to resist the draft and had found work in Windsor, was a key caucus member, according to one interview. This is an example of the flow of radical workers and ideas across the border. Unlike Local 444's publications and the writings of other dissident groups, the caucus-produced *Rank and File Bulletin* criticized racism in Windsor Chrysler plants. When replacement workers were brought into the V8 block department because the workers there refused to work overtime, the *Bulletin* observed, "These 3 scabs from the V8 blocks were all 'good Canadians' – one young, two older. This is mentioned because of the racist remarks that are heard daily in the plants and the common belief that it is the immigrants that do all the overtime."[89] The *Bulletin* also charged that "the racist attitudes of Canadian workers" were a contributing factor in a stabbing in Plant 2 and that the UAW was guilty of "outright neglect to combat racism and prejudice in the plants."[90]

Like the RUMs, the *Wildcat,* and the *Spark,* the *Bulletin* contended that worker violence arose from in-plant pressures and the "violent nature of assembly lines."[91] One article argued that layoffs and speedups would lead to violent reprisals:

> Autoworkers are some of the most distressed workers. The daily monotony of the job 5 days a week is and the ever increasing speedup is bad enough,

> but throw these guys out on the street who "worked steadily and haven't gotten into trouble before" and many flip out ...
>
> The auto worker isn't a criminal but pressure him, threaten him, and push him around and then the auto companies have a problem. For example, tell him he'll work through Xmas then tell him he won't. Tell him he'll get Xmas pay then tell him he won't. Tell him he'll be called back then tell him they won't. With psychiatric facilities strained to capacity this is hardly a game the company should be playing ...
>
> The company has S and A [sickness and accident] benefits for any worker that is driven nuts in the plant, but we find it ironic since they caused the situation. The problem is getting out of hand and if anyone does flip out he should know he'll be among other friends – autoworkers.[92]

Although the *Bulletin* offered a more radical take on auto work than Local 444 leadership, the two were much less divided than DRUM and Local 3, reflecting the greater cohesion in Windsor plants. The violence of the labour process was central to the *Bulletin*'s understanding of auto work, but the Rank-and-File Caucus stopped short of advocating or celebrating violence. Perhaps this was because, compared with the black Detroit workers who joined the RUMs, caucus members faced far less violence both on the job and from police and the state in their neighbourhoods. Their greater exposure to violence that was inextricably linked to structural racism and to their unbearable working conditions was likely the major reason why the RUMs celebrated violence and adopted it as a part of a revolutionary identity. RUM members believed that only violence would ultimately achieve black liberation and that to think otherwise was a delusion. As DRUM argued, "the factory is the tool of violence used by the union and management to crush all resistance put up by the workers." To DRUM, nonviolence was a dead end that would cause black workers to "be uncomplaining to their destiny" when the situation demanded any means necessary to force management and the union to change their policies. Comparing DRUM members and Windsor workers illuminates that the level of workers' exploitation and the power disparity between workers and leaders, whether in the union or on the job, influenced how likely they were to advocate violence as a solution to workplace grievances.[93]

The *Wildcat*, the *Spark*, and the *Bulletin*, like the RUMs, understood auto work, capitalism, white supremacy, and imperialism as violent processes, but they stopped short of celebrating individual violence. Although cognizant of the violence that beset workers on all sides, the *Wildcat* stressed organization and solidarity, not individual violence. One week after the Johnson murders, the *Wildcat* argued, "his solution was wrong, not because it was violent, but because it was aimed at the individuals involved, and not at changing the basic situation." After his trial ended, the *Wildcat* summed up its position:

> Most of us can understand how Brother Johnson felt, and why he struck back at his foreman, the daily symbol of his oppression. But he fought alone, as an individual. And now he is out of our fight, but the problems are still here. Individually we can do little to change a giant corporation like Chrysler, United, there is no limit to what we can do. Maybe even build a world in which men like James Johnson can be allowed to live in peace.[94]

Despite their differing judgments of whether violence was an efficacious solution to problems on the job, radical workers shared an understanding that violence in their plants was a fundamental reality of their working lives. Violence at work was a major influence on their consciousness and a central aspect of their critique of Chrysler, auto work, and capitalism.

Was Chrysler listening? The RUMs certainly had the company's attention because of their wildcat strikes, their challenges to the UAW power structure, their support among Chrysler's black workers in Detroit, and, not least, their threats of a violent reckoning with Chrysler and the UAW. Chrysler's responses to violence and militancy indicate that, like the UAW and the radical workers, the company saw in-plant violence as a serious concern. I have discussed how unionists and radical workers defined and responded to violence. Understanding how Chrysler perceived the violence in and around its factories is more difficult. Unlike Local 3's Ed Liska, Chrysler has not made any of its internal files from the period available. Unlike DRUM and the Rank and File Caucus, Chrysler was not in the habit of publishing and distributing its take on everyday in-plant incidents. Much of what we know about Chrysler in the period is reflected, having been taken from media accounts and the critiques of hostile organizations. The second challenge is discerning what elements of Chrysler's response were directed at violence in the plant generally and what ones were attempts to head off the radical Black Power organizing of the RUMs.

There was significant overlap between the two objectives. Like the UAW, Chrysler often conflated in-plant violence with the RUMs and crime. This overlooked relevant facts. The vast majority of in-plant violence had nothing to do with the RUMs, whose members were dedicated to political change, not illicit gain. Workplace violence, crime, and militancy occasionally overlapped, but they were distinct phenomena. Still, Chrysler was extremely concerned about the RUMs not only because of the widespread support they attracted among black workers but also because of their willingness to advocate violence and the commission of violent acts by DRUM members.[95]

So what did Chrysler do in response to the violence raging inside its Detroit assembly plants? In important ways, it did nothing. As discussed in greater detail in the next two chapters, an awareness of "workplace violence" as a specific issue did not exist at that time. Nevertheless, in-plant violence at Chrysler was an issue so serious that it prompted articles in *Time* and *Newsweek*. Yet there is little evidence that Chrysler acted to address issues that caused much of the in-plant violence, such as sped-up assembly lines or dangerous working conditions, during the 1970s. Nor were there specific programs aimed at tackling workplace violence or protecting workers. Asked why Chrysler did not do more to protect workers from violence, General Baker replied, "I don't think they really gave a damn."[96] As long as output could be maintained, Chrysler saw all other issues as being of secondary importance.

Output was the point on which Chrysler's concern over in-plant violence pivoted. Chrysler may have been largely unconcerned with the well-being of its production workers, yet it is clear from its actions that it took the violence and disorder in its plants seriously, as a phenomenon that hampered production and threatened industrial order. In the late 1960s, Chrysler invested heavily in weaponry and surveillance equipment for its plants and placed itself in the vanguard of a nervous US capitalist class that was deeply concerned about violent revolution. The National Association of Manufacturers held a counterinsurgency seminar in Detroit in 1968, one of fifteen seminars that the association conducted around the nation. In addition to conducting the seminars, they distributed 600,000 copies of a pamphlet titled "Industrial Planning Guide against Civil Disorders."[97]

The Detroit conference included speakers from the US military, Federal Bureau of Investigation, and Detroit police. DRUM reported,

> The Association plans such things as new higher fences and windows as is already recently constructed at Dodge Main and Eldon Ave. New security

> identification systems with photographs on badges, electric eye spy systems and this will probably lead to strip down searches at the gates as was used in atomic plants during W.W. II. They further projected arming the plant protection guards with revolvers and in the key areas guard towers with semi-automatic rifles.[98]

Although some of these measures did not come to pass, by January of the next year, the Eldon Axle Plant had electric devices to close plant doors, special camera equipment, new fences, and searchlights. Because of high tensions that month, Detroit police were patrolling the plant twenty-four hours a day, and its Tactical Mobile Unit was on standby.[99] Chrysler also provided steward rooms with the locking doors, in-plant phones, and fans mentioned above. The safety and comfort that these additions provided were likely welcomed by stewards, but they increased the distance, both actual and metaphorical, between workers and their representatives.[100] Although Plant Protection officers were never armed with guns, DRUM claimed that they were provided with teargas grenades, riot helmets, and batons, all stored on plant property.

Despite the increased security, a poem in the *Inner City Voice* warned that such measures directed at Students for a Democratic Society (SDS) or the Socialist Workers Party (SWP) would be useless in plants where the greatest threats came from the very workers who passed through the gates every day. The poem, printed beside pictures of new fences at Eldon Axle and a newly covered window at Dodge Main, stated:

> FENCES CAN STOP SDS OR THE SWP
> BUT THEY CANNOT STOP A DRUM WORKER
> ARMED WITH TNT.[101]

At the same time it was building new fences and stocking up on teargas, Chrysler was attempting to improve relations with black Detroiters in the factory and the city at large, primarily by increasing its hiring of the so-called "hard-core unemployed": jobless young black males who were seen as the principal drivers of the 1967 uprising. Although maintaining the order needed for production was Chrysler's main concern, the politics of the era, exemplified by black organizing and the uprising, pressured Chrysler to make gestures toward being a good corporate citizen in the Detroit community. Thus Chrysler, along with General Motors and Ford, participated in a program to recruit workers from the ghettoes. Chrysler began ignoring some criminal records during the hiring process, suspending a traditional barrier to the hiring of young black men. Chrysler also held racial-sensitivity seminars for foremen.

However, Chrysler's efforts to combat racism were themselves based on a racist assumption: that black workers were wide-eyed simpletons unable to manage the transition to industrial life. To Chrysler, the primary issue facing black workers was not structural racism but the unsuitability of blacks for modern industrial life, or what a *Saturday Evening Post* article on Chrysler's programs termed "the gap between White America and Poor Black America." According to the article, Chrysler learned of this gap when 60 percent of the first 600 new hires failed to show up at their assigned factories and when others quit after a day or two. According to one Chrysler official, "the first inclination of many people here was to use the old cliché about the Negro being too lazy to work. But then someone higher up decided to look into it, and we realized how wrong we were."[102]

That "someone" was Chrysler chairman Lynn Townsend, a "new-breed executive with a master's degree from the University of Michigan." According to Townsend, he chose to discard racist stereotypes and approach the issue as though it were a "marketing problem." He sent investigators from Chrysler's Personnel Department to interview each absentee, and the results were, in the *Post*'s estimation, "pathetically revealing. Many men who didn't show up for work were immigrants from the South who couldn't read and who never before traveled out of the ghetto." These men couldn't navigate the bus system, "and they ended up in distant sections of the city. They became discouraged, and thinking they had already lost their new jobs they went home." Those who did make it to the factories were overwhelmed by "the complexity of the industrial process" and by their inability to read or count to ten. "We found out," Townsend said, "that they quit because they simply were terrified."[103]

Townsend's assessment that ignorance and naiveté were the primary problems faced by these new workers is puzzling, considering that black and white workers had made the transition from the rural South to the auto factories for decades. Moreover, many of the new hires were likely Detroit natives who would have had little difficulty navigating the city. Chrysler preferred to frame the problems faced by black workers as rooted in their own cultural underdevelopment, not as the product of racial inequality in Detroit's streets and factories.

Therefore, Townsend hired fifty high school teachers as counsellors, who "led the men by the hand through the transportation system. They taught them just enough to identify signs and numbers." They provided alarm clocks so that workers could get up on time. According to Chrysler, these trained "ghetto men returned to their Chrysler jobs and most of them have stayed there." The article describes a training class funded by the new public-private Job Opportunities in the Business Sector program, where a black adviser named Al McPherson taught men between the ages of eighteen and thirty "personal hygiene, industrial responsibility, and punctuality ... 'He even teases the men about their Bushman haircuts, referring to them by such names as "Bramblebush," and the trainees usually cut their hair.'" This adviser, together with a "pretty blond" teacher named Marlene Jackson, taught the men to count, follow directions, and "adapt to the disciplines of the factory. Then they go to work on the assembly line as 'entry workers' and earn up to $3.50 an hour, more than they had ever dreamed of making in their lives."[104]

The Big Three chose mentors capable of deploying a rough, violent masculinity to get through to the "hard-cores." Ed Spicer, whom Chrysler selected to help integrate "hard-cores" into the plants, was a burly white man with eighteen years of boxing experience. In the 1969 documentary *Do You Think a Job Is the Answer?* Spicer is shown hitting the heavy bag and doing roadwork while talking about how he is well suited to reach out to ghetto youth. Ford held out Harry Palmer as a success story. After being hired through an outreach program, Palmer rose to a semi-skilled job and began saving money for a ranch house in the suburbs. Ford hoped he would serve as a model for its young black workers. The *Post* marvelled at Palmer, a man with a criminal record for breaking into a jewellery store, especially his "influence on younger, more militant Negroes. In a strange way, he is a folk hero to them because of his prison record for a daring crime, and this awe is being transmuted into further admiration for the way he has reorganized his life." According to Ford, "if we can develop a lot of Harry Palmers to influence the others, we *may* have the situation licked."[105] The Palmer example is a fascinating insight into how management approached the radical challenge in auto factories. Ford hoped to leverage the respect that it thought a worker of Palmer's criminal past and prison experience commanded in the factory to inculcate respectable values and habits.

Chrysler's outreach efforts may have provided some good publicity for the company, but the initiatives also had many critics. DRUM noted that the program showed Chrysler was willing to hire blacks to work on the assembly line, but the hiring of black foremen, skilled trades workers, and salaried employees was still virtually nonexistent. *Do You Think a Job Is the Answer?* argued that the efforts of the auto companies did not do enough to address the structural racism, underdevelopment, and poverty faced by Detroit blacks. In fact, Rev. William Fitch, a member of the Detroit Industrial Mission, a religious group attempting to heal race and class conflict in Detroit, argued that hiring black workers at the bottom of an industrial system that oppressed them was reinforcing racism, not transcending it.

The film also noted that the splashily publicized hard-core hiring initiative coincided nicely with a period of peak auto demand and a high need for workers among the Big Three. This criticism is borne out by Liska's diary. In 1969 he wrote of meeting with Labor Relations head William Prokopy, who was "IN A VERY SAD AND BEGGING MOOD" and upset about poor car quality. "PROKOPY SAID THAT WE CAN'T EVEN GET NEW GUYS TO HIRE. WE GET TRUCKS TO VISIT THE INNER CITY TO SEEK OUT GUYS WHO WANT A JOB."[106] As *Do You Think a Job Is the Answer?* shows, after the articles had been written, and perhaps after the demand for employees had peaked, Ford stopped sending buses into the ghetto to pick up workers.

Chrysler approached the challenge of the RUMs with a similar mix of repression and outreach. After DRUM's May 1968 wildcat strike, Chrysler fired several workers, including General Baker. According to Jefferys, black workers were "hit disproportionately."[107] According to Baker, after DRUM organized a picket of the Eldon Axle Plant, Chrysler roused a judge in the middle of the night to issue a warrant for Baker's arrest, as the picket violated a previous injunction that prohibited Baker from being at Chrysler plants.[108] Yet Chrysler also maintained back-channel communication with DRUM. According to Baker, he and other DRUM leaders would meet informally with a black community relations employee; it was this Chrysler man who told Baker that the shooting that paralyzed Detroit housing activist Fred Holsey, an attack likely targeting Baker, was the responsibility of the UAW, not Chrysler. There is evidence that Chrysler management and DRUM activists also communicated at the in-plant level. In 1970 Liska complained of "MANAGEMENT CUDDLING DRUM ORGANIZATION AND ITS LEADERS IN PLANT." He feared that DRUM activists like Ron March were usurping union stewards in representing workers and that DRUM had more access to the Labor Relations office than did elected union representatives.[109]

Although programs such as Job Opportunities in the Business Sector may have been window-dressing, Chrysler combined these public relations initiatives with more concrete responses to the demands of DRUM and other dissidents. It promoted several of Local 3's black activists, including those who had almost joined DRUM or who echoed similar positions, to foreman. It also stopped defending in-plant racism.[110] Some foremen were trained in people skills, or as *Dodge Workers Speak* charged, "instead of harassing the workers, Chrysler decided to try to trick the workers into getting out more production. They are training the foremen how to psyche the workers out when threats don't work. It's a con game."[111] Chrysler also built up conservative black unionists in Local 3, "allowing them to 'win' a few victories," as Jefferys states. These wins undercut DRUM's position that it was the only force capable of getting results for black workers.[112] By the time Andy Hardy succeeded Liska and became Local 3's first black president, DRUM, like the RUMs elsewhere, was a spent force, thanks in part to Chrysler's 1969 layoffs. Once in power, Hardy proved a pliant ally, enthusiastically helping the UAW break a wildcat strike at the Mack Avenue Stamping Plant, and he "got on very well with Clancy," the Dodge Main superintendent.[113] Through this combination of approaches, Chrysler outlasted the RUMs. At Dodge Main the company regained effective control of the plant and production. Workplace violence, however, continued to occur regularly right up until Dodge Main's closing. This again indicates that workplace violence had many causes and was an issue before and after the heyday of Black Power unionism at Chrysler. At Chrysler Windsor, where the UAW more successfully integrated militant perspectives, a much more militant orientation persisted. In the late 1970s and early 1980s, when the UAW in the United States acquiesced to concessions, its Canadian counterpart was much better placed to resist. The American UAW's more cooperative stance may have been influenced by its collaboration with Chrysler to quash violence and militant challenges.

Whether left or right, white or black, union or management, workplace violence affected the consciousness, strategy, and actions of those working in the Detroit and Windsor auto industry during the 1960s and 1970s. The impact of workplace violence did not end when a fight was broken up, a worker discharged, or a union election won and lost. Because workplace violence was not meaningfully reduced by the discipline and grievance systems of Chrysler and the UAW, violence remained part of the experience of working at Chrysler. Therefore, it remained active in the hearts and minds of the assembly line workers, radicals, unionists, foremen, guards, and executives who went to work at Chrysler every day. It affected the families and friends of victims and perpetrators – of those fired, suspended, threatened, injured, and killed.

Violence was the most important factor shaping Liska's outlook during his tenure as Local 3 president. It alienated him from his membership, infected him with fear and despair, and pushed him closer to management. Throughout his tenure, Liska saw himself not as the elected leader of a dynamic workers' organization pressing to improve conditions at Dodge Main but as an embattled figure trying desperately to keep the barrel of dynamite at Hamtramck from exploding. This perspective pushed him toward collaboration and identification with Chrysler management, whom he saw as his partner in keeping order in the plant. In Windsor a more effective union leadership, operating under better conditions and with a closer connection to its workers, often took a position on the everyday violence of health and safety conditions in its plants that was similar to the views of radical workers.

Chrysler executives in Detroit, while making a more serious effort to combat racial inequality in the plant than Liska, combined practical measures and public relations to tamp down the flames of workplace violence and Black Power organizing. In doing so, they deployed machismo as one way to win alienated workers over to their way of thinking. They also combined reform with repression, firing many workplace activists. These strategies, combined with the slowdown in the auto industry in the first half of the 1970s, enabled Chrysler to retain effective control of its shop floor, although violence was never totally eliminated.

Radical workers on both sides of the Detroit River responded to the situation in their factories by presenting a conception of workplace violence that was much broader than the one shared by Chrysler and Local 3 and the one formalized and accepted by corporations, unions, experts, and policy makers in the 1980s and 1990s. Their definition identified the labour processes of the auto companies as inherently violent and as the cause of much of the individual violence in the plants. Some radicals advocated violence as a way to reclaim dignity and manhood on the job and to obtain better treatment, better working conditions, and perhaps even a revolutionary awakening at the point of production. In Windsor and especially in Detroit, there was a crucial linkage between workplace violence and radical consciousness and practice.

A few high-profile incidents of violence in these plants had an even greater impact, sparking wider struggles in the cities of Detroit and Toronto. These struggles attracted national and international media investigation and made this link between workplace violence and political struggle even more apparent. It is to those incidents that I now turn.

5

Chrysler Pulled the Trigger

The Courts and the Press

What did people beyond the factory gates make of this violence at work? Long before incidents of workplace violence became regular features of cable news, before "going postal" became a macabre punch line of late-night monologues, three workplace shootings sent shockwaves through the automotive industry and the cities of Detroit and Windsor: the shootings of two foremen and a coworker at Chrysler's Eldon Axle Plant by worker James Johnson in 1970, the shooting of skilled trades worker William Harrell by United Automobile Workers (UAW) Local 600 executive David Mundy in 1973, and the murder of UAW Local 444 president Charlie Brooks by fired Chrysler worker Clarence Talbot in 1977. They were cases that produced remarkable outpourings of emotion, resulted in important legal struggles, and attracted national media attention.[1]

In the auto industries of Detroit and Windsor, as previously shown, these cases were notable but not unique. Interpersonal violence, including fights, beatings, and stabbings, was a regular part of the auto-workplace culture in both cities, being a recognized way to settle disputes between workers or to strike out against an oppressive boss. What made the Johnson, Mundy, and Talbot cases different was not their violence but that they attracted widespread, sustained attention beyond the factory or the union hall. These incidents had the power to shape broader understandings of workplace violence because of the attention they received in the cities where they took place, cities marked, to varying degrees, by class divides, racial stratification, and conflict. These shootings posed troubling questions for Detroiters and Windsorites. They took the issue of workplace violence beyond the plant gates and brought a larger group of people into the debate over how to explain and understand individual violence at work. Therefore, they allow us the chance to investigate what understandings of workplace violence were possible during the 1970s, just before workplace violence became a widely recognized societal issue, as well as what forces and factors determined their conditions of possibility.

How did observers, both within the automotive workplace and in the wider public, understand these incidents of workplace violence? How was violence defined, and what causes were incriminated? To what extent did these incidents prompt Canadians and Americans to look at the objective and symbolic violences that produced them? Here, I consider what was said and done in the wake of three workplace shootings and what remained unsaid and undone. The cases of James Johnson, David Mundy, and Clarence Talbot indicate that although workplace violence arose from work-related conflict and workplace power hierarchies, the understandings of this violence outside the workplace varied widely depending on the historical context in which that violence occurred and the nature of the cases themselves. These understandings of workplace violence, in turn, tell us much about the workings of class and race in the communities affected. Finally, at no time during the 1970s did the media or stakeholders define workplace violence as a problem in and of itself, much less devise solutions.

The anthropologist Begoña Aretxaga observed debates over violence's meaning in the aftermath of the 1995 murders of two Basque Country police officers by Mikel Otegi. Like her study of political violence and the unconscious, which argues that the significance of the Otegi case "is manifested in the proliferation of narratives it engendered," these three cases demand our attention because they too "became a battleground where the media and different political formations took their positions."[2] In each case, legal proceedings were at the heart of this process. In both Canada and the United States, the courtroom has been a crucial site of struggle against the inequities of capitalism, racism, and patriarchy. Scholars have demonstrated that legal contests shaped Canadian industrial relations, free speech and dissent within unions, and the rights of women at work.[3] An increased emphasis on individual rights and activism through legal challenges has been a critical feature of politics in the United States since the 1970s. American left legal scholars have pointed out both the opportunities and pitfalls of this turn to legalism. Although its focus on rights can produce legitimate victories for marginalized groups, critics such as political scientist Wendy Brown and legal scholar Janet Halley caution that the law is ultimately a liberal structure that works to co-opt or stunt left aims. Even when successful, these "left-endorsed liberal legalist" projects, such as the fight for affirmative action rights or against sexual harassment often "generate troubling new subjects and subjectivities" that actually delay social justice and strengthen reactionary forces.[4]

However, historians remind us that the courtroom has not only been a site of liberal cooptation but also one of radical possibility. In her study of labour defence campaigns and lynching prosecutions, historian Rebecca Hill notes that defence campaigns have been "the place where radicals most directly attack the power of the state, and the representative claims of the mass media."[5] Radical legal practice of the kind that Hill notes was used in defences by the Industrial Workers of the World in the early twentieth century, and in the cases of Nicola Sacco and Bartolomeo Vanzetti in the 1920s and the Scottsboro Boys in the 1930s has been an important element of left struggles and "one of the most popular elements of leftist politics."[6]

Indeed, attorneys and defendants have often succeeded in using the legal process to advance radical critiques. Hill observes that defence campaigns and anti-lynching campaigns have worked to "defend and resuscitate people who come to symbolize their communities in the mass media and to criticize the moral systems of law and the media."[7] In so doing, they have created and sustained "a new popular counter-history of the United States."[8] Radical legal practice advances arguments about justice and history that present alternative understandings of class, race, and gender, understandings that reverberate far beyond the walls of a courtroom. In the 1970s radical lawyers were key figures in the contests that resulted from high-profile incidents of workplace violence, although the success of their critiques was heavily influenced by the local political context.

"What Manner of Man Is James Johnson Jr.?" asked the *Michigan Chronicle* in July 1970, shortly after his shootings made headlines.[9] "Who is James Johnson?" echoed the radical black newspaper *Inner City Voice*.[10] In the wake of Johnson's murder of three men at the Chrysler plant where he worked, it was a question that the media, lawyers, unions, liberals, radicals, and conservatives all grappled with. An extremely quiet and reserved man, immediately tagged with the label of "loner" that would come to be a cliché in workplace shootings, Johnson seemed to offer a blank canvas upon which observers could project their own ideologies, fears, and dreams. He spoke little during the aftermath of the shootings and the trial. Like Otegi, Johnson claimed not to remember the shootings and offered little of his own explanation for why he had done it. He had simply "lost control." No matter what one's interpretation of Johnson's actions, however, it was clear that his life history was marked by several of the major factors that had shaped the African American experience in postwar Detroit. His was not the shocking crime of an unrecognizable outsider. He was a product of the city, and his rampage challenged Detroiters to understand why it had happened. As they would in the case of Otegi, observers rushed in to explain the causes of his shocking act of violence in the workplace, the perpetrator being defined primarily as a "displaced sign of something else."[11] Johnson was, depending on the telling, a disturbed perpetrator, a helpless victim, and a black working-class hero.

Heather Ann Thompson, who uses Johnson's story as a recurring motif in her compelling study *Whose Detroit? Politics, Labor, and Race in a Modern American City*, writes that Johnson's life was "a metaphor for all of the disappointments, frustrations, and hopes that had characterized their [black Detroiters'] lives in the Jim Crow South, the Motor City, and the auto plants between 1945 and 1985."[12] Thompson perceptively draws out many of the different grievances and anxieties that were highlighted by the Johnson case, notably the ongoing frustration with institutional racism and shop floor unrest in the city's auto industry. She demonstrates that the Johnson case was a key battleground in the ongoing struggle between liberals, conservatives, and radicals for control of the city. She also establishes that the defence of Johnson at trial demonstrated the power and effectiveness of a radical critique of racial hierarchies and the practices of the automakers in early 1970s Detroit.

My purpose here in considering the Johnson case is different. This chapter focuses on the competing understandings of workplace violence produced in the aftermath of Johnson's shootings and on their reception. Reading Johnson's case not only highlights conflicts over race, class, labour, and urban politics in Detroit but also provides evidence of how Detroiters and the media understood workplace violence in the early 1970s. The reactions to the Johnson case reveal that many recognized that individual violence at work was an outgrowth of the brutal processes of Detroit factory labour and the racial and other hierarchies that were central to how this labour was organized and carried out. However, many others resisted this interpretation, insisting that workplace violence was a product of individual pathology and the pernicious influence of radical organizations active in the auto factories.

The factory where Johnson had worked, Chrysler's Eldon Axle Plant, was a dirty, dangerous place of great unhappiness, where workers clashed with managers, union reps, the unforgiving line, and themselves. In May 1970, two months before Johnson's killings, a twenty-two-year-old Vietnam veteran named Gary Thompson was killed at the plant when his jitney, which was not in safe working condition, overturned and crushed him under a massive pile of scrap metal. Rose Logan and Mamie Williams, two black women workers at the plant, had also died in work-related incidents in the weeks previous to Thompson's death.[13] In response to the racism, speedup, and unsafe conditions, workers led wildcat strikes and created insurgent worker organizations like the Eldon Safety Committee and the Eldon Avenue Revolutionary Union Movement (ELRUM).

Despite the toxic atmosphere at the Eldon Plant, when Johnson was suspended and sent home from his job unloading brake shoes from an oven on July 15, 1970, he was devastated. Working at Eldon was the best job he had ever had, and he desperately wanted to keep it. It may have been "the worst job at the plant,"[14] as a quality control auditor later described it, but Johnson saw it as his "only source of survival."[15]

Johnson, an employee of the plant since 1967, had recently returned to work after a four-month layoff. On July 15 he was at work in the cement room when a temporary foreman, Hugh Jones, ordered Johnson off his job to go work the brake shoe oven, the hot, dirty, and dangerous assignment that Johnson believed he had escaped when he was promoted to the cement room. According to Heather Ann Thompson, the fact that Jones, like Johnson, was a black man added the sting of betrayal to a work order he already felt was unfair.[16]

Johnson reported to the oven but, because he was not provided with the proper safety gloves for the job, refused to start working. Johnson had his union steward, Clarence Horton, summoned to mediate the situation. The temperature at the oven that July day was over 120 degrees Fahrenheit, so Horton tried to secure a "heat pass" for Johnson. He was unsuccessful, and Jones suspended Johnson for "insubordination."[17]

To Johnson, the suspension was the final indignity in a history of racist and degrading treatment by Chrysler. Two months earlier, Johnson had suffered head and neck injuries in a car accident. Taking time off to heal, he was ordered back to work by the company against his doctor's wishes, under threat of firing. This was a common Chrysler practice. His request to have his health benefits cover his medical bills was denied. Later that month, he took a few days of vacation with a supervisor's permission. But upon returning to work, he found that he had been charged with absenteeism. The next month, an arranged temporary promotion for Johnson was quashed when his white foreman, Bernard Owiesny, placed a white friend in the job instead. These incidents fed a growing feeling of harassment and racial persecution in Johnson even though, after contesting the discipline meted out to him, it was reversed. The work reassignment and suspension of July 15, which he feared was a dismissal, accelerated a smouldering frustration into a bonfire of rage and despair.[18]

An hour after he was sent home, Johnson returned to the plant gate. He told the guard that he was arriving late for his shift. The guard called the plant foreman and learned of Johnson's suspension. The guard denied Johnson entry to the plant and confiscated his employee badge. Johnson left the gate and climbed over a fence surrounding the plant. At 4:55 p.m., he reappeared in his department, demanding to see the man who had suspended him: "Where's Jones?"[19]

When he found him, Johnson removed a lightweight, short-barrelled rifle he had stashed in his coveralls and shot the foreman in the leg, knocking him to the floor. Johnson then continued to shoot Jones as he lay prone on the factory floor. Edward Lacey, an autoworker who witnessed the shootings, recalled, "He was standing over him, pumping bullets into him. He was going to make sure he was dead."[20]

Johnson reloaded his gun and turned a corner around a group of bins. A co-worker then attacked Johnson in an attempt to stop him. "I gave him all I had, right from the floor," said the unnamed witness. "The gun flew out of his hands in one direction and he [Johnson] went in another direction."[21] The gun loose, fellow workers shouted to foreman Gary Hinz, "Get it Gary, get it!" Hinz and Johnson both dived for the weapon. Johnson wrestled it free and shot Hinz twice in the chest, killing the man who two years earlier had sold Johnson a lawn mower at a bargain price.[22] Johnson then killed job setter Joseph Kowalski, shooting him as he tried to find shelter under a time clock, before eventually being persuaded to stop by Local 961 steward John Moffett.[23]

Johnson's rampage was a major news story. It made national headlines in the *New York Times* and covered the front page of the next day's *Detroit Free Press,* jarringly juxtaposed with a photo of UAW president Leonard Woodcock shaking hands with General Motors executive Earl Bramblett, their performance of industrial peace in the auto industry subverted by the news of Johnson's one-man war. Detroiters, workers, union leaders, and media all struggled to answer the *Michigan Chronicle*'s question: "What Manner of Man Is James Johnson Jr.?" The *Inner City Voice* had an answer: "James Johnson is you and me." The violence that erupted from Johnson, the *Voice* argued, could have come from anyone exposed to the racism, harassment, and "inhumane conditions" at the Eldon Plant. The article went on to detail the circumstances that had led to the shootings, claiming that "in a manner which all of us oppressed by the foul, racist machinery of Capitalism, are capable, of being driven James Johnson was pushed to the breaking point."[24] Because any black worker could have been Johnson, it was incumbent on all black workers to resist his prosecution for murder:

> All of us, and not just James Johnson, are on trial beginning April 26. And that is why all of us in turn must put Chrysler on trial that day, put the sell-out UAW on trial, must put the vicious system of Capitalist exploitation on trial, must put US "homegrown" racism and imperialism on trial. We cannot afford any more James Johnsons to be "judged" and sentenced by the same racist dogs who daily push the James Johnsons in us to the breaking point.[25]

The radical narrative that any black worker could have been James Johnson existed literally side by side with a more active, heroic portrayal of his actions. Beside the article was a poem, "The Ballad of James Johnson," which praises Johnson as a man who "does what he has to do," a martyr who "has given his soul." The poem concludes with the cry "James Johnson needed a Thompson!,"[26] referring to the machine gun.

The newsletter of the Dodge Revolutionary Union Movement (DRUM) also featured the narrative of Johnson as a heroic black workers' avenger who "supposedly asked all of his fellow workers to stand back for he was not going to hurt them. Who ended his rampage by coolly throwing down his gun and saying 'I'm satisfied.'" Johnson, according to DRUM, "has moved the Black Workers struggle at the point of production to a new and higher level." DRUM explicitly placed Johnson in a lineage of other black workers who had employed violence in the workplace, including Rushie Forge, Chuck Wooten, Sidney Lewis, and "another black worker in Dept. 9150 at Dodge" who "became outraged and locked his foreman in the trunk of a car on the assembly line."[27]

The DRUM article also included Ike Jernigan on its list of heroic black workers. Jernigan, a member of the International Association of Machinists, was working at an aerospace plant in California, where he helped to organize a dissident worker caucus, the Lockheed Employees Unity Association. In 1970 Jernigan shot and killed his foreman and two union executives after repeated conflicts with management and his union. All of the people mentioned by DRUM, with the exception of the unnamed individual from Department 9150, were either DRUM members or, in the case of Jernigan, consciously political black worker activists, unlike the quiet, apolitical Johnson.[28]

DRUM's construction of Johnson's violence as a heroic act of rebellion makes sense when one considers that the newsletter was primarily designed as propaganda meant to inflame and inspire black workers inside the plant. General Baker, one of the leaders of DRUM, recalled that when violence broke out in the factory, DRUM would get behind it, viewing violent incidents as an opportunity to craft a revolutionary consciousness among black autoworkers.[29]

It was certainly true that Johnson's murders had an immediate impact on relations in the workplace. Journalist William Serrin's book about the 1970 negotiations between the UAW and the automakers quotes a militant worker who told of the day after the shooting. He said a fellow worker returned to his plant after skipping two days of work. When the worker was confronted by his foreman, the militant claimed, "I took the front page of the fucking *Free Press* and I went over there and held it up to his fucking face. He turned his back."[30] Union officials, meanwhile, were concerned that workers seemed to enjoy the fear that foremen now had of them.[31]

Radicals were not the only ones who saw deeper meanings in Johnson's murders. Although others stopped far short of calling him a hero, they asserted that Johnson's rampage was a logical consequence of racism and working conditions in Detroit's auto plants. Bill Black was a prominent writer for the *Michigan Chronicle,* a progressive newspaper of Detroit's African American community. Black argued, much like the writer of the *Voice* article, that Johnson was an ordinary workingman pushed into a horrific outburst, a "man-machine, ready and willing to perform his hard, hot, heavy, dirty, and dangerous job." Black refused to condone violence, but he concluded, "Anyone familiar with conditions on Detroit's auto plantations would not be entirely surprised by what James Johnson did" because "work in Detroit's auto shops, particularly for black men, breeds violence."[32]

One of the factors breeding violence was in-plant racism. Black located evidence of Chrysler's racist practices in the very victims of Johnson's attack. He pointed out that Jones, the black foreman Johnson killed, had put in twenty-two years of service to the company; by contrast, Hinz, the white foreman, had been promoted to the same position in less than six years. Kowalski, who held the semi-skilled position of job setter, was white, whereas almost all eighty workers in Johnson's department, the "worst job in the plant," were black. To Black, they were flesh and blood examples of "the hoax known as 'Equal Employment Opportunity,'"[33] the name of a federal commission that had been established five years earlier to end discrimination based on race, among other factors, in the American workplace. Black held that Johnson's murders were an indictment of the commission's failure to change the racial calculus of auto work.

Much like the disgruntled workers in the auto shops, Black directd his criticism at both the company and the union. Black opined that the union had failed Johnson in not vociferously defending him against his suspension. He concluded that Johnson, whom he quoted a co-worker describing as "a good man who got pushed too far," therefore "went home and got his gun."[34] Black's criticism of the union and working conditions at the Eldon Plant attracted a rebuke from Local 961 officials, who issued a written statement, signed by the local's president, secretary, and Region 1 representative, that accused Black of "playing up Johnson as a hero."[35] As Johnson's union remained largely silent during the trial, the statement is a rare indication of UAW and Local 961 attitudes toward the Johnson incident and wider issues of race, gender, and conflict in the plant. In response to the structural issues raised by radicals and liberals alike, the union countered with a narrative that stressed that Johnson's murders were the product of his own individual pathology.

That the union contested Black's claim that Johnson's steward did not represent Johnson adequately before the shootings was to be expected. Historians have shown that the UAW leadership of the day combated black radicals with ferocity, while largely ignoring other dissident groups. UAW leadership called DRUM members "fanatics" and "black fascists" and consistently denounced them in union publications. It employed violence and harassment against black leaders, forcibly broke the picket lines of DRUM-led strikes, and underhandedly interfered in union elections to sink black radical candidates.[36]

In this context, the union's criticisms of Johnson as a "sick" man and a loner who often did not get along with his co-workers emerge as elements of a counternarrative contesting the adoption of Johnson as a symbol by black radical elements opposed to Local 961's leadership. Both Black and those radical elements would have been bitterly amused by the statement's defence of working conditions in the plant itself. The union heads acknowledged that Johnson's job in the brake shoe department was the lowest-paying work in the plant but defended the department by claiming that it had fewer requests for transfers out than any other department. "'If it's such a rugged place to work,' they asked, "why do they have women working there – and contented?"[37] This complacent approach to both working conditions and the struggles of black and women workers illustrates why so many production workers had become dissatisfied with a local union leadership that they saw as uninterested in improving the jobs of black, female, and lower-status workers.

At Johnson's trial, his defence lawyers, Ken Cockrel and Justin Ravitz, expertly blended the narratives of radicals and progressives to construct a narrative that made Johnson's acts explicable, and excusable, to a jury. The two were political radicals, Cockrel being one of the leaders of the League of Revolutionary Black Workers, who were also able attorneys. Cockrel and Ravitz were uniquely suited to the task of making radical critiques palatable, both in a courtroom setting and to the media. Exploring the racism and poor working conditions that Johnson endured was the foundation of their defence. As Cockrel said, "the trial gives us a chance to question both the auto companies and the union."[38] Cockrel and Ravitz would stress Johnson's lifelong struggles with mental illness, arguing that it predisposed him to snap under the strain of racist mistreatment at Chrysler that another worker might have endured. They emphasized the racism that shaped Johnson's life at every turn. Cockrel and Ravitz also took pains to demonstrate that workplace violence at the Eldon Axle Plant contributed to an intolerable situation that sparked Johnson's violent reaction. They presented an understanding of workplace violence as caused in large part by structural factors.

Through the testimony of Johnson's co-workers, Cockrel and Ravitz demonstrated that work at the Eldon Plant was defined by racism. One of the first witnesses called, production worker William Threet, testified that a foreman had called Johnson "boy." When asked whether the foreman had ever spoken to him in that way, Threet replied, "He hasn't yet – I hope he don't, because there'll be trouble."[39] Witnesses revealed that racism at the plant worked both structurally and informally. In his own testimony, Johnson alluded to this situation, discussing his frustration both with the racialized hierarchy of work at the Eldon Plant and with the countless small insults and indignities that contributed to his fraying mental state.[40]

The second major element of Cockrel and Ravitz's defence was a sustained presentation of the poor working conditions and violence experienced

Ken Cockrel (pictured) and Justin Ravitz's radical defence of James Johnson at his criminal trial argued racism and brutal working conditions were to blame for Johnson's workplace violence. Photo courtesy of Walter P. Reuther Library, Archives of Labor and Urban Affairs, Wayne State University.

by Johnson and other Chrysler workers. Tom Ricke, who covered the trial for the *Detroit Free Press,* wrote that "working conditions and treatment of workers by foremen have become the main issues of the trial." A parade of witnesses testified to the epidemic of shop floor violence at the Eldon Plant. John Moffett, the union steward whose intervention helped to end Johnson's rampage, said he was "shot at by a worker two weeks ago as he tried to defend another man who was in trouble for not coming back from lunch on time." He also told of "dangerously greasy floors, unprotected conveyers, and dangerous aisles crowded with workers and hi-low trucks at the same time."[41] Quality control auditor Don Thomas called Johnson's job "the worst job at the plant" and said he "has frequently witnessed foremen pick on workers who are doing the best they can." Suspending workers for refusing to work the brake shoe ovens, which precipitated Johnson's shootings, was common.[42] That Thomas, who claimed to be a friend of all three men murdered, offered such testimony speaks to his understanding of how fundamental exploitation and harassment were to the production of Chrysler automobiles. Clemens Fitzgerald, a psychiatrist called by the defence, identified the entire environment at Chrysler as toxic, citing the "total despair and frustration" felt by workers "with no chance of upward achievement."[43]

Moffett indicated that little had changed at the Eldon Axle Plant since the day of Johnson's terrible vengeance. This situation was corroborated by the testimony of others. Foreman John Pietrziewicz "told how he was attacked by a worker he suspended last week. He said he was hit on the head from behind and knocked into a 'skid box.'"[44] In fact, according to the testimony of Ellsworth J. Rhodes, the plant's general foreman and an apparent target of Johnson on July 15, the problem was getting worse, not better. Rhodes testified "that violence has been 'rather markedly increasing' at the factory for the past few years, especially since the Johnson shootings, including 'workers hitting foremen with iron bars and things like that. There's been fights between workers too.'"[45] Rhodes's testimony underlined the defence's point that violence was an everyday part of the Eldon Plant environment. This enabled the jury to understand Johnson's shootings as a reaction to the everyday racism and violence at the plant, not a shocking revenge murder from outside the bounds of comprehensibility.

To counter Cockrel and Ravitz's structural explanation of Johnson's killings, prosecutors attempted to personalize and pathologize his actions. In cross-examining Johnson, Wayne County assistant prosecutor Avery Weiswasser focused on the fact that Johnson left the plant and then returned with a hidden weapon. This conduct showed, he argued, that Johnson acted as a rational individual perpetrating a crime. To Johnson's definition of committing the murders and other violent incidents of his life as "losing control," Weiswasser countered that Johnson was actually "losing his temper." The prosecution also called its own psychiatrist, who opined that Johnson was capable of distinguishing right from wrong at the time of the shootings. This construction of Johnson's mental state replaced an explanation that identified him as a man driven beyond reason by the strains of the factory with one that identified him as an actor in full control of his faculties and wholly responsible for his violent crimes. He called Johnson "evil" and said, "his soul is sick, not his head."[46]

Weiswasser did include one outside factor in the understanding of Johnson's shootings that he presented to the jury. During his cross-examination, he asked Johnson whether he read dissident newspapers like the *Eldon Wildcat* or the *Inner City Voice:* "Was your attitude created in any way by some of the things you read in the newspapers?"[47] He also pressed Johnson as to whether he belonged to ELRUM, DRUM, or the League of Revolutionary Black Workers. These questions appear to be part of a strategy by Weiswasser to undercut the defence's argument that racism contributed significantly to Johnson's actions.[48] The defence, he charged, was being used as a "cat's paw" by "revolutionary elements."[49] In Weiswasser's telling, in-plant racism was nothing more than the persecution complex of a violent paranoiac.

However, Weiswasser's dismissal of racism as a factor in the murders would dramatically backfire:

> Under cross-examination by Assistant Wayne County Prosecutor Avery Weiswasser, Johnson testified to incidents he considered "harassment" by company foremen, "no job upgrading ... no consideration" and a "conspiracy to get me fired." "They were all just picking on you, I suppose," Weiswasser said. "Not just me," Johnson answered. "It happened to a lot of people there." "How do you know?" Weiswasser asked." "I saw it all with my own eyes," Johnson said. "I supposed you mean all the black boys [were being harassed]," Weiswasser snapped. Groans rose from many of the courtroom spectators and jurors. Weiswasser was silent. Defense attorney Kenneth Cockrel stood up slowly and said calmly: "Your honor, I object to the word 'boys.'" Judge Kenneth Colombo agreed.[50]

Nevertheless, Weiswasser continued to explain Johnson's violence along personal lines, concluding on the final day of the trial that he was "just a big baby."[51]

The prosecution's explanation of Johnson's workplace violence as essentially the product of his own individual agency was further weakened by the jury's visit to the Eldon Axle Plant, an event that radical attorney Paul Harris concludes "had the most profound impact"[52] and that Heather Ann Thompson calls "the most important moment of the trial."[53] Chrysler had done its best to whitewash the plant for the visitors. "Eldon Avenue looked as if Mr. Clean, Snow White and the Seven Dwarfs and the White Tornado had gone through it," the *Michigan Chronicle* reported.[54]

Nevertheless, jurors were moved by the solemnity of the workers who stood silently as the jurors, court officials, and press toured the plant and by the expression of support from one young black worker who called out to the defendant, "Hey Brother Johnson." Jurors tried loading and unloading the brake shoes. Although Johnson remarked, "it wasn't like this when I was here," the jurors' view of the plant deeply affected their understanding of Johnson's actions. The trip, Thompson concludes, "impressed upon the jury the alienating and dangerous nature of the oven job" in a way that even the eloquence of Cockrel and Ravitz could not.[55] As *Time* reported, during deliberations one member commented, "Did you see that cement room?

Working there would drive anyone crazy."[56] Although the jurors' deliberations were heated, they arrived at a decision in less than four hours. They found Johnson not guilty due to insanity.

Why did the understanding of workplace violence as a product of structural racism and exploitative work presented by Johnson's defenders resonate with Detroiters inside and outside the courtroom? Race has rightly been identified as a major factor in the Johnson defence and its understandings. Thompson sees the Johnson verdict as primarily a symptom of the changing alignment of forces in the struggle for control of Detroit. Pressed by the actions of black radicals, she argues, city liberals moved leftward during the late 1960s and 1970s. The Johnson verdict was one of a series of high-profile acquittals that infuriated white conservatives, who believed that "liberals [were] now in cahoots with radicals to promote black interests over white."[57] However, there is an important class element of the acquittal that must also be considered. Although Cockrel and Ravitz had to win over a jury that was made up of both blacks and whites, class was also a key factor in the jury's makeup. Ten of the twelve had worked in the city of Detroit, two as autoworkers. Three more were married to autoworkers.[58] *Time* noted that even Judge Colombo's working-class sympathies were engaged by the defence strategy:

> A villain to many liberals for having once sentenced a marijuana defendant to 9½ years, Judge Colombo was nonetheless scrupulously fair to the defense. "I used to work on the line in an auto plant during the summers," he recalls. "That's a lot of what persuaded me to go to law school. I hated the men who wore white shirts and always knew how to do your job better than you."[59]

As Dan Georgakas and Marvin Surkin write in *Detroit – I Do Mind Dying: A Study in Urban Revolution,* Cockrel turned "defense into offense" by "emphasizing class" in a true "jury of your peers" strategy that meant "the Chrysler corporation was put on trial."[60] Attorney Paul Harris writes that "the genius of these two young lawyers was in creating a strategy to help the jurors understand how race and class destroyed a fellow human being."[61]

Further evidence of the effectiveness of this radical, structural critique of workplace violence was attorney Ronald Glotta's 1973 suit against Chrysler seeking worker's compensation for Johnson. Glotta argued that Johnson was in the Michigan mental health system, where he had been ever since his trial, because of a mental illness that had been caused by Chrysler's inhumane working conditions; therefore, his mental illness was as much a workplace injury as a slipped disc suffered lifting an overloaded box. The 1960 case of *Carter v. General Motors* had established a precedent for compensating workers for mental disabilities stemming from employment in Michigan.[62] In March 1973 Judge John Conley decided that Chrysler was responsible for Johnson's predicament. He awarded Johnson benefits of $75 a week, effective from the day of the shootings.[63]

The precedent-setting ruling underlined the ability of radical legal practice to define workplace violence as a phenomenon stemming from racism and poor conditions in the workplace. Glotta declared after the ruling, "Chrysler pulled the trigger which resulted in Johnson's insanity and the death of the three men."[64] Conservatives expressed shock and dismay at such arguments, finding Johnson's 1973 award for mental disability disturbing. A suburban Detroit editorial reiterated the argument that only Johnson was responsible for the killings, claiming that "the same working conditions did not drive other employees insane" and that Johnson's very real experiences with racism and harassment at work were "contrived grievances conjured up by a sick mind."[65] The *Detroit Free Press* argued that Chrysler's suspension of its personnel test, a measure aimed to facilitate the hiring of more African American workers after the 1967 uprising, resulted in the hiring of a worker who was "insane to begin with."[66] The *Detroit News* claimed that Johnson's court award would leave workers with a history of mental illness "virtually unemployable," leading to higher worker's compensation premiums. Ironically, this critique of the verdict echoed the perspective of radicals in its understanding of the intersection of trauma and workplace stress as widespread. Detroit's mainstream press asked, "Who among us hasn't had some trauma that work might 'aggravate?' Who among us, far short of killing or violence, couldn't claim an impairment of earning ability as a result of this 'aggravation?'"[67]

Despite the outcry, however, the wider impact of the verdict fulfilled neither the dreams of radicals nor the nightmares of conservatives. After the verdict, Glotta issued a press release that directly linked the verdict to the political struggle and wildcats led by radical workers at Eldon: "It is hoped that the Johnson case will become the spearhead for a new effort to improve working conditions not only in the Eldon Plant but in all plants across the United States."[68] This hope was in vain. As Thompson notes, the UAW, "blinded by political paranoia," was completely uninterested in using Johnson's case to pressure the automakers on race, safety, or violence.[69]

Cockrel, Ravitz, and Glotta's radical legal practice effectively defended Johnson by advancing a structural understanding of their client's violent actions at work. However, the aftermath of the Johnson ruling reflected the limits of radical legal practice in creating durable understandings of violence at work as a structural phenomenon. That Judge Conley ordered Chrysler to pay James Johnson, a man who had killed three people at work, $75.00 a week in worker's compensation was certainly an important, precedent-setting ruling. Glotta called it "an important case for people in the plants" that made it much easier to receive compensation for psychiatric conditions caused by job stress.[70]

Once the criminal and workplace compensation cases were over, however, public concern about workplace violence evaporated. In an age of crusading journalism and muckraking, few observers, aside from the occasional journalist like Bill Black or Rachel Scott, who featured the Johnson case in her book *Muscle and Blood,* called for any action to curb the violence that was common in Detroit auto factories.

How prevalent was it? What caused it? Did workers in other sectors face violence on the job? What could be done to reduce the levels of violence at work? These questions remained unasked. Although many people understood that Johnson's violence was partly the product of his experiences at Chrysler, the concept of workplace violence as a discrete issue, much less as a problem that could be solved, simply did not exist in the 1970s. Little was done in the plants to reduce the high risk of violence that autoworkers faced on the job. Nor was there any consideration outside the factories of the true scope of violence, either in the auto industry or in the wider working environment. In a real sense, Johnson was excused for his violence in a way that allowed such violence to continue.

In 1973 Black wrote, "The only thing unusual about the Johnson case is the fact that such tragedies don't happen more often. Conditions in the auto plants are such that on any working day one or several auto workers could be impelled to do exactly what James Johnson did."[71] As little was done to reduce violence at work, the violence – including the homicides and attempted homicides – continued. In the automotive industries of the United States and, in at least one instance, Canada, there were several more work-related shootings during the 1970s. As two of the most prominent cases show, it was often difficult to present the structural understanding so effectively employed in Johnson's legal battles.

Nine months after Johnson's victory in the worker's compensation case, an auto-industry shooting in Detroit would again make national headlines.

David Mundy, the African American chairman of UAW Local 600's casting centre and foundry unit, which had 5,900 members, stood trial, accused of shooting white skilled trades worker William Harrell. Once again, Cockrel led the defence of the accused. Unlike in the Johnson case, however, Cockrel largely eschewed placing structural factors and workplace issues at the centre of his defence. The Mundy case shows that, for radical attorneys and others, diagnosing workplace conflict, racism, and stress as a precipitator of violence was not equally possible in every case of violence at the automotive workplace, even if these factors were present. The specifics of the case mattered a great deal to which understandings of workplace violence were possible.

The shooting occurred in the context of a historic struggle within the UAW. Skilled trades workers were vigorously contesting the union's proposed contract with Ford. They objected to provisions that would allow production workers to replace them on overtime shifts if they refused to work them. At a time when automakers were attempting to squeeze as much production as they could from their workforce, overtime emerged as a major factor affecting quality of life. Workers were forced to work hours and hours of overtime a week as the Big Three opted to combat foreign automakers by squeezing maximum production from aging plants through speedup and extended hours.[72] Ford's skilled trades workers felt that a provision allowing management to put production workers into their jobs if they refused overtime was a backhanded way to erode their job security and force them to accept longer workweeks. The disagreement exposed deep fissures within the union. Skilled tradesman Louis Rucker, a worker with fifteen years at Detroit's Ford Rouge Plant, said, "Just because I don't want to work overtime, that shouldn't give the company the right to bring in a production guy to fill my job."[73] Asked to comment on the skilled trades revolt, UAW president Leonard Woodcock averred, "I'm not a psychiatrist. I'm just a collective bargainer."[74]

This tension erupted into open conflict after the skilled trades workers rejected the contract by a margin of four to one. It was the first time that a UAW contract had ever been rejected by the rank and file. The Detroit workers were the only workforce in the country to vote against the contract, an indication of the local nature of the grievances and the serious problems with working conditions in Detroit plants. In an article headlined "Labor Rebellion Stuns UAW Leadership," *Detroit Free Press* labour reporter Ralph Orr portrayed the union as out of touch: "The UAW, which had its roots in dissent, now faces dissent in its own ranks and appears bewildered by it." He said that the union was now looking for "scapegoats" to blame for the ballot box defeat, notably "the media, outsiders, and agitators," but that this response had come after the vote, when it was too late. During the lead-up to the vote, a picture of the formerly revered union leader Walter Reuther was torn from the wall at one Local 600 debate. One picket smashed a lock to attempt to get into Solidarity House, the enclave of UAW leadership. Yet these leaders were slow to react to the forces trying to scupper the deal. Woodcock did not make a statement arguing in favour of the contract's ratification until 25 per cent of the vote was already in, well after members had made up their minds against the contract.[75]

According to Orr, this inaction cost the leadership. He concluded, "tradesmen appear to have turned down the contract mainly because the leadership did so little to sell it."[76] And although the UAW directed concerted acts of repression at the radical, race-based challenge of the revolutionary union movements, it was caught flatfooted by the grassroots protest of mostly white skilled workers, supported by the United National Caucus, a reform body within the UAW. The leadership's response to its developing crisis of authority in Detroit among skilled trades workers would place an enormous amount of pressure on local union leadership and spark interunion violence.[77]

After the initial defeat of the deal with Ford, the UAW decided to issue a call for a second round of balloting of the skilled trades unit; in essence, it asked for a do-over. Behind the scenes, top leadership exhorted local leaders to bring the skilled trades workers into the fold. The situation was contentious. Trades workers were irate at a leadership they saw as unconcerned with their best interests. As one worker said, "Forty years ago you could lead people around by the nose. Now they're educated. You can't do that anymore."[78] The call for another vote added to workers' feelings of being unheeded by leadership. At Local 600 offices in Dearborn, Michigan, where workers and leadership had gathered in preparation for the ratification revote, "there were fistfights and bitter exchanges between dissidents protesting overtime rules for skilled tradesmen in the new agreement with Ford."[79]

In the hallway, David Mundy argued with a group of workers. It was about 2:30 p.m., after what had been a long and grinding day. Mundy and one of the workers, a twenty-seven-year-old white millwright named William Harrell, began shouting at each other. "Why don't you go out and negotiate a contract?" Mundy challenged. "OK. I could. I could," Harrell responded. What happened next is a matter of some dispute. Harrell tried to assault Mundy but was initially held off by some of Mundy's assistants.[80] After that,

Harrell was able to punch Mundy in the face, severely injuring his eye. Harrell fled the offices on foot, pursued by Mundy, who was a former heavyweight boxer, and three other men. Mundy took out a pistol. He would later say at trial that he had been carrying the gun because of death threats he had been receiving that week.[81]

Mundy allegedly fired two shots at Harrell, missing both times. Harrell ran down the streets of Dearborn, eventually seeking sanctuary inside the Hi Tower gas station. "Call the police. Call the police. They're going to kill me. They're going to kill me," Harrell implored Walter Hopper, the attendant. As Harrell attempted to call police from a phone inside, Mundy and the three other men arrived at the station. Also present was a camera operator from a Detroit television station, who captured a clip of the incident. Mundy allegedly fired three shots through the window of the station, hitting Harrell once. After Harrell fell to the ground, the four men walked away calmly. Hopper said, "They walked away like they owned the place."[82] Harrell, fortunately, had been only slightly injured by the shot that hit him in the buttock. Meanwhile, the second balloting for the skilled trades unit had been cancelled.

The shooting added a tragic and bizarre element to the dispute, guaranteeing that it made even bigger news. Agis Salpukas, a *New York Times* reporter who witnessed most of the altercation, called it "an extreme example of the intensity of feeling that has been evident on both sides during and after the negotiations."[83] The camera footage appeared on several local newscasts. Woodcock weighed in on the outcry, calling one account of the shooting "sensationalism."[84] Media observers connected the shooting to the struggle over the new contract, diagnosing the incident as a symptom of UAW dysfunction. In an editorial, the *Detroit Free Press* stated, "The problems for the UAW leadership in securing ratification of its contract settlement with Ford have only been heightened by the tragic, senseless shooting that took place Tuesday ... Guns should not replace reason in the heat of debate at the union hall, and local union leaders should be as aware of that as anyone else."[85]

The *Free Press*'s editors, like Orr, thought that the debacle demonstrated that UAW leadership was largely out of touch, not understanding its members' positions and issues: "There is a restlessness among the auto worker force that has caused Leonard Woodcock, the UAW president, and his key aides, to take a new and proper look inside the plants and to form a better understanding of those who work in them." The controversy showed that "UAW leadership needs to work even harder towards that goal."[86] In the headline of its story on the dispute and the shooting, the *Times* appeared to offer its own wry comment on an incident that occurred at a time of widespread grassroots worker action against management: "They Can Wildcat the Union, Too."[87]

In January 1974 Mundy's trial on a charge of assault with an attempt to commit murder began. The trial started on a note of low comedy, prosecutor Robert Healy cracking that "the saving grace is apparently Mundy is a lousy shot."[88] Many witnesses stepped forward during the next three weeks to reiterate the facts of the case: the argument in the hallway at Local 600 offices, the scuffle, the chase through Dearborn streets, and finally, the shooting at the service station. As in the Johnson case, the details of the matter were little disputed.

However, whereas in the Johnson case Cockrel painted his client as the victim of degrading work, as well as racism and violence both in the plant and out, he offered little of that type of defence here. Perhaps Mundy's position as a union leader made this critique more difficult to advance, although it is clear that local union leaders like him were being squeezed between the pressure of UAW leadership to bring the skilled trades workers onside and the desire of skilled trades workers to have leadership hear their demands. Cockrel did mention external factors, arguing before the trial that the videotape of the shooting was "only a segment. It does not show the racial implications ... It does not show the other implications."[89] However, Cockrel's defence of Mundy pivoted instead on a technical point: that, as reported in the *Free Press,* "after receiving the blow to the face, Mundy, a former professional heavyweight fighter, was 'out on his feet' and was mentally incapable of forming the intent to commit murder."[90] Mundy himself testified that he had no memory of the shooting, saying "I just don't remember pulling a gun ... I don't deny it, but I don't remember it, either."[91] After deliberating for two and a half hours, the jury convicted him of the most serious charge available to it, assault with the attempt to commit murder.

The transcript of Mundy's sentencing hearing reveals that the UAW's reaction to Mundy's crime was vastly different from its reaction to Johnson's. Whereas Johnson was largely forsaken and the criticisms of his working conditions rebuffed by Johnson's local leadership, UAW brass rushed to Mundy's defence. At his sentencing hearing, several prominent UAW leaders asserted that a man like Mundy, who had escaped a harsh upbringing in the Cincinnati ghettos to become a respected union leader, was a man needed in the streets of Detroit and the union hall, not locked up in prison. Even Leonard Woodcock sent a letter of support. Despite their forceful testimony on behalf of Mundy's character, Judge James Canham said that he was unable to overlook the fact that the jury had convicted on the most serious charge and that this verdict must be taken into account. Mundy was sentenced to a minimum of five years in prison.[92]

It is somewhat ironic that a political defence of Mundy was not really attempted given that Mundy was politically active, whereas Johnson was reclusive and withdrawn. Furthering the irony was Local 600 vice-president Buddy Battle's testimony that he would call Mundy in the middle of the night to act as a peacemaker when racial tensions exploded in Detroit neighbourhoods. Another major factor in Mundy's sentencing was gun violence, which was an increasing concern in Detroit. Here, too, David Mundy had attempted to stop the violence. In the early 1970s, a police unit named Stop the Robberies Enjoy Safe Streets (STRESS) conducted particularly aggressive and controversial police incursions into Detroit's black neighbourhoods, raiding properties without warrants and practising entrapment. During STRESS's first year of operation, Detroit had the highest rate of civilians killed by police of any US city, with STRESS responsible for over one-third of these deaths.[93] Mundy was a speaker at a major rally against STRESS. Battle, an important figure in Detroit's black liberal community and later UAW Region 1A director, said that "it would be an injustice to the community and a loss to me and the membership" if Mundy were jailed.[94]

Unlike Johnson, an isolated worker who became a hero to many radical workers, Mundy was an integral part of mainstream black unionism in Detroit, and his shooting of Harrell was condemned by radicals. Mundy had been a member of Battle's Trade Union Leadership Council, the moderate, leadership-aligned black faction of the UAW. After the shooting incident, the *Eldon Spark,* generally no friend of the almost exclusively white workers in the skilled trades, claimed Mundy's shooting of Harrell was part of a wider UAW campaign against dissidents and democracy: "How can the UAW bureaucrats be surprised if local bureaucrats end up shooting at UAW members? These little bureaucrats are only following the example of the big bureaucrats in Solidarity House!"[95]

Like James Johnson, dynamics of race, workplace violence, and job stress were present in the case of David Mundy. The violence of both men sprang directly from stressful job situations and a workplace marked by conflict. The case of Mundy shows that workplace violence did not just flow in a simple direction from "exploited worker" to "boss" but, reflecting the contentious union situation of the time, also came out of the UAW's conflicts with its own rank and file. Mundy's position as both a black worker and a union leader placed him at the centre of a conflict between skilled trades workers and the UAW leadership. This hybrid position may have been why Cockrel opted for a relatively apolitical defence. With no widely understood framework of "workplace violence" into which to place the incident, and no simple narrative of worker versus company to present, Mundy's action was seen as symptomatic of workplace conflict, not produced by it.

The deployment of radical legal practice in response to an incident of workplace violence, then, depended on both the political context surrounding the case and the specific facts of the case itself. This situation is underlined by the final case considered here, the 1977 murder of UAW Local 444 president Charlie Brooks by fired autoworker Clarence Talbot in Windsor, Ontario. Because of Brooks's widely beloved status in the community, Talbot's history of violent criminality, the differing racial and political context of Ontario, and the conventional defence of Talbot pursued by his attorneys, the question of whether workplace conflicts, racism, and interunion politics may have played some role in Talbot's actions was largely ignored at trial. Nevertheless, some of the public discussions of the case indicated that issues of union conflict and racial friction were not unknown in Windsor or in the Canadian auto sector. Radical legal practice primarily intersected with the Talbot case not at his trial but in the Law Society of Upper Canada's prosecution of two civil rights lawyers who attempted to assist Talbot after his arrest. This prosecution resulted in a public clash over the Talbot case and a notable victory for radical, anti-racist legal practice in Canada.

As previously shown, Windsor was marked by racism and racial inequality. In a 1965 report for the newly formed Ontario Human Rights Commission, which made Windsor the site of its very first field office, anthropologist Rudolf Helling concluded that "Negroes in Windsor are at the base of the city's social structure." This racial hierarchy was deeply established. Despite the longstanding presence of African Canadians in Windsor, "newcomers have advanced more rapidly."[96] Among all nonmajority groups in Windsor, "Negroes have experienced the greatest difficulties. They encountered problems in restaurants, taverns, with law enforcement officers, educational officers, employers, fellow workers, and previous employers."[97]

This racialized hierarchy was clearly visible in Windsor's workplaces. Among the city's fifteen largest companies, Helling found that nine had zero black employees and that none had a black manager.[98] Helling wrote, "the marginality of Negroes can be seen in the considerably high rate of unemployment even through generations."[99] Compared with workers of Italian and Chinese descent, blacks reported trouble finding employment in much higher numbers and were much more likely to attribute the cause to discrimination.[100] For those black workers who made it past racial bias and into a job, further racism abounded at work. Thirteen of eighty-seven workers reported unfair treatment by fellow workers, and fourteen of eighty-eight said that supervisors had treated them unfairly. Helling recommended that "union programs to increase the acceptance of minority group members among fellow employees might be appropriate."[101] Noting that blacks of varying income levels reported the same incidence of discrimination, Helling concluded that Windsor's problems "were race problems, not social class problems."[102]

This was the city where Clarence Talbot grew up as a young black man in the 1960s. Years later, a friend would describe his upbringing as "brutal," marked by prejudice, violence, and paranoia. A gifted artist, he had dropped out of school by Grade 7, apparently over the frustration of being illiterate. He began to box. He was talented and powerfully built. In 1972, after over a decade of amateur boxing, he was headed to a pre-Olympic qualifying tournament in northern Ontario. However, the month before the tournament, he clashed with a man at a Windsor bar. They went outside to the parking lot, and when Talbot assumed his boxer's crouch, the man shot him four times, a response that a jury later ruled was self-defence.[103]

Talbot's work in the auto industry was also marked by conflict. Employed at Chrysler for over a dozen years, he had been fired several times and had then returned to work after successfully grieving his dismissals. In January 1977 he was out of work again, fired for lateness and absenteeism. The father of ten children, he arrived at the offices of UAW Local 444 to discuss getting his job back.[104]

As noted in Chapter 3, Talbot had a reputation as a bully in the plant and had been involved in at least one major brawl with a co-worker. For his part, Talbot saw himself as being discriminated against racially, and had complained about how his union was not doing enough to reinstate him.[105] That January morning, Talbot spoke to local leaders, including president Charlie Brooks, about his dismissal. The union had initially grieved Talbot's firing, but there are conflicting accounts as to the fate of that grievance: whether the grievance had been dropped, unbeknownst to Talbot, during contract negotiations with Chrysler in November 1976, or whether the grievance was still active. Others insist that the grievance was still in process.[106] At trial, UAW second vice-president Gerry Bastien, present at the fatal meeting, recalled that although Talbot felt he was being discriminated against, he "calmly discussed"[107] the problem and "only showed emotion during a brief dispute with Mr. Brooks over whether the union president had promised to get the job back."[108]

Talbot, however, certainly had strong feelings about his firing. Recounting a discussion with Talbot in November or December 1976, Bastien testified, "He felt he was being discriminated against. He described to me how he felt as a black and said he felt he was not properly represented concerning his dismissal." According to Bastien, at the January meeting, Brooks insisted that he had only promised to try to get Talbot's job back. After this discussion, Talbot left the office. He went to his car and got a rifle. He returned, forced his way into the office, and shot Charlie Brooks to death. Police arrested Talbot immediately afterward.

The killing of Brooks sent Windsor into a state of shocked grief. Charlie Brooks was a locally beloved and revered figure. A UAW member for over forty years, he was serving his eleventh consecutive term as Local 444 president. He had fought for the Auto Pact and for wage parity between Canadian and American autoworkers. He was also a strong social unionist, who used his platform to press for wider transformations of society. Current members of Unifor/Canadian Auto Workers (CAW) Local 444 remember him as a "visionary."[109] He helped to create co-op housing for Windsor workers and pressed for reductions in the workweek. A particular passion was nuclear disarmament, a controversial cause to spearhead in the repressive climate of the 1950s. John McArthur, publisher of the district's UAW newspaper, remembered, "He always believed strongly in that, even when he was branded left-wing and pro-communist."[110] In the 1960s Brooks pushed the Canadian branch of the UAW to oppose the Vietnam War, a stance credited by later president Ken Lewenza as establishing an anti-war orientation for the CAW.[111] He was a tough-minded leftist, perhaps a Communist, who often clashed with national and international UAW leadership and who seemed beloved by his 13,000-member local. The day of his funeral, workers shut down four Chrysler plants by leaving the line to pay their respects.[112]

Mournful messages and tributes appeared in the local and national media. UAW International president Leonard Woodcock and Canadian president Dennis McDermott said Brooks's "tragic and senseless" death "diminishes us all – because Charlie Brooks is gone and because of the way he died."[113] In addition to scores of Local 444 members, McDermott and the mayor of Windsor were at the funeral. UAW International vice-president Doug Fraser, soon to take over as UAW head, spoke to the mourners.[114]

Local 444 members pause to remember murdered president Charlie Brooks. Photo courtesy of Unifor Local 444.

Meanwhile, Clarence Talbot sat in a Windsor jail. Newspaper articles reporting Talbot's arraignment stated that Talbot did not have a lawyer. These articles came to the attention of Toronto civil rights lawyer Charles Roach. Roach, together with his partner Michael Smith, had been active in civil rights law and anti-racist activism in Ontario for several years. Both were members of the International Committee against Racism, an affiliate of the Progressive Labor Party. The two lawyers earned national headlines in early 1978 when they challenged the federal government's deportation of seven Jamaican-born women working in Canada. The government was deporting them on the grounds that they had lied about having children before entering the country. Roach and Smith countered that the women were encouraged to do so by Jamaican and Canadian officials because their labour was in demand in Canada. When unemployment rose, they alleged, the government used the child issue as a pretext to discard women workers who were no longer needed in the labour market.[115]

According to Roach, it was through their contacts in the anti-racist community, who feared for the plight of a black defendant in a city marked by racism, that Roach and Smith were prompted to look into the case.[116] In Roach's telling, he and Smith, together with a social worker named Owen Leach, travelled to the Windsor jail to visit Talbot and to see whether there was any assistance they could offer him. After informing the officer on duty of the purpose of their visit, they sat down to wait for Talbot to be brought out. After about forty minutes, a Jaguar pulled up outside the courthouse. According to Roach, the car's driver, a Windsor attorney named Harvey Strosberg, said to Roach and Smith, "'Are you folks here to see Talbot?' I said yes. He said: 'I'm representing Talbot.' I tried to shake his hand. He didn't shake my hand." Talbot's brother Clayton Talbert accompanied Strosberg. Roach, Smith, and Leach left the jail without seeing Talbot and drove back to Toronto. Roach recalled,

> Coming back with my two friends ... we in some kind of way figured what was going to happen. They're going to put this guy in an asylum and say that he's crazy. We hadn't even seen him! But what tipped us off was when Harvey Strosberg says "professional," used the word "professional assistance," some word like that. It's like a code word for lawyers saying they'll come in here and do something.[117]

After consulting Toronto lawyer Edward Greenspan and John Laskin, Strosberg recommended charges against Roach and Smith to the Law Society of Upper Canada, the professional body that regulates lawyers in Ontario.[118] Roach and Smith were charged with attempting to poach another attorney's client. Roach was also charged with misconduct in an older case. According to Roach, because of these professional charges, neither Roach nor Smith had involvement with Talbot's criminal trial, although Roach recalled being "really keen to get into the depths of this case."[119] Talbot's trial took place in Toronto. Public outcry over the murder was so great that the trial had been moved from Windsor, as it was believed that it was impossible for Talbot to receive a fair trial there.[120]

The moved venue was not the only unusual aspect of the trial. There was a disagreement between Talbot and his attorney, the renowned Canadian trial lawyer Edward Greenspan, about how Talbot should plead. As in the Johnson and Mundy cases, the facts of the trial were not in any real dispute. Talbot told Greenspan that "he would not allow a defence of insanity."[121] Whatever the reason, there was a serious dispute between Talbot and his legal counsel as to what explanation of his violent act they would present to the court.

The debate was so intractable that Judge Patrick Galligan took the rare step of calling witnesses from the bench to testify to Talbot's mental condition.[122] In effect, Talbot was forced to plead insanity over his own objections. This practice was infrequently employed. According to Roach, Talbot would later tell him that he had been denied the chance to tell his side of the story at trial.[123]

With the judge and defence attorney focused on the issue of Talbot's mental state, little else was brought into the trial's consideration of how this act of violence occurred. Unlike Cockrel and Ravitz's defence of Johnson, as well as the defence Roach and Smith would have likely put forth for Talbot, Greenspan presented a medical, nonstructural claim for Talbot's insanity. This defence defined Talbot's act of workplace violence as a purely internal, psychological matter. Therefore, other factors that may have contributed to Talbot's mental instability, like past experiences of racism in Windsor and the plant or conflict between Talbot and his managers or union representatives, were considered largely irrelevant.

The only mention of racism or union-worker conflict at trial to appear in the media was Bastien's testimony that Talbot felt "discriminated against" and "not properly represented."[124] In the context of Windsor Chrysler, however, this evidence was understood as proof of Talbot's disorder – a paranoid persecution complex arising from within – not as evidence of a lifetime of racism and on-the-job stress that had created an uncontrollable violent reaction to a contentious situation, as radical attorneys like Cockrel, Glotta, Roach, or Smith may have argued.

Talbot was duly found not guilty by reason of insanity and committed to a provincial mental health facility at Penetanguishene. However, the Law Society's hearing into the charges against Roach and Smith remained active. The prosecution of Roach and Smith for attempting to provide aid to Talbot is evidence of the legal profession's resistance to radical legal practice in 1970s Ontario. Ironically, however, although issues of race and workplace conflict were never raised at Talbot's trial, the Law Society's proceeding against Roach and Smith, despite being intended to chill their oppositional legal practice, brought these issues into public discussion. Even more ironic was that Roach, Smith, and their supporters turned the hearing, ostensibly a weapon of the establishment, into a politicized environment that directly challenged the Law Society's practices and biases. In doing so, they won a significant victory for the anti-racist movement in Ontario.

In November 1978, almost one year after the conclusion of Talbot's trial, the Law Society of Upper Canada's hearing began. Roach and Smith's supporters formed a defence committee to apply political pressure to the Law Society. The committee appears to have been comprised of allies gained by Roach and Smith through their work as civil rights lawyers and anti-racist activists.[125] Each of the committee's publications highlighted Roach and Smith's previous work. Peter Rosenthal, a University of Toronto professor and later a lawyer and anti-racist activist in his own right, was one prominent member. The defence committee produced a pamphlet titled "ORGANIZE TO DEFEND CIVIL RIGHTS LAWYERS," which alleged that suppressing anti-racist legal activism was the real purpose of the Law Society's charges against Roach and Smith: "It is clear that certain members of the legal establishment are determined to curtail the fight that Charley Roach and Mike Smith are waging against racism and for civil liberties."[126]

To fight the charges against them, Roach, a member of the National Conference of Black Lawyers, drew on his contacts in North America's radical, anti-racist law community. The conference was the leading anti-racist legal organization in North America, with experience defending high-profile political clients, including Angela Davis and the Black Panthers. Arriving from the United States to lend their skills to the defence were attorneys Lennox Hinds, the conference's director, who had defended Assata Shakur at her murder trial in 1973; Leonard McMann, of the Michigan Alliance against Racial Oppression; conference member Victor Young; and Leora Mosston. Joining the defence team in Canada was James Lockyer, who would later help to exonerate David Milgaard and Guy Paul Morin, both wrongfully convicted of murder in 1970 and 1992 respectively. The participation of these attorneys in the case is an example of a transnational anti-racist legal practice that was forged in struggles around the continent and deployed in opposition to Ontario's legal establishment.[127]

The crucial tactic in Roach and Smith's wider political campaign against the charges was to open the hearing to the public. According to Roach, the Law Society wanted to conduct the hearing *in camera*. Roach and Smith demanded the press be accommodated. The Law Society acceded to this request but insisted on holding the hearing in a small room that held no more than thirty spectators. When Roach and Smith's lawyers requested a room big enough to accommodate a public audience, the Law Society responded that, in Roach's words, "For 135 years we've held hearings in this room, in Osgoode Hall ... This is where it's going to be held."[128]

However, Roach and Smith's supporters overwhelmed the Law Society's attempt to control the space and the parameters of the hearing. They vocally demanded entry and defied the Law Society's attempts to prohibit them from attending the proceedings or to constrain and limit their presence by the size of the room. Once they gained admission, they filled a large meeting room with around 200 people, some sitting in the aisles. Throughout the hearings, supporters would regularly interrupt the proceedings with heckles for the prosecutors and applause for Roach and Smith.[129] The pressure succeeded in destabilizing the Law Society's normal way of doing business, brought external issues into the deliberations, and took away the Law Society's home-field advantage.

Before the hearing's second day, demonstrators carried signs reading "anti-racist lawyer harassed," "defend civil rights lawyers," and "fight racism." Inside, the Law Society's lawyer told the hearing that the pair failed to follow "reasonable steps to ask whether Mr. Talbot was already represented."[130] Roach and Smith's attorney disputed this claim. Furthermore, Roach and Smith insisted that their motivation for action in the Talbot case was not to gain financially by poaching a client but to intervene constructively in a racially combustible situation. As Smith wrote to Rosenthal, one of the organizers of the defence committee,

> I should make it clear that our interest in the Clarence Talbot case was related to our involvement with the International Committee against Racism and the anti-racist movement generally. We wanted to insure that the charges made against Clarence Talbot did not become the source of increased racism in Canada. We wanted to investigate the circumstances of the shooting because we suspected that elements of racism were aggravating Talbot's problems and frustration. Finally, we wanted to insure that Talbot was not further victimized by the trial process because of his race. We had no intention of representing Mr. Talbot.[131]

Roach and Smith's defence team contended that this trial was not an isolated prosecution of two attorneys for violating the accepted rules of professional conduct but rather part of a pattern of persecution of radical and anti-racist advocates by bar associations and law societies in the United States and Canada. Hinds viewed Roach and Smith's prosecution as an example of "the increasingly widespread use of professional sanctions to muzzle legal advocates who espouse unpopular clients and causes throughout the world."[132] Hinds was speaking from direct experience, having faced a disbarment hearing in New Jersey that he believed was racially motivated. Hinds had been charged after referring to an in-progress murder trial as a "legalized lynching" by a "kangaroo court." These comments, and a trip

Hinds took to Iran to participate in a conference on American involvement there, also led a New York judicial committee to recommend that he not be allowed to practice in that state. As with Roach and Smith, a group of Hinds's supporters formed a committee in his defence.[133]

The Law Society denied any racial bias or political animus. Strosberg testified, "I don't care if Mr. Roach had been pink, I would have sent the letter."[134] Criticisms of Strosberg and Greenspan's handling of Talbot's defence emerged at the hearing. Strosberg insisted there was no racial dynamic to the situation. In his view, there was no "racist tinge to the way community was inflamed." Windsor was simply "enraged that a beloved person in the community generally was shot down."[135]

Exchanges at the hearing pitted Smith's critique against Strosberg's depoliticized view of the Talbot case. Whereas Smith argued that Talbot was merely being processed through the justice system with little concern for his desires or defence, Strosberg paid little attention to issues of race or union conflict. Of their conversation at the Windsor jail, Smith asked, "Did you say that: 'We are trying to keep a lid on it?'" Strosberg denied making this statement but admitted, "I certainly wasn't looking to add any more material to the public position that was being set out as a precedent."[136]

That position was to treat Talbot's slaying of Brooks as arising only from Talbot's own psyche and not to raise any other factors, such as race or union conflict, that might have had any bearing on the case – factors that Roach and Smith would likely have made a cornerstone of their approach. Asked why he rejected offers of assistance from Roach and Smith's organizations, Strosberg blandly replied, "this was a proceeding on the basis of insanity."[137] No other issues, he seemed to be saying, were worth mentioning, or as he put it in another answer, "the only question was one of capacity and intent."[138]

However, it was not only Roach and Smith's attorneys and political allies who felt that a concern with the racial context of the Talbot case was warranted. Talbot's brother Clayton, himself a former UAW local leader in Windsor, commented that Windsor was "a very, very bad place to live if you are black." Noting that his family had been threatened and that a general atmosphere of racial hostility existed, Clayton Talbert asserted, "it was pretty nice of these guys [Roach and Smith] to see if there was anything they could do to assist my brother in his time of need."[139] Roach highlighted his attention to factors that other lawyers may not have considered, especially the extralegal situation faced by Talbot and his family. According to the *Globe and Mail,* Roach "suggested bitterly to the discipline panel that there were some members of the society whose sole motivation was not personal gain and that there could be 'humanitarian missions outside the strict legal capacity they have.'"[140]

After three sessions, the touting charges against Roach and Smith were dismissed due to an absence of adequate evidence. The outcome was a significant victory. Anti-racist activists in Toronto, helped by their American allies, had rallied around two of their standard-bearers and had effectively taken control of the Law Society's process, legally and politically. Rosenthal recalled that Roach and Smith's defenders "felt very good about this victory. The Law Society, with all its power, came after Mike and Charlie in a big way, and they were very successfully resisted."[141]

The Talbot, Johnson, and Mundy cases show how, during the 1970s, notable incidents of workplace violence were catalysts that touched off contests over race, work, violence, and the law in both the United States and Canada. Like the Mikel Otegi case, these cases dealt with controversial events that prompted different parties to struggle over establishing what understanding of these violent acts would be adopted. How workplace violence was understood was not stable but was determined in part by clashes in the courtroom, in the media, and in the streets. In the Talbot and Johnson cases, radical legal practice was a crucial part of this struggle. Like earlier courtroom crusades over free speech or lynching, trials in response to workplace violence have been an important forum for radical law.

However, it must be remembered that radical legal practice, although important, was just one factor among many that shaped understandings of workplace violence in the 1970s. The Johnson, Mundy, and Talbot cases demonstrate that understandings of workplace violence – what it is, why it happens, and who is responsible – are historically contingent. The local, national, and legal contexts in which these incidents occurred, the life histories of the perpetrators and victims, the media construction of the cases, and the strategies of attorneys all helped to determine how a particular incident of workplace violence was understood. Over time, the understandings of a particular case could also change. In the early 1980s, the Michigan legislature rewrote its worker's compensation laws to exclude more workers with emotional and cardiac conditions, citing the Johnson case as evidence that workers were abusing the system.[142]

In the 1980s incidents of workplace violence became more spectacularly violent and thus more widely reported. Now carrying automatic weapons, violent workers committed acts that killed scores of people. A spate of killings at US post offices thrust workplace violence permanently into the national consciousness. These killings did what the incidents of workplace violence in the 1970s, although widely publicized, had not done: they prompted a widespread understanding of workplace violence as a discrete social problem that required the deployment of knowledge and policies aimed at its eradication. Yet even though awareness of the problem widened, the understanding of the causes of workplace violence narrowed in the 1980s and 1990s. Policies tended to focus on violent workers as crazy, paranoid loners, ignoring the factors that created the conditions for workplace violence, such as class conflict, the labour process, unsafe workplaces, racism, and patriarchy. As shown in the final chapter, workplace violence was simultaneously everywhere and nowhere, a terrifying "new" phenomenon occurring all over North America, whose causes were troublingly buried in the unknowable hearts and minds of workers themselves. As Ronald Glotta reflected in 2012, "I couldn't win James Johnson today."[143]

6

Out of the Back Streets and into the Workplace

The Discovery of Workplace Violence in the 1980s and 1990s

On the morning of September 10, 1994, the executives of the operations and maintenance unit of United Automobile Workers Local 600 wrapped up their weekly committee meeting at Ford. Most of them then walked from their portable trailer at the River Rouge complex in Dearborn, Michigan, to a second trailer, where they began working on an informational pamphlet. Another executive member, Oliver French, soon joined them. French, a forty-seven-year-old black man, was a member of a unity slate which had just lost power to a slate headed by white workers. French believed, as did other unionists, that the new slate was pushing black workers out of positions of power.

French's frustration with the situation was boiling over. On the previous Thursday, French, who would later be described as "a damn good guy" and "always a gentleman," had kicked down a door at the office trailer, claiming he needed to use a fax machine. Others had a key to the door but not French. This Saturday, he stalked into the trailer with a gun. French shot four of his fellow union members, killing Ron McTasney and Greg Couls. French then walked to an adjacent building and handed over his .357 Magnum to a worker there. "I just shot four people," he said. When the Dearborn police arrived, an officer asked French, "Why did you do it?" French's reply could have come straight from the Dodge Main of the 1970s: "Because they fucked with me."[1]

Auto work, race, union politics, masculinity: the tragedy of Oliver French's murderous rampage carried many echoes of the violence that reverberated through auto plants in the 1970s. But when French left the Rouge building in handcuffs, he was walking out into a world very different from that of James Johnson, one that had different concerns and would understand his violent rage in a different way. The *Detroit Free Press*'s story on the shootings was accompanied by a sidebar titled "Deadly Trail in the Workplace Keeps Growing," which argued that "murder in the work place has become the fastest growing type of homicide in America." Below, it listed several examples of deadly shootings on the job both in Michigan and across the United States. In 1994, the United States was gripped by the troubling "new" phenomenon of workplace violence. At the time of French's shootings, officials at the Ford Rouge Plant and members of Local 600 were preparing to meet to discuss on-the-job violence, twenty years after David Mundy chased Billy Harrell from the Local 600 hall and shot him in the street. In Detroit this concern created novel alliances. Mike Hamlin recalls being brought in by Ford in the aftermath of the French shooting to help lead the healing process. In the late 1960s, Hamlin was a leader of Detroit's radical black worker insurgencies. Now, he was a social worker specializing in the troubles of autoworkers.[2]

As discussed in the previous chapter, when violent incidents occurred in Detroit's and Windsor's auto plants during the 1960s and 1970s, they occasionally grabbed national headlines and pressed observers to consider the role of working conditions, racism, union politics, and alienation in producing these violent explosions on the job. Yet never was "workplace violence" understood as a pressing social issue, a problem in itself, to be investigated, analyzed, and solved. In the 1980s, however, the age of workplace violence arrived. Although the identification of workplace violence as a specific, solvable issue was in one sense a step forward, the framing of the problem often ignored the actual nature of violence at work and its causes. The solutions advanced by experts, employers, and governments therefore failed to address the totality of the problem. The definition of workplace violence that they established has resulted in the pursuit of solutions such as enhanced surveillance and security measures at work as well as additional layers of bureaucracy, but it has not done enough to address the root causes of workplace violence. An appreciation of the history of workplace violence, something this study has attempted to further, would have produced a much richer understanding of violence at work and likely resulted in better solutions. It is unwise to try to solve a problem in the present while remaining ignorant of its past.

In the United States, workplace violence became an issue of nationwide concern following a series of deadly shootings at post offices by postal workers, including the 1986 massacre of eighteen people in Edmonds, Oklahoma, by former postal worker Patrick Sherrill. The post office shootings were accompanied by multiple-victim shootings in other workplaces across the nation: offices, factories, and stores.[3] In 1992, for the first time, the Occupational Health and Safety Administration began tracking workplace violence fatalities.[4] Major media outlets across North America ran stories on the terrifying new threat in the nation's workplaces: your co-worker. A typical piece, from the *St. Petersburg Times* read,

> "Look who is doing the firing now."
>
> That thought, says a criminologist who studies mass murder, is often in the minds of men who slaughter their bosses and co-workers.
>
> "Workplace homicide has doubled in about a decade," said James Alan Fox, dean of the College of Criminal Justice at Northeastern University in Boston. "More and more baby boomers are losing jobs. They're facing unemployment, they're angry, and they want revenge.
>
> "More and more they are willing to take out the boss, as a way of saying, hey, look who's doing the firing now."[5]

A *Globe and Mail* piece began, "Surviving the working day can be a matter of life and death for some Americans, as murder on the job rises at an alarming rate." The article quoted Bruce Blythe, president of Crisis Management International, who contended that "workplace murder is now the fastest-growing kind of homicide in America."[6] A chorus of voices echoed Blythe's conclusion. *USA Today* reported, "'We like to think the workplace is safe,' says Peggy Lawless, research project director for Northwestern National Life. Her company releases the survey 'Fear and Violence in the Workplace' today. 'The reality is that violence in America is spilling out of the back streets and into the workplace.'"[7]

Note the construction of workplace violence as something invading peaceful workplaces from the outside. *USA Today* cited a survey of 600 workers that found that one in four claimed to have been attacked, threatened, or harassed on the job in the past year. It quoted Mark Braverman, president of the Crisis Management Group: "There's enormous rage being directed at the American workplace now."[8] Nowhere in these stories were names like James Johnson, Clarence Talbot, or David Mundy mentioned. Workplace violence was something happening strictly in the present tense.

Concern about workplace violence did not stop at the 49th parallel. In 1992, suspended Ontario Glove employee Patrick Dombrowskie shot and killed a co-worker, a supervisor, and the company's co-owner.[9] The Canadian media regularly published articles on the subject. Women's groups and union groups regularly launched campaigns to end violence against women and violence at work, often in tandem. A crucial event that sparked such activism was the 1989 École Polytechnique massacre, in which a prospective student denied admission entered a Montreal university building and murdered fourteen women studying to become engineers.[10] The date of the murders, December 6, became a sombre anniversary and a rallying point, a time to remember and to combat violence against women. Two years after the killings, activists entered subways and boardrooms to demand action on violence against women, including violence on the job. In response, at least one employer, Ontario Hydro, developed an educational program designed to address violence against women both at home and in the workplace.[11]

In 1992 Leo Gerard, the Canadian director of the United Steelworkers, announced the union's pledge to fight violence against women in the home and at work: "In order to change the behaviour of violent men, we must also change our own behaviour. We can no longer turn our backs."[12] In 1994, on the fifth anniversary of the École Polytechnique massacre, the Quebec Federation of Labour announced its own campaign against workplace violence.[13] Throughout this period, according to interviewees, the Canadian Auto Workers succeeded in getting language about workplace violence into contracts, winning workers protections such as the right to refuse work if a risk of violence was present.[14] In Canada, then, the struggle against violence in the workplace has intersected with the struggle against violence against women.

In the United States, conversely, a variety of causes for workplace violence were identified by a panoply of experts offering books, seminars, and videocassettes that promised to help companies combat the threat of "ticking time bombs" in the workplace. The causes that they identified were both psychological and structural, but generally all constructed the problem and its causes as contemporary, ignoring the longstanding presence of violence in North American workplaces. Job stress, substance abuse, and the greater availability of guns were all often identified as contributing factors. The shattering stress of layoffs was also a popular culprit.[15]

Layoffs were a major and often discussed aspect of middle-class life during the 1980s, but it is important to remember that they had been a regular experience of blue-collar workers for decades, as had autocratic workplaces and high levels of job stress. Indeed, one reason for the greater concern about workplace violence in the 1980s and 1990s, beyond the higher body counts that were the legacy of the availability of automatic and semi-automatic weapons, was that shootings were now occurring in occupations more typically considered middle-class, such as post offices and white-collar office buildings. Viewed in this light, the concern about workplace violence is a powerful symbol of anxieties over the proletarianization and degradation of middle-class work in the early neoliberal period.[16] A *Newsweek* piece on the phenomenon raised the spectre of class war:

> But in a flat economy, many people with mounting bills, a pressured job or the loss of one see their employers and other organizations as the source of the problem. Last week a man who officials said had lost his disability pay stormed a state insurance office in Las Vegas. Most employees who kill managers or colleagues have been fired or feel mistreated. When "employees are treated as disposable commodities," says Bruce Blythe, president of Crisis Management International, the company loses moral authority. Reports of sky-high executive salaries exacerbate such anger, says a compensation expert. "We have a war of haves and have-nots," says Ira A. Lipman, chairman of Guardsmark, Inc., a security firm. The have-nots probably won't rise up and revolt. But the workplace has become an ad hoc battlefield.[17]

The article's next question was not why toxic workplaces and inequality were accepted or how dignity and fairness could be restored to workers. Instead, it asked, "When does someone angry become murderous, and who is likely to explode?" This question perfectly reflected the main response to workplace violence: the profiling of potential problem individuals by creating a picture of the person most likely to "snap" or to "go postal."

Although variations on the profile existed, the experts presented a general image that was remarkably consistent. Violent workers were white men in their late thirties or forties, socially maladaptive "loners" with few human connections. *Newsweek* confidently concluded, "Those who target the workplace fit a general profile: they are primarily white males who have few social supports, tend to 'externalize' or blame others for their problems and are preoccupied with weapons." The magazine quoted a Palm Springs security consultant: “His primary anchor to society is his job. When he loses his job, he goes ballistic.”[18] In a sense, these experts asked the same question that the *Michigan Chronicle* had asked when it pondered, “What manner of man is James Johnson Jr.?”[19] Yet, unlike the *Inner City Voice,* none of the experts or media concluded that workplace shooters were “you and me.”[20]

Instead, experts created a portrait of a lunatic in the office. Michael Mantell, a leading workplace violence expert and author of *Ticking Bombs: Defusing Violence in the Workplace,* provided *Psychology Today* with a “Portrait of a Violent Worker”:

- White, male, 25–50
- Low self-esteem
- Loner
- Fascination with the military and/or guns.[21]

Although Mantell and other experts also discussed workplace factors such as layoffs and toxic job stress, this individual profile became iconic. The figure of the homicidal loner, exemplified by Michael Douglas’s rage-filled laid-off engineer in the 1993 film *Falling Down,* emerged as a cultural archetype and dominated the thinking about workplace violence.

The fixation on profiling possible shooters was a mistake. Journalist Mark Ames, who studied workplace and school shootings for his book *Going Postal: Rage, Murder, and Rebellion – From Reagan’s Workplaces to Clinton’s Columbine and Beyond,* characterizes such an approach as extremely unhelpful in reducing the level of workplace violence. Although hundreds of profiles were created, none effectively identified and predicted which workers would commit violent acts.[22] Furthermore, focusing only on shooting incidents and shooters dramatically distorted the true picture of workplace violence, which included fistfights, stabbings, bullying, harassment, unsafe work, and institutional and managerial violence, all of which were far more common than a shooting rampage.

The obsession with “loners” and “ticking time bombs” put the focus on a feared and despised boogeyman figure and moved it away from the workplace. Because the problem was defined as something emanating from individuals, so were the solutions. Many workplace violence policies were designed more to protect the company from the elusive violent individual than to make the overall workplace healthier and safer. Consider, for example, Polaroid’s influential workplace violence policy. Copies of it were requested by hundreds of companies. Although the policy had some useful initiatives, such as counselling for abusers and abused and short-term paid leaves of absence for emotional distress, it also emphasized identifying and stopping problem individuals, including training managers to "recognize signs a worker could become violent and to look for signs of domestic violence."[23]

Mantell's model for "defusing the bomb" included extensive psychological screening of all prospective employees, a "golden rule attitude" at work, training supervisors to identify potentially violent workers, counselling, and security measures. The individual-focused prescriptions of these newly minted experts were duly enacted by many workplaces. Concern over workplace violence played a key role in justifying the encroaching securitization of the North American workplace, exemplified by the "perp walk": security personnel escorting fired employees out the door like criminals.[24] This practice has made headlines in the white-collar world over the past two decades but, as previously shown, was standard practice at Dodge Main at least as far back as the 1960s.

When postal massacres and other office shootings captured North American attention during the 1980s, the rush to name and understand workplace violence distorted the issue in two important ways. First, the widespread belief that this problem was new meant that it was approached without the benefit of historical perspective. Just one decade earlier, cases like those of James Johnson, David Mundy, and Clarence Talbot had captured national and international attention. Yet they were completely forgotten during the workplace violence discussions of the 1980s and 1990s. Historical perspective would have enabled a consideration of whether violence in the workplace was actually increasing, what forms workplace violence had traditionally taken, whether changes in the workplace were contributing to the problem, and what methods workers, unions, companies, and governments had employed in the past to reduce the risk of violence at work.

Second, when we look closely at workplace violence, we learn that individual violence cannot be separated from structural factors. Ames points out that the US post office, the site of many of the workplace massacres of the 1980s and 1990s, was the first US government agency to be "subjected to what was essentially a semi-deregulation and semi-privatization plan," under which managers increased profitability by "pushing its workers to work harder and ... creating an increasingly stress-jammed atmosphere."[25] These tactics mirror the approach Chrysler took in its Detroit plants during the 1960s and 1970s, with similarly tragic results. Acting on information from workers, Michigan senator Carl Levin investigated conditions in the state's post offices. He was so alarmed by the brutal management style and toxic atmosphere that he wrote to the US postmaster general demanding action, only to be dismissed with a form letter. In 1991, postal worker Thomas McIlvane killed five people, including himself, at his workplace in Royal Oak, Michigan. Ames places the rise of workplace shootings squarely at the feet of Reaganomics and neoliberalism's destruction of the limited security, stability, and dignity of working people's lives. Ames argues that neoliberal government and corporate policies make the entire US working class disposable and precarious: a nation of outsiders.[26] More recently, Franco Berardi has contended that an age of constant online media flows and the triumph of the market in every aspect of social life have produced a "kingdom of nihilism" in which mass murder and suicide are responses to alienation and hyperindividualization.[27]

Indeed, although the focus on the individual obscured the structural dimensions of the issue, it was in another sense perceptive, if misdirected. Individual violence at work was a manifestation of one of the most important developments in how class was experienced in the postwar era and beyond: the replacement of notions of external, collective class struggle by an internal, individualized struggle, as chronicled by sociologists Richard Sennett and Jonathan Cobb in their 1972 book *The Hidden Injuries of Class*. They wrote of the "frustration" and "powerlessness" of Boston workers living in a society whose ideology insisted that opportunity and success were available to all who had the talent and initiative to grasp them: "All of [their] experience, which had to do with the structure of class, had presented itself to them as a problem in the structure of their own characters, and so there lay an unspoken distrust of themselves below the surface, a feeling of doubt."[28]

This dilemma of a structural experience of class felt as an individual tribulation can be seen in the Chrysler plants of the 1970s. In response to the structural problems they faced, some workers joined collective efforts to maintain dignity on the job, such as the Dodge Revolutionary Union Movement in Detroit or the walkouts and sit-downs in Windsor. But there were also many individual responses, actions that Sennett and Cobb would classify as motivated by "the internalizing of class conflict," a desire "to heal a doubt about the self rather than create more power over things and other persons in the outer world."[29] These individual responses to frustration and pain, guided by a "logic of discontent [that] leads people to turn on each other rather than on the 'system,'" are visible in many of the episodes of workplace violence recounted in the preceding chapters.[30] Again and again during the 1960s and 1970s, autoworkers lashed out individually at those they felt had wronged them, often insisting on their dignity and warning that the target of their violence "better quit fucking with me." Writing in 1972, Sennett and Cobb concluded that "the real oppression of the new working class" – an oppression rooted in the fact that when one experiences dissatisfaction with working life, "everything in the society prompts a kid to believe that his insides are therefore all messed up" – had created "a sense of mass bitterness and frustration that we believe will keep growing."[31]

The next two decades vindicated Sennett and Cobb's gloomy prognosis: collective workplace action stagnated, the working worlds of blue-collar and even white-collar workers became ever more precarious, and individual workplace violence became a major societal concern. The change from the late nineteenth and early twentieth centuries, when there was collective, sometimes revolutionary class violence, to today's era of worker atomization and anomic violence is striking and demands further research. This study suggests that the individualization of both working-class experience and the consciousness of workers, of which individual violence is just one particularly revealing example, is one of the most important dynamics of twentieth-century labour history. If we wish to understand the postwar stagnation of any collective politics based on class and the persistent tendency of workers to identify with the interests of capitalists, not each other's interests, further research and theorizing of the roots, manifestations, and consequences of worker individualization is crucial.

While I was working on this project, another historian asked what my category of analysis was: Class? Race? Gender? After thinking for a moment, I replied that it was violence. This question has been a helpful one. Researching and writing this book has been a complex undertaking, and when I found myself lost in the complexities, I returned again and again to the lens of violence to see what it revealed about these times, these places, these workplaces, and the lives of these workers. Looking through this lens revealed that postwar auto workplaces were suffused with violence. It showed me that workplace violence was a crucial variable in the labour processes and workplace cultures of the automotive industry. I was able to see a historical relationship between structural violence and individual violence in the workplace setting, as well as how levels of violence changed over time because of changes in the labour process.

Because violence was so strongly connected to workplace factors, it is crucial that we do not fall into the trap of naturalizing violence by essentializing working-class men as violent. Instead, we need look at the social structures and cultural contexts that have increased the likelihood of violent actions. Contemporary discussions of individual mass shootings often focus on mental health, the easy availability of guns, or a perceived conservative or misogynistic terror unleashed by disenfranchised men. Although these factors are important to consider with care, this study highlights the workplace as the historical setting in which individual mass violence became common and as the location of the class conflict that gave rise to it. The usually unnoticed structural violence of labour exploitation and workplace racism produced the spectacular examples of individual violence that did make headlines. The past few years have seen a proliferation of studies of violence, in tandem with a tragic persistence of individual mass violence. Such studies of violence past and present must account for the influence of social relations under capitalism and acknowledge the workplace as a crucial source of structural and individual violence in both the United States and Canada.

This study makes clear not only that the workplace shaped violence but also that violence shaped postwar workplaces. This violence needs to be accounted for in histories of postwar North America. The coruscating effect that violence had on plants in Detroit indicates that capital flight and the collapse of consensus liberalism were not hastened only by white backlash or a changing political economy. Rather, the violence produced by the American industrial labour processes that underwrote that liberalism may also have been a significant factor in deindustrialization. Much of this individual violence occurred in the context of automakers burning through the last years of older northern plants and their workforces before relocating.[32] The violence directed at nonwhite, female workers by industrial insiders in Windsor and Detroit suggests that intra-working-class violence mattered in labour's failure to move beyond a vision of a white, male working class and to stimulate a powerful, diverse worker identity in the 1970s. When we understand violence not just as a strange and troubling consequence of postwar class relations but also as something that shaped these relations, we can better appreciate its ongoing impact.

Looking through the lens of violence, I saw that place also mattered. In Detroit, where the prevailing conditions made labour exploitation more feasible and where class relations intersected with racism, high levels of violence were the result. This showed me that there was nothing inevitable about the violence in Detroit plants or in the city itself and that the strategies and actions of powerful actors like Chrysler need to be much more fully accounted for in histories of the city and its half-century of crisis. It taught me that everyday violence was a powerful factor in the life and culture of Windsor workers, especially the insider violence that they used to regulate their workplace and prove their manhood. Therefore, I encourage historians of Canada to account for the many ways that violent acts and discourses have historically constructed the experience and structured the power relations of a country often complacently understood as a largely peaceable place, especially in contrast with its neighbour to the south. In the same vein, I saw that the greater unity and militance of the United Automobile Workers in Canada were partly the legacy of racial exclusion and a nationalist orientation. Whiteness in Canada's postwar working-class history is another dynamic that needs much more critique and explication in order to determine both how it was created and maintained and to better contextualize anti-racist activism by Canadian workers and allies, whether radical or not. More generally, much of the history of Canada's radical workplace organizing in the 1960s and 1970s still needs to be recovered. Finally, as we continue to investigate workplace violence, comparative and transnational frames remain crucial. Management scholar Santanu Sarkar's analysis of recent autoworker murders of managers in India reveals that collective violence is the dominant mode there, underlining that varying expressions of capitalism embedded in specific national and local contexts play key roles in structuring levels and expressions of violence at work.[33]

In terms of place, the role of environmental factors in increasing historical violence by individuals demands further research and analysis. In 2007 economist Jessica Wolpaw Reyes advanced the hypothesis that given childhood lead exposure's link to poor impulse control and greater violent behaviour, reduced exposure is largely responsible for lower levels of violent crime in the United States since the 1990s.[34] Both Reyes's study and a paper published in 2000 by economic consultant Rick Nevin that claimed "lead exposure may have influenced crime rates throughout this century"[35] were brought to mainstream attention in a 2013 *Mother Jones* cover story by Kevin Drum.[36] The hypothesis has been disputed by other researchers, who claim that Reyes's reliance on Uniform Crime Reporting (UCR) data produced a false correlation between lead and crime in the 1970s and 1980s that disappears when National Crime Victimization Survey data are used. These researchers believe that UCR data are problematic for observing individual violence over time.[37] However, the correlation between lead exposure and violence was buttressed by a recent study by economist James J. Feigenbaum and sociologist Christopher Muller. They examined lead and crime during the 1920s and 1930s and concluded that American cities that used lead pipes for municipal water had homicide rates 24 percent higher than those that did not.[38] It is clear that environmental factors deserve further consideration, keeping in mind that environments, like workplaces, are conditioned by class, race, and gender, among other categories, and that there are many factors that increase the risks of individual violence in a given environment, whether the workplace or elsewhere. As previously shown, in Detroit and Windsor plants, workplace factors were very often the precipitating factors that sparked violent incidents.

Finally, I saw that easy definitions of what violence was and why it happened were elusive. The reception and understanding of incidents of violence at work during the 1970s were contested processes that depended a great deal on history, politics, and the nature of the incidents themselves. The contemporary definition of workplace violence was created at a specific historical moment in response to specific societal anxieties. This definition stressed individual and psychological factors and excluded workers' perspectives and a consideration of structural violence. Structural understandings of the causes of workplace violence were perhaps more widely accepted in the early 1970s than they would be twenty-five years later, when Oliver French stood trial. In the early 1970s, courts found James Johnson not guilty by reason of insanity for his workplace murders, even extending him worker's compensation for a mental illness that they judged had been precipitated by working conditions at Chrysler. In the 1990s, although media and experts gestured toward toxic workplaces and the culture of layoffs, they more often presented workplace violence as the terrifying revenge of the wackos in our midst. Breathless media coverage encouraged workers to fear each other. The *St. Petersburg Times* asked, "How can you be sure the person sitting next to you at work won't go over the edge and bring an Uzi to the office tomorrow? You can't."[39] This shift to a focus on individual actors demonstrates that to understand the history of violence, we need to understand how violence is defined in time and place.

In our own present time, the novelty and shock of workplace violence have faded. Workplace massacres still occur but are now seemingly a regular, if tragic, aspect of North American working life, joined by massacres in public schools, movie theatres, on college campuses, and at LGBT nightclubs. They have become a commonplace trope in our popular culture. In 1997 the videogame *Postal,* where the gamer played the role of a lone shooter gunning down his co-workers, attracted widespread censure. Almost twenty years later, a package delivery chain with outlets around

America bears the name Goin' Postal. This reflects a culture that has come to view violence at work as regrettable but normal.

The institutional expectation that certain levels of violence at work are a mundane cost of doing business is clearly apparent in a 2006 case adjudicated by the British Columbia Worker's Compensation Appeal Tribunal. A manager at a grocery store sought compensation after being graphically threatened and harassed by an employee she had disciplined. The employee's menacing gestures with a knife and threats to, for example, "cut open your jugular just to see what happens" had affected her ability to sleep and brought on acute anxiety.[40] The tribunal did not dispute that the woman's condition was a result of workplace violence, and was thus a workplace injury, yet it still denied compensation for her condition. The tribunal's reasoning was that the workplace violence she suffered was gradual and part of the normal work process. As it was not a "sudden and unexpected traumatic event," it was not compensable.[41] Only acute and unexpected workplace violence, such as the police chasing a suspect into the store and shooting that person in front of her, would have resulted in an acute and unexpected mental injury that was eligible for compensation. The tribunal held that fear and harassment, including experiencing death threats, were an expected part of working life.

In recent years, provincial and state governments, not individual employers, have taken the lead in combatting violence at work. In 2009 the Ontario government passed Bill 168 to address workplace violence and workplace harassment. The bill requires employers to assess the risk of violence in their workplace and to report those risks to workers. It also requires employers to post their workplace violence policy at the workplace. Finally, it protects the right of workers to refuse work that exposes them to a risk of workplace violence. According to interviewees, the Canadian Auto Workers, having been deeply affected by workplace violence due to the murder of Charlie Brooks, was instrumental in lobbying for this legislation. The final passage of Bill 168 was galvanized by the murder of nurse Lori Dupont.[42] Dupont was fatally stabbed at Windsor's Hôtel-Dieu Grace Hospital in 2005 by an anesthesiologist who also worked at the hospital.[43]

In the United States, meanwhile, twenty-two states have passed "Bring Your Gun to Work" legislation, discussed in Chapter 1, which forbids employers to bar workers from having firearms in their car. Employers argue that the closer proximity to guns will create more fatal incidents of workplace violence, whereas supporters of the legislation, such as the National

Local 3 workers walk the picket line, 1970. Violence at work was a significant dynamic shaping their lives on the job. Photo courtesy of Walter P. Reuther Library, Archives of Labor and Urban Affairs, Wayne State University.

Rifle Association, contend that it enhances workers' freedom and ability to protect themselves.[44]

Although this wave of legislation may, in time, reduce the risks of violence in the workplace, it generally fails to define violence broadly enough. As previously discussed, the definition of what constitutes workplace violence is always contentious. Studies have shown that "how violence in the workplace is defined depends on one's location in the organization." Much as radical autoworkers argued in the 1970s, scholars are increasingly calling for a greater understanding of how violence is "bred into the practices"[45] of workplaces before attention is turned to interpersonal violence, as the latter is often caused and constructed by the former.[46] Thus the editors of a recent volume on workplace violence in healthcare settings argue that a single-definition approach "has not provided a way into [violence's] chameleon-like characteristics."[47] Indeed, broad-minded approaches that consider a number of factors that increase the risks of violent outcomes offer our best hope for understanding violence. With that in mind, we see that naming violence is not enough; a detailed understanding of how violence actually operates at work is needed. This insight requires going beyond defining only single incidents as "violent" and acknowledging that violence operates as part of workplace systems in ongoing ways. To paraphrase E.P. Thompson, violence can be understood only in motion – that is, in terms of relationships between workers, managers, owners, and labour processes.[48]

History supports this conclusion. It teaches us that defining workplace violence as something outside the workplace itself, something that can be kept out by legislation or policy, fails to appreciate the true nature of violence in the workplace. For Detroit and Windsor autoworkers in the 1960s and 1970s, violence was ever present at work, whether in the foreground as a fight or a workplace injury or in the background as a subtle factor shaping work processes and culture. It injured and traumatized countless workers and even cost some their lives. A great many structural factors contributed to the risk of violence that workers faced on the job. The labour process, social relations at work, racism, gender, workplace culture, health and safety conditions, crime, the surrounding community, drug and alcohol abuse, political struggle, national and international labour relations, and employment contexts – all played a role. Many workers in Detroit and Windsor knew about this convergence of causes, spoke about it, and wrote about it. Workers were and are well placed to diagnose and explain workplace violence, yet the perspectives of workers are too often ignored in contemporary discussions about workplace violence.

Violence at work in Detroit and Windsor Chrysler factories during the 1960s and 1970s was not a flashpoint; it did not burst into flame and then disappear. Rather, it was an ever-present *current* that shaped the labour process, workplace culture, and the consciousness, ideas, and strategies of workers, managers, unionists, and executives alike. Violence, then, could not have been barred from Detroit and Windsor's Chrysler plants, because the labour process at these workplaces was the primary source of violence. It may be obvious, but it bears remembering that without workplaces, there would be no workplace violence. This means that, if we are to seriously confront workplace violence, we must interrogate the fundamentals of our working lives: how the work is done, by whom, and under whose control; how the work is organized and for whose benefit; and what kind of human interactions flow from these social relations. To be sure, this interrogation is much more difficult and requires much more soul searching than coming up with standard lists of policies and best practices. But if we truly want to live and work in peace, we must fully reckon with our history of workplace violence.

Notes

Chapter 1: Dripping with Blood and Dirt

1 Quoted in Sara Murray, "Guns in the Parking Lot: A Delicate Workplace Issue," *Wall Street Journal,* October 15, 2013, http://www.wsj.com/news/articles/SB10001424052702303983904579095532026750354. Item no longer available.

2 Online comment, in ibid.

3 Karl Marx, *Capital: Critique of Political Economy,* vol. 1, trans. Ben Fowkes (1976; reprint, New York: Penguin Classics, 1990), 926.

4 See ibid., 340–416.

5 Ibid., 389–90.

6 Ibid., 412.

7 Ibid., 416.

8 Upton Sinclair, *The Jungle* (1905: reprint, New York: Signet Classics, 1963); Eric Schlosser, *Fast Food Nation: The Dark Side of the All-American Meal* (New York: Perennial, 2002).

9 Important works concerning class, capitalism, and violence in North America include, but are in no way limited to, Louis Adamic, *Dynamite: The Story of Class Violence in America* (1931; reprint, New York: Chelsea House, 1958); Mark Ames, *Going Postal: Rage, Murder, and Rebellion – From Reagan's Workplaces to Clinton's Columbine and Beyond* (New York: Soft Skull, 2005); Thomas G. Andrews, *Killing for Coal: America's Deadliest Labor War* (Cambridge, MA: Harvard University Press, 2008); Michael Belleseilles and Christopher Waldrep, eds., *Documenting American Violence: A Sourcebook* (New York: Oxford University Press, 2006); Aaron Brenner, Robert Brenner, and Cal Winslow, eds., *Rebel Rank and File: Labor Militancy and Revolt from Below during the Long 1970s* (New York: Verso, 2010); Elizabeth Faue, *Community of Suffering and Struggle: Women, Men, and the Labor Movement in*

Minneapolis, 1915–1945 (Chapel Hill: University of North Carolina Press, 1991); Beverly Gage, *The Day Wall Street Exploded: A Story of America in Its First Age of Terror* (New York: Oxford University Press, 2009); Dan Georgakas and Marvin Surkin, *Detroit – I Do Mind Dying: A Study in Urban Revolution* (1975; reprint, Chicago: Haymarket Books, 2012); Aaron Goings, "Red Harbor: Class, Violence, and Community in Grays Harbor, Washington" (PhD diss., Simon Fraser University, 2011); David Goldberg and Trevor Griffey, eds., *Black Power at Work: Community Control, Affirmative Action, and the Construction Industry* (Ithaca, NY: Cornell University Press, 2010); Reinhold Kramer and Tom Mitchell, *When the State Trembled: How A.J. Andrews and the Citizens' Committee Broke the Winnipeg General Strike* (Toronto: University of Toronto Press, 2010); Paul F. Lipold and Larry Isaac, "'Striking Deaths' at Their Roots: Assaying the Social Determinants of Extreme Labor-Management Violence in US Labor History, 1877–1947," *Social Science History* 38, 3–4 (2014): 541–75; Steve Meyer, "Rough Manhood: The Aggressive and Confrontational Shop Culture of U.S. Auto Workers during World War II," *Journal of Social History* 36, 1 (2002): 125–47; Stephen Norwood, *Strikebreaking and Intimidation: Mercenaries and Masculinity in Twentieth-Century America* (Chapel Hill: University of North Carolina Press, 2002); David Roediger, *The Wages of Whiteness: Race and the Making of the American Working Class* (New York: Verso, 1999); Donald Wayne Rogers, *Making Capitalism Safe: Work Safety and Health Regulation in America, 1880–1940* (Champaign: University of Illinois Press, 2009); Joan Sangster, *Transforming Labour: Women and Work in Postwar Canada* (Toronto: University of Toronto Press, 2010); and Roger Stonebanks, *Fighting for Dignity: The Ginger Goodwin Story* (Edmonton: Athabasca University Press, 2004).

10 Lipold and Isaac, "'Striking Deaths,'" 541.

11 Bryan Palmer, *Working-Class Experience: The Rise and Reconstitution of Canadian Labour, 1800–1980* (Toronto: Butterworth, 1983), 143.

12 Richard Hofstadter, "Reflections on Violence in the United States," 1970, reprinted in *The Baffler,* 28 (2015), n.p., http://www.thebaffler.com/ancestors/reflections-violence-united-states.

13 Judy Fudge and Eric Tucker, *Labour before the Law: The Regulation of Workers' Collective Action in Canada, 1900–1948* (Toronto: University of Toronto Press, 2004); David Brody, "Workplace Contractualism in Historical Perspective," in *Industrial Democracy in America: The Ambiguous Promise,* ed. Nelson Lichtenstein and John Howell Harris, 176–205 (New York: Woodrow Wilson Center for International Scholars, 1993).

14 On Banks, see Peter Edwards, *Waterfront Warlord: The Life and Violent Times of Hal C. Banks* (Toronto: Key Porter Books, 1987). On *"les gars de Lapalme,"* see Desmond Morton, *Working People: An Illustrated History of the Canadian Labour Movement* (Montreal and Kingston: McGill-Queen's University Press, 1999), 284–86; and Bryan Palmer, *Canada's 1960s: The Ironies of Identity in a Rebellious Era* (Toronto: University of Toronto Press, 2009), 237. On the United Aircraft strike and the murders of the Robin Hood strikers, see Morton, *Working People,* 284–86, 292. Morton notes that these struggles prompted Quebec premier René Lévesque's Parti Québécois to pass legislation that forbade the use of replacement workers during

strikes, provided for automatic check-off of union dues, made certifying a union easier, and safeguarded workers' return to their job after a labour dispute.

15 On Teamster strikes in the 1970s, see Dan La Botz, "The Tumultuous Teamsters of the 1970s," in *Rebel Rank and File: Labor Militancy and Revolt from Below during the Long 1970s*, ed. Aaron Brenner, Robert Brenner, and Cal Winslow, 199–228 (New York: Verso, 2010). On violence and the United Farm Workers, see Frank Bardacke, *Trampling out the Vintage: Cesar Chavez and the Two Souls of the United Farm Workers* (New York: Verso, 2014), 426–37; and Miriam Pawel, *The Crusades of Cesar Chavez: A Biography* (New York: Bloomsbury, 2014), 269–71, 288–95, 404–5. On the decades of struggle between workers and capital in Harlan County, see Alessandro Portelli, *They Say in Harlan County: An Oral History* (Oxford: Oxford University Press, 2010). On King in Memphis, see Michael Honey, *Going down Jericho Road: The Memphis Strike, Martin Luther King's Last Campaign* (New York: W.W. Norton and Company, 2011).

16 Robert Michael Smith, *From Blackjacks to Briefcases: A History of Commercialized Strikebreaking and Unionbusting in the United States* (Athens: Ohio University Press, 2003).

17 Nelson Lichtenstein, *Walter Reuther: The Most Dangerous Man in Detroit* (Champaign: University of Illinois Press, 1995); Charles Williams, "Reconsidering CIO Political Culture: Briggs Local 212 and the Sources of Militancy in the Early UAW," *Labor* 7, 4 (2010): 17–43; Charles Brooks, "20 Years in the UAW," *444 News*, June 11, 1956, in Unifor Local 444 Private Collection, Unifor Local 444 Offices, Windsor, Ontario (hereafter UL444).

18 On racism within the plants and the UAW, see David M. Lewis-Colman, *Race against Liberalism: Black Workers and the UAW in Detroit* (Champaign: University of Illinois Press, 2008). On racialized and gendered conflicts within the plants during the Second World War, see Kevin Boyle, "The Kiss: Racial and Gender Conflict in a 1950s Automobile Factory," *Journal of American History* 84, 2 (1997): 496–523.

19 Lichtenstein, *Walter Reuther*, 398.

20 Charles Denby, *Indignant Heart: A Black Worker's Journal* (Detroit: Wayne State University Press, 1989), 35.

21 Georgakas and Surkin, *Detroit*, 85.

22 "Violence in the Factories," *Newsweek*, June 29, 1970, 66.

23 See, for example, Tod D. Rutherford and John Holmes, "Manufacturing Resiliency: Economic Restructuring and Automotive Manufacturing in the Great Lakes Region," *Cambridge Journal of Regions, Economy and Society* 7, 3 (2014): 359–78.

24 Steven High, *Industrial Sunset: The Making of North America's Rust Belt, 1969–84* (Toronto: University of Toronto Press, 2003); Tracy Neumann, *Remaking the Rust Belt: Space, Citizenship, and the Postindustrial Transformation in North America* (Philadelphia: University of Pennsylvania Press, 2015); Jason Hackworth, "Why Is There No Detroit in Canada?" *Urban Geography* 37, 2 (2016): 272–95. Other scholars who have looked at the Great Lakes region transnationally and historically include John J. Bukowczyk, *Permeable Border: The Great Lakes Basin as Transnational Region, 1650–1990* (Pittsburgh: University of Pittsburgh Press, 2005); Karl S. Hele, ed., *Lines Drawn upon the Water: First Nations and the Great Lakes Borders and*

Borderlands (Waterloo, ON: Wilfrid Laurier University Press, 2008); Robert Heuton, "Urban Sprawl: A Comparative Study of the Detroit-Windsor Region" (PhD diss., Wayne State University, 2005).

25 In this endeavour, I am mindful of the race and policing scholar Micol Seigel's observation that historians using comparative approaches often create or reinforce national mythologies rather than challenging them, although I remain convinced the comparative method, used with care, can illuminate and critique. See Micol Seigel, "Beyond Compare: Comparative Method and the Transnational Turn," *Radical History Review* 91, 1 (2005): 62–90.

26 Ames, *Going Postal,* 87–120.

27 Ronald D. Brown, *Dying on the Job: Murder and Mayhem in the American Workplace* (Lanham, MD: Rowman and Littlefield, 2012).

28 Norwood, *Strikebreaking and Intimidation,* 229.

29 Certainly, many American and Canadian historians, especially in recent years, have stressed the continuance and relevance of class conflict in this period, including the contributors to Brenner, Brenner, and Winslow, eds., *Rebel Rank and File;* the contributors to Goldberg and Griffey, eds., *Black Power at Work*; Heather Ann Thompson, *Whose Detroit? Politics, Labor, and Race in a Modern American City* (Ithaca, NY: Cornell University Press, 2004); Peter S. McInnis, "'Hothead Troubles': Sixties-Era Wildcat Strikes in Canada," in *Debating Dissent: Canada and the Sixties,* ed. Lara Campbell, Dominique Clément, and Gregory S. Kealey, 155–72 (Toronto: University of Toronto Press, 2012); Ian Milligan, *Rebel Youth: 1960s Labour Unrest, Young Workers, and New Leftists in English Canada* (Vancouver: UBC Press, 2014); Palmer, *Canada's 1960s;* Joan Sangster, "'We No Longer Respect the Law': The Tilco Strike, Labour Injunctions, and the State," *Labour/Le Travail* 53 (2004): 47–87.

30 On commonalities between workers and supervisors and the severing of these links in the 1960s, see Thompson, *Whose Detroit?* 60–63.

31 Ames, *Going Postal,* 119–20.

32 Richard Wright, *Black Boy (American Hunger): A Record of Childhood and Youth, 1945* (New York: Perennial Classics, 1998), quoted in Amy Louise Wood, *Lynching and Spectacle: Witnessing Racial Violence in America, 1890–1940* (Chapel Hill: University of North Carolina Press, 2009), 1.

33 Karl Marx, *The Eighteenth Brumaire of Louis Napoleon* (New York: International Publishers, 1963), 15.

34 There has been much outstanding recent work analyzing violence, both theoretically and historically. I have found the following particularly useful: David Graeber, *The Utopia of Rules: On Technology, Stupidity, and the Secret Joys of Bureaucracy* (Brooklyn, NY: Melville House, 2015); Neil L. Whitehead, ed., *Violence* (Santa Fe, NM: SAR Press, 2004); Wood, *Lynching and Spectacle;* and Slavoj Žižek, *Violence* (New York: Picador, 2008). In Canada scholars are producing work that highlights violence as more influential than previously considered, especially Dimitry Anastakis, *Death in the Peaceable Kingdom: Canadian History since 1867 through Murder, Execution, Assassination, and Suicide* (Toronto: University of Toronto Press, 2015). Finally, scholars who have expanded our understanding of the workings of violence on the automotive shop floor include Meyer, "Rough Manhood"; Steve

Meyer, "Workplace Predators: Sexuality and Harassment on the U.S. Automotive Shop Floor, 1930–1960," *Labor: Studies in Working-Class History of the Americas* 1, 1 (2004): 77–93; Sangster, *Transforming Labour;* and Thompson, *Whose Detroit?*

35 Neil L. Whitehead, "Introduction," in *Violence,* ed. Neil Whitehead, 3–24 (Santa Fe, NM: SAR Press, 2004), 9.

36 Graeber, *Utopia of Rules,* 66–69.

37 Pat Cunningham, interview with author, February 25, 2013.

38 Graeber, *Utopia of Rules,* 57–61.

39 Žižek, *Violence,* 2.

40 Ibid.

41 "What Makes a Story 'NEWS'?" *Eldon Wildcat* 72 (October 5, 1972), Unprocessed Manuscript Box, Walter P. Reuther Library of Labor and Urban Affairs, Detroit.

42 Grievance 72–551–387, Box 95, File 3, UAW Local 3 Collection, Walter P. Reuther Library of Labor and Urban Affairs, Detroit; *Rank and File Bulletin,* November 7, 1973, in UL444.

43 Hofstadter, "Reflections on Violence."

44 Katalin Fabian, "Introduction: The Politics of Domestic Violence in Postcommunist Europe and Eurasia," in *Domestic Violence in Postcommunist States: Local Activism, National Policies, and Global Forces,* ed. Katalin Fabian (Bloomington: Indiana University Press, 2010), 26–30.

Chapter 2: Fights and Knifings Are Becoming Quite Commonplace

1 Although the increasing numbers of grievances related to violence might partly be a product of the much higher numbers of grievances overall, it is worth noting that there is a noticeably greater severity of violent incidents in the grievances. It is also crucial to remember that in the 1950s, violence at work was not a major concern of unionists and workers, nor was it the topic of investigations in the mass media.

2 For more on the Johnson shootings, see Chapter 5. The James Netter incident is detailed in Grievance 72–551–387, Box 95, File 3, UAW Local 3 Collection, Walter P. Reuther Library of Labor and Urban Affairs, Detroit (hereafter UL3C).

3 Frank Menendez to George Merrelli, February 18, 1969, Local Union 3 DRUM Activities 1968, UAW Region 1 Collection, Walter P. Reuther Library of Labor and Urban Affairs, Detroit (hereafter UR1C).

4 "Violence in the Factories," *Newsweek,* June 29, 1970, 66–67.

5 Report quoted in Liska Reports, May 1971, Box 2, File 22, Ed Liska Papers, Walter P. Reuther Library of Labor and Urban Affairs, Detroit (hereafter ELP).

6 On the 1967 uprising, the fundamental reference remains Sidney Fine, *Violence in the Model City: The Cavanagh Administration, Race Relations, and the Detroit Riot of 1967* (Ann Arbor: University of Michigan Press, 1989).

7 Kevin Boyle, "The Kiss: Racial and Gender Conflict in a 1950s Automobile Factory," *Journal of American History* 84, 2 (1997): 496–523. The best study of the challenges and conflicts faced by Detroiters in the 1950s and 1960s remains Thomas Sugrue, *The Origins of the Urban Crisis: Race and Inequality in Postwar Detroit* (Princeton, NJ: Princeton University Press, 2005). See also David Freund, *Colored Property:*

State Policy and White Racial Politics in Suburban America (Chicago: University of Chicago Press, 2007).

8 Boyle, "Kiss," 499, 500.

9 An excellent summary of the multiple interpretations of the Fordist accord can be found in Joan Sangster, *Transforming Labour: Women and Work in Postwar Canada* (Toronto: University of Toronto Press, 2010), 4–6.

10 An example of a mass confrontation with a supervisor at Dodge Main in 1944 can be found in Steve Meyer, "Rough Manhood: The Aggressive and Confrontational Shop Culture of U.S. Auto Workers during World War II," *Journal of Social History* 36, 1 (2002): 138. The article as a whole is a revealing account of the belligerent, male work culture of the American automotive industry during the Second World War. On mid-century masculinity and the US auto industry, see also Steve Meyer, "Workplace Predators: Sexuality and Harassment on the U.S. Automotive Shop Floor, 1930–1960," *Labor: Studies in Working-Class History of the Americas* 1, 1 (2004): 77–93; and Steve Meyer, "Work, Play, and Power: Masculine Culture on the Automotive Shop Floor, 1930–60," *Men and Masculinities* 2, 2 (1999): 115–34. Examples of bullying, horseplay, and violence against women at Dodge Main during the 1950s can be found in Grievance R.M. 7, Box 43, File 8, UL3C; Grievance R.M. 50, Box 46, File 22, UL3C; Grievance R.M. 44(a), Box 49, File 3, UL3C; Grievance R.M. 4(b), Box 46, File 7, UL3C; Grievance R.M. 37(a), Box 49, File 9, UL3C; F247–4, Box 61, File 23, UL3C.

11 Tim Rhodes, "The Risk Environment: A Framework for Understanding and Reducing Drug-Related Harm," *International Journal of Drug Policy* 13, 2 (2002): 85–94; 85.

12 Rhodes, "The Risk Environment," 87, emphasis in original.

13 Rhodes, "The Risk Environment," 88.

14 Jefferys, *Management and Managed,* 68–148.

15 Ibid., 144–45.

16 Sangster, *Transforming Labour,* 196–97.

17 Boyle, "Kiss," 504.

18 Jefferys, *Management and Managed,* 163–64.

19 Boyle, "Kiss," 506.

20 Ibid., 507.

21 Ibid., 514.

22 Ibid., 510–15.

23 Jefferys, *Management and Managed,* 162.

24 A.C. Jones, "Rank-and-File Opposition in the UAW during the Long 1970s," in *Rebel Rank and File: Labor Militancy and Revolt from Below during the Long 1970s,* ed. Aaron Brenner, Robert Brenner, and Cal Winslow (New York: Verso, 2010), 284.

25 Jefferys, *Management and Managed,* 161–62.

26 Jones, "Rank-and-File Opposition," 283.

27 Heather Ann Thompson, *Whose Detroit? Politics, Labor, and Race in a Modern American City* (Ithaca, NY: Cornell University Press, 2004), 59.

28 The best discussions of the deteriorating conditions at Chrysler are Dan Georgakas and Marvin Surkin, *Detroit – I Do Mind Dying: A Study in Urban Revolution* (1975;

reprint, Chicago: Haymarket Books, 2012), 85–100; Thompson, *Whose Detroit?* 58–63; and Rachel Scott, *Muscle and Blood* (New York: E.P. Dutton, 1974), 119–73.

29 Thompson, *Whose Detroit?* 107.

30 "MEETING – TUESDAY, APRIL 10, 1973," Box 44, Local 3 UAW General File, 1973, UR1C.

31 Scott, *Muscle and Blood,* 162.

32 "TB at Dodge Main," *Eldon Wildcat* 71 (September 7, 1972), Unprocessed Manuscript Box, Walter P. Reuther Library of Labor and Urban Affairs, Detroit (hereafter EW-UMB).

33 Richard David Riddle, "The Rise of the Reagan Democrats in Warren, Michigan, 1964–1984" (PhD diss., Wayne State University, 1998), 263, http://digitalcommons.wayne.edu/cgi/viewcontent.cgi?article=2188&context=oa_dissertations.

34 Scott, *Muscle and Blood,* 126.

35 Ibid., 163.

36 Georgakas and Surkin, *Detroit,* 87.

37 Ibid., 88.

38 Jefferys, *Management and Managed,* 154.

39 Thompson, *Whose Detroit?* 60–61.

40 Jefferys, *Management and Managed,* 149.

41 Georgakas and Surkin, *Detroit,* 85.

42 Thompson, *Whose Detroit?* 68.

43 "Foremen Layoffs," *Eldon Spark* 108 (February 13, 1974), EW-UMB. This publication appeared first under the name *Eldon Wildcat* and later under the name *Eldon Spark.*

44 Grievance AD706–791, Box 69, File 19, UL3C.

45 Grievance AD857–922, Box 70, File 11, UL3C.

46 Grievance AD733–713, Box 72, File 12, UL3C.

47 Grievance AF209–213, Box 75, File 9, UL3C.

48 Grievance AF1203–948, Box 78, File 24, UL3C.

49 Grievance 72–108–72, Box 95, File 13, UL3C.

50 Grievance HC658–497, Box 91, File 7, UL3C.

51 Grievance 70–330–211, Box 90, File 6, UL3C.

52 Grievance AF531–497, Box 77, File 10, UL3C.

53 Grievance HC245–188, Box 84, File 16, UL3C.

54 Grievance HB340–235, Box 80, File 6, UL3C.

55 Grievance 73–726–592, Box 100, File 8, UL3C.

56 Grievance AF126–138, Box 76, File 18, UL3C.

57 Grievance HB352–255, Box 84, File 14, UL3C.

58 Liska Reports, June–July 1969, Box 2, File 2, ELP. Liska's accounts of his day-to-day work as Local 3 President have been an invaluable resource for me, but his unconventional prose style presented challenges in terms of how best to render his words in this text in a way that balances accuracy and readability. I have chosen to retain the all-capitals style in which Liska wrote, but edit the ellipses he often used between sentences into periods. Spelling and grammar errors have been left in at times, edited at others.

59 Jones, "Rank-and-File Opposition," 282.

60 Ibid., 285.
61 Scott, *Muscle and Blood,* 158.
62 Jones, "Rank-and-File Opposition," 285.
63 David M. Lewis-Colman, *Race against Liberalism: Black Workers and the UAW in Detroit* (Champaign: University of Illinois Press, 2008), 93.
64 Jefferys, *Management and Managed,* 165.
65 Scott, *Muscle and Blood,* 164–65.
66 Jones, "Rank-and-File Opposition," 285.
67 "Prepare for the Worst," *DRUM* 1, 8. On DRUM, in addition to the work of Georgakas and Surkin, Jefferys, Jones, Lewis-Colman, and Thompson, each cited earlier in this chapter, other important studies of the revolutionary union movements and the League of Revolutionary Black Workers include James A. Geschwender, *Class, Race, and Worker Insurgency: The League of Revolutionary Black Workers* (Cambridge, UK: Cambridge University Press, 1977); Elizabeth Kai Hinton, "The Black Bolsheviks: Detroit Revolutionary Union Movements and Shop-Floor Organizing," in *The New Black History: Revisiting the Second Reconstruction,* ed. Elizabeth Kai Hinton and Manning Marable, 211–28 (New York: Palgrave McMillan, 2011); Nicola Pizzolato, *Challenging Global Capitalism: Labor Migration, Radical Struggle, and Urban Change in Detroit and Turin* (London: Palgrave McMillan, 2013); and Kieran Taylor, "American Petrograd: Detroit and the League of Revolutionary Black Workers," in *Rebel Rank and File: Labor Militancy and Revolt from Below during the Long 1970s,* ed. Aaron Brenner, Robert Brenner, and Cal Winslow, 311–34 (New York: Verso, 2010). For a recent account that significantly expands our understanding of independent black workplace organizing in Detroit; the relationship between the League of Revolutionary Black Workers, DRUM, and the independent black construction workers' union Local 124; the role of violence in creating a space for construction work struggles; and how these struggles unfolded, see David Goldberg, "Community Control of Construction, Independent Unionism, and the 'Short Black Power Movement' in Detroit," in *Black Power at Work: Community Control, Affirmative Action, and the Construction Industry,* ed. David Goldberg and Trevor Griffey, 90–111 (Ithaca, NY: Cornell University Press, 2010).
68 Thompson, *Whose Detroit?* 69.
69 Grievance AD5–2, Box 70, File 5, UL3C.
70 Grievance 72–1333–973, Box 97, File 15, UL3C.
71 Grievance 71–1021–820, Box 95, File 22, UL3C.
72 Grievance 73–298–251, Box 99, File 11, UL3C.
73 Heather Ann Thompson, "Unmaking the Motor City in the Age of Mass Incarceration," *Journal of Law and Society* 15 (2013): 41–61; 43.
74 Jefferys, *Management and Managed,* 164.
75 Grievance A69–899–617, Box 88, File 14, UL3C.
76 *Click* 13, pen-dated April 13, 1972, Box 44, File 3, UR1C; William K. Stevens, "In a Dodge Plant, Long Days of Heat, Noise, and Violence," *New York Times,* September 14, 1973.
77 Liska Reports, September 1970, Box 2, File 16, ELP.
78 *Click* 13, pen-dated April 13, 1972, Box 44, File 3, UR1C.

79 "ROBBERY," *DRUM* 1, 8, Box 44, Local Union 3 DRUM Activities 1968, UR1C.
80 Scott, *Muscle and Blood,* 159.
81 Jefferys, *Management and Managed,* 164.
82 Liska Reports, March 1971, Box 2, File 20, ELP.
83 CHIP Board Meeting Minutes, June 19, 1974, Box 39, File 3, UR1C.
84 Jefferys, *Management and Managed,* 164.
85 Liska Reports, May 1971, Box 2, File 22, ELP.
86 Liska Reports, September 1969, Box 2, File 4, ELP.
87 Scott, *Muscle and Blood,* 156–57.
88 Grievance 73–929–710, Box 100, File 3, UL3C.
89 Scott, *Muscle and Blood,* 157.
90 Stevens, "In a Dodge Plant."
91 Heather Ann Thompson, "Why Mass Incarceration Matters: Rethinking Crisis, Decline, and Transformation in Postwar American History," *Journal of American History* 97, 3 (2010): 703–34.
92 Grievance AE329–337, Box 74, File 4, UL3C.
93 Liska Reports, October 1969, Box 2, File 5, ELP.
94 Grievance AE197–194, Box 77, File 2, UL3C.
95 Grievance AF439–391, Box 77, File 4, UL3C.
96 Ibid.
97 Grievance [number missing], Box 79, File 20, UL3C.
98 Grievance HB663–401, Box 86, File 17, UL3C.
99 Grievance A70–1200–747, Box 90, File 2, UL3C.
100 Jefferys, *Management and Managed,* 179.
101 Liska Reports, March 1971, Box 2, File 20, ELP.
102 Thompson, *Whose Detroit?* 108–9; Georgakas and Surkin, *Detroit,* 21–22.
103 Georgakas and Surkin, *Detroit,* 20.
104 Grievance HD163–103, Box 92, File 28, UL3C.
105 "Will You Be Next?" *DRUM* 1, 5, Box 44, Local Union 3 DRUM Activities 1968, UR1C.
106 Grievance HD163–103, Box 92, File 28, UL3C.
107 Grievance A69–128–122, Box 85, File 12, UL3C. The information about Forge fleeing the city is from General Gordon Baker, interview with author, July 26, 2012. Baker said that Forge eventually returned to Detroit and was murdered in a drug-related incident.
108 Grievance A69–128–122, Box 85, File 12, UL3C.
109 Baker, interview; The full quotation is "We finally got the news of how our dues are being used," which protesters are seen chanting in the documentary. Stewart Bird, Rene Lichtman, Peter Gessner, and John Louis Jr., dirs., *Finally Got the News,* documentary, produced in association with the League of Revolutionary Black Workers (Detroit: Black Star Productions, 1970), https://www.youtube.com/watch?v=RgJd_MvJVzg.
110 Jefferys, *Management and Managed,* 176.
111 Riddle, "Rise of the Reagan Democrats," 269. On the other historians who have covered the Merrelli raid, see ibid., 269n30, where Riddle notes that Geschwender,

Class, Race, and Worker Insurgency, "seems to believe that, although some voting improprieties probably occurred, not all of the League's charges were factual." There are more details on DRUM's charges of violence during the election in Thompson, *Whose Detroit?* 160–61.

112 "ELECTION NOTES," Local Union 3 Election 1970, UR1C.

113 Baker, interview.

114 Trevor Griffey, "History Declassified: Using U.S. Government Intelligence Documents to Write Left History," *Left History* 16, 1 (2012): 115–28.

115 Jones, "Rank-and-File Opposition," 294.

116 Jefferys, *Management and Managed,* 181; Thompson, *Whose Detroit?* 168–73.

117 Grievance 72–1073–756, Box 99, File 5, UL3C.

118 Grievance 74–1112–883, Box 103, File 13, UL3C.

119 An excellent discussion of how this dynamic was treated by intellectuals of the 1970s can be found in Jefferson Cowie, *Stayin' Alive: The 1970s and the Last Days of the Working Class* (New York: New Press, 2010), 216–21.

120 Jones, "Rank-and-File Opposition," 284.

121 Baker, interview.

122 Grievance AE104–104, Box 74, File 4, UL3C.

123 Grievance AE677–633, Box 76, File 16, UL3C.

124 Grievance AG831–68, Box 80, File 2, UL3C.

125 Grievance HB336–158, Box 83, File 2, UL3C.

126 Grievance A70–601–359, Box 92, File 25, UL3C.

127 Grievance A71–293–228, Box 38, File 25, UL3C.

128 Grievance A71–1021–820, Box 95, File 22, UL3C.

129 Grievance 74–389–271, Box 102, File 2, UL3C.

130 Grievance 72–674–482, Box 95, File 9, UL3C.

131 Liska Reports, August 1969, Box 2, File 3, ELP; Liska Reports, July 1969, Box 2, File 2, ELP.

132 Liska Reports, August 1969, Box 2, File 3, ELP.

133 Ibid.

134 Liska Reports, November 1969, Box 2, File 6, ELP.

135 "Violence in Chrysler Plants," undated handout, Box 31, File 10, Arthur Hughes Collection, Walter P. Reuther Library of Labor and Urban Affairs, Detroit (hereafter AHC).

136 Jefferys, *Management and Managed,* 179.

137 Baker, interview.

138 *Engle v. Koehler,* 707 F.2d 241, United States Court of Appeals, 6th Circuit, 1983, https://law.resource.org/pub/us/case/reporter/F2/707/707.F2d.241.82-1470.html.

139 Grievance A71–179–127, Box 93, File 8, UL3C.

140 Grievance [number missing], Box 102, File 14, UL3C.

141 Grievance 73–1788–1405, Box 102, File 16, UL3C.

142 Grievance 74–533–405, Box 104, File 3, UL3C.

143 Grievance A69–1207–917, Box 91, File 3, UL3C.

144 "Confidential Statement from Foreman M.D. Blount," September 16, 1970, Box 31, File 10, AHC.

145 Liska Reports, September 1970, Box 2, File 15, ELP; Liska Reports, December 1971, Box 3, File 7, ELP.
146 Grievance 70–1436–1015, Box 90, File 2, UL3C.
147 Grievance 73–1413–1102, Box 100, File 2, UL3C.
148 Liska Reports, May 1971, Box 2, File 22, ELP.
149 Grievance 74–105–79, Box 102, File 8, UL3C.
150 Grievance [number missing], Box 97, File 12, UL3C. Turner later returned to work.
151 Liska Reports, March 1970, Box 2, File 10, ELP.
152 Liska Reports, May 1971, Box 2, File 22, ELP.
153 Scott, *Muscle and Blood,* 162.
154 Liska Reports, March 1970, Box 2, File 10, ELP.
155 Grievance 74–812–625, Box 104, File 8, UL3C.
156 Gina Braxton to Local 3, Box 45, File 13, UR1C.
157 Grievance 73–725–591, Box 100, File 3, UL3C.
158 This account and all quotations regarding the incident are in Wesley's grievance or in the attached letter he submitted in support of his grievance. Grievance 73–1785–1402, Box 97, File 10, UL3C.
159 Stevens, "In a Dodge Plant."
160 "Worker Slain at Dodge Plant," *Detroit Free Press,* February 3, 1973.
161 Material on the incident appears in Box 45, File 13, UR1C.
162 Larry Hartman to Ken Morris, December 12, 1979, Box 114, File 26, UAW Region 1B Collection, Walter P. Reuther Library of Labor and Urban Affairs, Detroit (hereafter UR1BC).
163 Barrett Seaman, "In Michigan: Goodbye, Dodge Main," *Time,* February 11, 1980, 10.
164 "Dec. 7, the Day the 'Bomb' Fell on Hamtramck," *Detroit News,* December 8, 1979.

Chapter 3: The Way Boys and Men Took Care of Business

1 "Horseplay, Violence," *444 News,* May 16, 1975, in Unifor Local 444 Private Collection, Unifor Local 444 Offices, Windsor, Ontario (hereafter UL444). Although the "two brothers" incident likely refers to the stabbing mentioned below, it is unclear what the "violent situation" was.
2 *Rank and File Bulletin,* May 7, 1975, UL444.
3 Ashley Johnson, "Illegal Detroiters: Undocumented Europeans and Unions in America's Motor City, 1924–42," paper presented at the North American Labor History Conference, Wayne State University, Detroit, October 2012; Holly Karibo, "Detroit's Border Brothel: Sex Tourism in Windsor, Ontario, 1945–1960," *American Review of Canadian Studies* 40, 3 (2010): 362–78.
4 Charles Brooks, "20 Years in the UAW," *444 News,* June 11, 1956, UL444.
5 Ibid.
6 Gary Parent and Rick Laporte, interview with author, October 17, 2012.
7 A revealing analysis of why capital flight and racialization produced different outcomes on either side of the Canada-US border can be found in Jason Hackworth, "Why Is There No Detroit in Canada?" *Urban Geography* 37, 2 (2016): 272–95.
8 Rudolf A. Helling, *The Position of Negroes, Chinese, and Italians in the Social Structure of Windsor, Ontario* (Toronto: Ontario Human Rights Commission, 1965); H.C.

McNeil, "Target of Wrath," *Guardian* (London), May 15, 1964, UL444; Brandi Lucier, "'The Black Man Doesn't Present a Problem until He Presents Himself': The Windsor Council on Group Relations, UAW Canadian Region 7, and the Hiring Policies of Chrysler Canada, 1944–54," unpublished paper in author's possession, 2015.

9 Lucier, "'Black Man Doesn't,'" 4.

10 Pamela Sugiman, "Privilege and Oppression: The Configuration of Race, Gender, and Class in Southern Ontario Auto Plants, 1939 to 1949," *Labour/Le Travail* 47 (2001): 86.

11 Ibid., 91–94.

12 Lucier, "'Black Man Doesn't,'" 9–10.

13 Ibid., 20.

14 Ibid., 21–22.

15 Sugiman, "Privilege and Oppression," 97, 105–8.

16 Ibid., 102–3, 109.

17 Ibid., 103–7, 110.

18 Detroit homicide statistics are from Peter Gavrilovich and Bill McGraw, eds., *The Detroit Almanac: 300 Years of Life in the Motor City* (Detroit: Detroit Free Press, 2000), 484–85. Windsor homicide statistics are from Statistics Canada, *Publication Crime Statistics 85–205* (Ottawa: Statistics Canada, 1962–76). Computing and comparing homicide rates are difficult, given the different methods of collecting and calculating population and homicide statistics. However, it is clear that, estimating Detroit's population to be just less that ten times Windsor's during this period, its number of homicides and its homicide rate were far greater.

19 Gord Gray, interview with author, February 25, 2013.

20 Chris Roberts, "Harnessing Competition? The UAW and Competitiveness in the Canadian Auto Industry, 1945–90" (PhD diss., York University, 2002), 234.

21 Charles Brooks, "Membership Determined to Correct Company Abuses," *444 News*, March 10, 1960, UL444.

22 "Company Charges Fall Flat," *444 News*, March 14, 1957, UL444; "Layoffs Due to Poor Public Relations," *444 News*, June 6, 1957, UL444.

23 Brooks, "Membership Determined."

24 Roberts, "Harnessing Competition?" 517.

25 On the era's militancy and worker resistance, see Peter S. McInnis, "'Hothead Troubles': Sixties-Era Wildcat Strikes in Canada," in *Debating Dissent: Canada and the Sixties*, ed. Lara Campbell, Dominique Clément, and Gregory S. Kealey, 155–72 (Toronto: University of Toronto Press, 2012); Bryan Palmer, *Canada's 1960s: The Ironies of Identity in a Rebellious Era* (Toronto: University of Toronto Press, 2009), 211–41; and Joan Sangster, "'We No Longer Respect the Law': The Tilco Strike, Labour Injunctions, and the State," *Labour/Le Travail* 53 (2004): 47–87.

26 "CHRISTMAS SCHEDULE, SABOTAGE," Box 27, File 3, United Automobile Workers Chrysler Department Collection, Walter P. Reuther Library of Urban and Labor Affairs, Detroit (hereafter CDC).

27 "Special Union-Management Conference," November 19, 1965, Box 27, File 3, CDC.

28 John Horne, election handout, UL444.

29 Local 444 election handout, UL444.

30 Roberts, "Harnessing Competition?" 510.
31 Ibid., 532.
32 Ibid., 510.
33 Ibid., 513.
34 Charles Brooks, "Chrysler Presses Vigorously – Again??" *444 News*, September 3, 1970, UL444.
35 Intolerably hot conditions were a constant summertime issue in Chrysler plants. Heat walkouts were wildcat strikes that occurred when workers walked off the job because of the sweltering conditions.
36 "For A Canadian Contract," handout, Box 20, File 17, CDC.
37 Gray, interview.
38 See Steve Meyer, "Rough Manhood: The Aggressive and Confrontational Shop Culture of U.S. Auto Workers during World War II," *Journal of Social History* 36, 1 (2002): 125–47; Steve Meyer, "Work, Play, and Power: Masculine Culture on the Automotive Shop Floor, 1930–60," *Men and Masculinities* 2, 2 (1999): 115–34; Steve Meyer, "Workplace Predators: Sexuality and Harassment on the U.S. Automotive Shop Floor, 1930–1960," *Labor: Studies in Working-Class History of the Americas* 1, 1 (2004): 77–93.
39 Parent and Laporte, interview.
40 Pat Cunningham, interview with author, February 25, 2013; Jim O'Neil, interview with author, April 24, 2013.
41 Gray, interview.
42 Wayne Lewchuk, "Men and Monotony: Fraternalism as a Managerial Strategy at the Ford Motor Company," *Journal of Economic History* 53, 4 (1993): 824–56. The quoted passage appears on page 833.
43 Gray, interview; Parent and Laporte, interview.
44 Monk shared these reminiscences in an interview with Gerald Hannon, "Gay on the Line," *Toronto Body Politic*, September, 1978. I read of Monk and the interview thanks to Miriam Frank, *Out in the Union: A Labor History of Queer America* (Philadelphia: Temple University Press, 2014), 39. Frank shared this material with me via private correspondence before publication of her book. I am truly grateful for her generosity.
45 Frank, *Out in the Union*, 40.
46 Cunningham, interview.
47 Ibid.
48 "Rank and File Reply to Plant 2 Bulletin," March 10, 1972, UL444.
49 Cartoon, *444 News*, May 31, 1973, UL444.
50 Frank, *Out in the Union*, 40.
51 Meyer, "Work, Play, and Power," 124.
52 Gray, interview.
53 Parent and Laporte, interview.
54 Gray, interview.
55 Ibid.; Parent and Laporte, interview.
56 Gray, interview.

57 Parent and Laporte, interview.
58 Ibid.
59 Ibid.
60 Ibid.
61 "Blue and White Bulletin," 1968, UL444.
62 Ken Gerard, "Blue and White Slate Opposition News and Facts," pamphlet, 1966, UL444.
63 Parent and Laporte, interview.
64 Ibid.
65 O'Neil, interview. Whether or not the story about the supervisor's murder is true, such a story is a powerful indicator of what type of workplace culture prevailed at the plant.
66 Gray, interview.
67 Cunningham, interview.
68 Gray, interview.
69 "Watch That Language ...," *444 News,* January 12, 1968, UL444.
70 Dan Georgakas and Marvin Surkin, *Detroit – I Do Mind Dying: A Study in Urban Revolution* (1975; reprint, Chicago: Haymarket Books, 2012), 85.
71 Gray, interview.
72 "Gate-Line Misery," *Official Bulletin,* November 16, 1966, UL444.
73 "Wright Is Wrong," *444 News,* October 9, 1969, UL444.
74 Charles Brooks, "New Contract Geared to Solve In-Plant Problems," *444 News,* February 22, 1968, UL444.
75 John Horne, election handout, UL444.
76 Cunningham, interview.
77 Gray, interview.
78 Charles Brooks, "Chrysler Goes on Legal Kick," *444 News,* June 4, 1967, UL444.
79 "Plant 2 – Not Again, Edgar?" *Workers' Unity,* October 1970, UL444.
80 "Engine Plant Report," *444 News,* August 21, 1969, UL444.
81 Parent and Laporte, interview.
82 Charles Brooks, "Full Force of UAW to Correct Grievances," *444 News,* October 17, 1963, UL444.
83 Charles Brooks, "Improvement in Management's Attitude," *444 News,* July 15, 1966, UL444.
84 Brooks, "Chrysler Goes."
85 Ibid.
86 Ibid.
87 Ibid.
88 Parent and Laporte, interview.
89 Gray, interview.
90 Ibid.
91 Ibid.
92 *444 Engine Plant Bulletin,* April 26, 1970, UL444.
93 *Plant 3 Bulletin,* October 3, 1978, UL444.

94 Gray, interview.

95 Jim Monk, "Working on an Assembly Line," in *Working in Canada,* ed. Walter Johnson (Montreal: Black Rose Books, 1983), 49.

96 Box 253, File 8, Canadian Auto Workers Fonds, Library and Archives Canada, Ottawa (hereafter CAW).

97 Monk, "Working on an Assembly Line," 53.

98 Ibid., 53–54.

99 McGivney to McDermott, October 20, 1971, Box 253, File 8, CAW.

100 McGivney to McDermott, February 4, 1973, Box 253, File 7, CAW.

101 On racism in Windsor auto plants, see *Naraine v. Ford Motor Co. Ltd.,* BOI 96–023 (1996), https://archive.org/details/boi96_023.

Chapter 4: The Constant Companion of All That Earn Their Living Here

1 This account of the Brookins case is based on Brookins's grievance, found in Box 79, File 12, UAW Local 3 Collection, Walter P. Reuther Library of Labor and Urban Affairs, Detroit (hereafter UL3C); "Will You Be Next?" *DRUM* 1, 1.

2 "Racicm [sic] Costs," *DRUM* 1, 13.

3 "Will You Be Next?" *DRUM* 1, 1; "Racicm [sic] Costs,"*DRUM* 1, 13.

4 Tony Conole to Doug Fraser, October 8, 1968, Box 24, File 31, Local 3 Correspondence 1968–69, United Automobile Workers Chrysler Department Collection, Walter P. Reuther Library of Urban and Labor Affairs, Detroit (hereafter CDC). The letter also notes that UAW International never received material from the local after Brookins's first grievance, which may suggest that the local was lax in grieving his firing. It may also suggest that UAW International was considering going over the heads of local leadership on the matter.

5 "Guide to Good Conduct for Chrysler Employees," Box 121, File 5, UAW Region 7 Collection, Walter P. Reuther Library of Labor and Urban Affairs, Detroit.

6 Of course, not every incident of workplace violence resulted in discipline; many were likely never witnessed or reported. Nor did the union grieve every disciplinary action meted out for a violent incident. Probationary employees were new hires who had yet to accrue ninety days of service at Chrysler, so they were not officially UAW members. If fired for a violent incident, these workers would lose their jobs without a grievance being filed on their behalf.

7 "Pressure," *DRUM* 1, 2.

8 "DRUM Demands," *DRUM* 1, 9.

9 Liska Reports, November 1969, Box 2, File 5, Ed Liska Papers, Walter P. Reuther Library of Labor and Urban Affairs, Detroit (hereafter ELP). When black workers were moved out of Plant Protection, radicals propagandized that this was a precursor to a violent campaign against black workers by Plant Protection staff: "Well DRUM has proof that they now have teargas, night-sticks, riot helmets and the new untested chemical MACE which might blind you on plant property ... They know no true black brother would use this gas and mace on his own brothers." "Prepare for the Worst," *DRUM* 1, 8.

10 It is impossible to exactly track the success of the grievances filed by Local 3, as most of the grievance records do not include a statement of the grievance's eventual

outcome. However, enough of them contain handwritten notes and other information about their disposition to enable the drawing of some general conclusions about the responses to violent incidents that were brought to the grievance arena.

11 Liska quoted in Steve Jefferys, *Management and Managed: Fifty Years of Crisis at Chrysler* (Cambridge, UK: CUP Archive, 1986), 165.
12 Joan Sangster, "Just Horseplay? Masculinity and Workplace Grievances in Fordist Canada, 1947–1970s," paper presented at the Annual Meeting of the Labor and Working Class History of the Americas, New York City, June 7, 2013.
13 Grievance AE104–104, Box 74, File 4, UL3C; Officer Level Grievance Meetings, August–September 1965, Box 1, File 8, ELP.
14 Grievance 72–1073–756, Box 99, File 5, UL3C.
15 Grievance 71–572–438, Box 94, File 5, UL3C.
16 Officer Level Grievance Meetings, August–September 1965, Box 1, File 8, ELP.
17 Liska Reports, March 1970, Box 2, File 10, ELP.
18 Liska Reports, October 1969, Box 2, File 5, ELP. The same report notes that in Tiny's area, one worker had been fired for being abusive toward a supervisor and another fired for beating up a plant guard. The union got both back to work.
19 "Is It Chrysler Policy to Have Mad-Dog Foremen?" *Dodge Workers Speak* 61 (March 14, 1973), Box 44, Local 3 – UAW – General, 1973, UR1C.
20 "A Letter," *Dodge Workers Speak* 67 (1973), Unifor Local 444 Private Collection, Unifor Local 444 Offices, Windsor, Ontario (hereafter UL444).
21 "Racism at Chrysler," *Inner City Voice,* March 1968.
22 "Black Rage on the Auto Lines," *Time,* April 11, 1969, 109.
23 Quoted in "Jordon Sims Appeal Board Case 5351," Box 27, File 22, CDC.
24 Gary Parent and Rick Laporte, interview with author, October 17, 2012.
25 Jordon Sims, "Employee-Foreman Confrontation Points Up Need for Improvements," *Criterion,* February 12, 1969, Box 27, File 22, CDC.
26 Liska Reports, August 1969, Box 2, File 3, ELP. See also Liska Reports, June–July 1969, Box 2, File 3, ELP.
27 Liska Reports, August 1969, Box 2, File 3, ELP.
28 Liska Reports, September 1969, Box 2, File 5, ELP.
29 Liska Reports, November 1969, Box 2, File 6, ELP.
30 Ibid.
31 Ibid.
32 Liska Reports, February 1970, Box 2, File 9, ELP.
33 Ibid.
34 Liska Reports, September 1969, Box 2, File 4, ELP.
35 Liska Reports, November 1969, Box 2, File 6, ELP.
36 Liska Reports, July 1970, Box 3, File 1, ELP.
37 Liska Reports, November 1971, Box 3, File 6, ELP.
38 Jefferys, *Management and Managed,* 166.
39 Liska Reports, February 1970, Box 2, File 9, ELP.
40 Liska Reports, March 1970, Box 2, File 10, ELP.
41 Ibid.
42 Liska Reports, September 1970, Box 2, File 16, ELP.

43 Ibid.
44 Liska Reports, February 1971, Box 2, File 16, ELP.
45 Liska Reports, February 1970, Box 2, File 9, ELP.
46 Liska Reports, April 1970, Box 2, File 11, ELP.
47 Liska Reports, March 1970, Box 2, File 10, ELP.
48 Liska Reports, July 1970, Box 3, File 1, ELP.
49 Liska Reports, February 1970, Box 2, File 9, ELP.
50 Liska Reports, March 1970, Box 2, File 10, ELP.
51 Liska Reports, September 1970, Box 2, File 16, ELP. The incident proved unpopular with Dodge Main workers, and Steve Jefferys identifies it as a turning point for the "new relationship" between Chrysler executives and Local 3 leadership in the campaign against DRUM, as a larger group of anti-militant, anti-strike workers mobilized against the wildcatters. Jefferys, *Management and Managed,* 183.
52 Liska Reports, September 1970, Box 2, File 15, ELP.
53 Liska Reports, September 1970, Box 2, File 16, ELP.
54 Ibid.
55 Liska Reports, October 1970, Box 2, File 17, ELP.
56 "UAW Contract Talks," *Inner City Voice,* October 1970.
57 Ibid.
58 Jefferys, *Management and Managed,* 158–59.
59 Joseph Elliott to Steve Yokich, June 13, 1977, Box 45, File 13, UR1C.
60 John Smith to Emil Mazey, March 26, 1979, Box 46, File 14, UL3C. On safety at the local hall, see letters from Joseph Elliott to Steve Yokich and Donald Riegle, June 13, 1977, Box 45, File 13, UR1C. Elliott's letter to Riegle objects to the move of Hamtramck police station further away from the factory, another indication of the ongoing role the police played in keeping order at the plant.
61 Liska Reports, October 1969, Box 2, File 5, ELP.
62 "Bonus vs. an Ass Kicking," *DRUM* 1, 10.
63 "Unite Against Violence," *Eldon Wildcat* 36 (May 12, 1971), Unprocessed Manuscript Box, Walter P. Reuther Library of Labor and Urban Affairs, Detroit (hereafter EW-UMB). On the outlook and practices of the *Wildcat* group, see the interview with John Taylor in Georgakas and Surkin, *Detroit,* 96.
64 "Murders for Profit," *Eldon Spark* 167 (March 25, 1976), EW-UMB.
65 "Fewer Jobs, More Machines," *Eldon Spark* 126 (November 13, 1974), EW-UMB.
66 Is It Chrysler Policy to Have Mad-Dog Foremen?" *Dodge Workers Speak* 61 (March 14, 1973), Box 44, Local 3 – UAW – General, 1973, UR1C.
67 "TB at Dodge Main," *Eldon Wildcat* 71 (September 7, 1972), EW-UMB.
68 *Rank and File Committee Bulletin,* May 7, 1975, UL444.
69 "Rumblings from the Lines," *Workers' Unity,* May 1971, UL444.
70 "'Het' ... Two ... Three: Bolder Than Bold," *Eldon Ave. Liberator,* n.d., ELRUM Police File, in author's possession.
71 "Foremen Layoffs," *Eldon Wildcat* 108 (February 13, 1974), EW-UMB.
72 "Foreman Packs Pistol," *Eldon Spark* 90 (June 14, 1973), EW-UMB.
73 "Yellow Badges," *Eldon Wildcat* 120 (August 21, 1974), EW-UMB.
74 General Gordon Baker, interview with author, July 26, 2012.

75 "Rebellion inside the Gates," *DRUM* 2, 27.
76 Ibid.
77 "Hail James Johnson," *DRUM* 3, 1.
78 "Letter to Editor," *DRUM* 1, 15.
79 "300 Years Ago," *DRUM* 2, 25.
80 "What Has DRUM Done?" *DRUM* 2, 13.
81 For more on DRUM turning off many potential allies and DRUM's gender politics, see Heather Ann Thompson, *Whose Detroit? Politics, Labor, and Race in a Modern American City* (Ithaca, NY: Cornell University Press, 2004), 168–72.
82 Quoted in Georgakas and Surkin, *Detroit,* 92.
83 "B.X.9," *DRUM* 1, 7.
84 "Pressure on Women," *Eldon Spark* 122 (September 18, 1974), EW-UMB.
85 Gary Parent, "At the Truck Plant," *Local 444 News,* August 29, 1975, Unprocessed Manuscript Box (hereafter 444-UMB), Walter P. Reuther Library of Labor and Urban Affairs.
86 Charlie Brooks, "United Action: The Only Way to Fight Bosses' Abuse!" *Local 444 News,* April 15, 1974, 444-UMB, Walter P. Reuther Library of Labor and Urban Affairs.
87 Gerry Bastien, "Management on Collision Course with Workers," *Local 444 News,* May 25, 1979, 444-UMB, Walter P. Reuther Library of Labor and Urban Affairs.
88 "Rumblings from the Lines," *Workers' Unity,* May 1971, UL444.
89 *Rank and File Bulletin,* March 28, 1973, UL444.
90 *Rank and File Bulletin,* May 7, 1975, UL444.
91 Ibid.
92 *Rank and File Bulletin,* November 7, 1973, UL444.
93 "Negro Lovers," *DRUM* 2, 5.
94 "James Johnson Found 'Not Guilty,'" *Eldon Wildcat* 37 (May 25, 1971), EW-UMB.
95 See Thompson, *Whose Detroit?* 118–19.
96 Baker, interview.
97 "Plants Arm against Worker Struggle," *Inner City Voice,* October 1968.
98 "N.A.M.," *DRUM* 2, 20.
99 "Calling Black Workers Everywhere!" League of Revolutionary Black Workers Police File, in author's possession.
100 "The 1970 UAW Contract Settlements," *DRUM* 3, 15.
101 "Fences Can Stop" poem, *Inner City Voice,* October 1969, Box 17, File 10, Detroit Revolutionary Movements Collection, Walter P. Reuther Library of Urban and Labor Affairs, Detroit. On increased security at Dodge Main, see "N.A.M.," *DRUM* 2, 20.
102 Bill Davidson, "If We Can't Solve the Problems of the Ghetto Here, God Help Our Country," *Saturday Evening Post,* October 5, 1968, 31.
103 Quoted in ibid. Townsend's master's degree was in business administration. See Melody Petersen, "Lynn Townsend, Ex-Chrysler Chief, Dies at 81," *New York Times,* August 22, 2000, http://www.nytimes.com/2000/08/22/business/lynn-townsend-ex-chrysler-chief-dies-at-81.html.
104 Davidson, "If We Can't Solve," 31.
105 Quoted in ibid., 32, emphasis in original. Gary Gilson, dir., *Do You Think a Job Is the Answer?* documentary (1969), in author's possession.

106 Liska Reports, November 1969, Box 2, File 6, ELP.
107 Jefferys, *Management and Managed,* 172–74.
108 Baker, interview; Baker said he was told of Chrysler's actions regarding his arrest warrant by attorney Ken Cockrel.
109 Ibid.; A. Muhammad Ahmad, *A Study of the League of Revolutionary Black Workers* (Baltimore, MD: Collective Action Notes, 1979), 10; Liska Reports, September 1970, Box 2, File 16, ELP.
110 Jefferys, *Management and Managed,* 181.
111 "Why Foremen Go to School," *Dodge Workers Speak* and *Eldon Spark,* February 6, 1974, Box 44, Local 3 1974 General File, UL3C.
112 Jefferys, *Management and Managed,* 181.
113 Ibid., 185.

Chapter 5: Chrysler Pulled the Trigger

1 A version of this chapter, as well as some material that appears in Chapter 1, was published as "'Chrysler Pulled The Trigger': Competing Understandings of Workplace Violence During the 1970s and Radical Legal Practice," *Labour/Le Travail* 74 (Fall 2014): 51–88. I am grateful to *Labour/Le Travail* for permitting me to reproduce that material in this book.
2 Begoña Aretxaga, "Before the Law: The Narrative of the Unconscious in Basque Political Violence," in *Violence,* ed. Neil Whitehead (Santa Fe, NM: SAR Press, 2004), 135.
3 See, for example, the articles collected in Judy Fudge and Eric Tucker, eds., *Work on Trial: Canadian Labour Law Struggles* (Toronto: Irwin Law for the Osgoode Society for Canadian Legal History, 2010).
4 Wendy Brown and Janet Halley, eds., *Left Legalism/Left Critique* (Durham, NC: Duke University Press, 2002), 18.
5 Rebecca Hill, *Men, Mobs, and Law: Anti-lynching and Labor Defense in U.S. Radical History* (Durham, NC: Duke University Press, 2009), 16.
6 Ibid., 1.
7 Ibid., 15.
8 Ibid., 1.
9 Bill Black, "What Manner of Man Is James Johnson Jr.?" *Michigan Chronicle,* July 25, 1970.
10 "Hail Brother Johnson," *Inner City Voice,* April 1971.
11 Aretxaga, "Before the Law," 142–43.
12 Heather Ann Thompson, *Whose Detroit? Politics, Labor, and Race in a Modern American City* (Ithaca, NY: Cornell University Press, 2004), 228. This book contains a superlative summary of Johnson's case and the contests that surrounded it. My account of both the case and the reaction to it owes a substantial debt to Thompson's research and analysis, especially her presentation of the case itself, her explanation of the major figures, and most of all, her perceptive rendering of the historical context of Detroit factories, courtrooms, and politics during the 1970s. Particularly helpful was her analysis of how radical attorneys were able to leverage these dynamics to win several high-profile criminal cases and to push for their political objectives.

13 Kieran Taylor, "American Petrograd: Detroit and the League of Revolutionary Black Workers," in *Rebel Rank and File: Labor Militancy and Revolt from Below during the Long 1970s,* ed. Aaron Brenner, Robert Brenner, and Cal Winslow (New York: Verso, 2010), 323.
14 Tom Ricke, "Worker on Trial for Three Killings at Plant," *Detroit Free Press,* April 26, 1971.
15 Tom Ricke, "Murder Trial Witnesses Tell of Violence at Auto Plant," *Detroit Free Press,* May 6, 1971.
16 Thompson, *Whose Detroit?* 125.
17 Ibid.
18 Ibid., 124–25.
19 "Ousted Worker Kills Three in Chrysler Plant Shooting," *Detroit Free Press,* July 16, 1970.
20 John Griffith and Louis Heldman, "Worker Kills Three in Plant," *Detroit Free Press,* July 16, 1970.
21 Ibid.
22 Thompson, *Whose Detroit?* 142.
23 Ricke, "Murder Trial Witnesses."
24 "Hail Brother Johnson," *Inner City Voice,* April 1971.
25 Ibid.
26 "The Ballad of James Johnson," *Inner City Voice,* April 1971.
27 "Hail James Johnson," *DRUM* 3, 13.
28 Ibid.; "League of Revolutionary Black Workers," *Inner City Voice,* June 1970, http://www.freedomarchives.org/Documents/Finder/Black%20Liberation%20Disk/Black%20Power!/SugahData/Journals/League.S.pdf.
29 General Gordon Baker, interview with author, July 26, 2012.
30 William Serrin, *The Company and the Union: The "Civilized Relationship" of the General Motors Corporation and the United Automobile Workers* (New York: Vintage Books, 1974), 235.
31 Thompson, *Whose Detroit?* 179.
32 Black, "What Manner of Man?"
33 Ibid.
34 Ibid.
35 "Unionists Dismiss Johnson Story as 'Distorted Facts,'" *Michigan Chronicle,* August 8, 1970.
36 On UAW and company attacks against radical black organizations, see Thompson, *Whose Detroit?* 117; A.C. Jones, "Rank-and-File Opposition in the UAW during the Long 1970s," in *Rebel Rank and File: Labor Militancy and Revolt from Below during the Long 1970s,* ed. Aaron Brenner, Robert Brenner, and Cal Winslow (New York: Verso, 2010), 293–94.
37 "Unionists Dismiss Johnson Story."
38 Tom Ricke, "Trial Opens in 3 Slayings," *Detroit Free Press,* April 26, 1971.
39 Bill Black, "Word Battle Marks Opening of Axle Plant Slaying Trial," *Michigan Chronicle,* May 8, 1971.
40 Tom Ricke, "Worker Tells Why He Killed at Plant," *Detroit Free Press,* May 12, 1971.

41 Ricke, "Murder Trial Witnesses."
42 Ibid.
43 Tom Ricke, "Old Mental Scars Blamed in Killing of 3 at Factory," *Detroit Free Press,* May 19, 1971.
44 Ricke, "Murder Trial Witnesses."
45 Lee Winfrey, "Witness Reveals Violence in Plants," *Detroit Free Press,* May 4, 1971.
46 Tom Ricke, "Killer of 3 Called Evil," *Detroit Free Press,* May 21, 1971.
47 Paul Harris, *Black Rage Confronts the Law* (New York: NYU Press, 1997), 100.
48 Thompson, *Whose Detroit?* 141.
49 Ibid.
50 Ricke, "Worker Tells Why."
51 Thompson, *Whose Detroit?* 144.
52 Harris, *Black Rage,* 108.
53 Thompson, *Whose Detroit?* 143.
54 Bill Black, "Murder Plant Revisited by Chrysler Slayer," *Michigan Chronicle,* May 22, 1971.
55 Thompson, *Whose Detroit?* 143.
56 "Hell in the Factory," *Time,* June 7, 1971, 41–42.
57 Thompson, *Whose Detroit?* 155.
58 Dan Georgakas and Marvin Surkin, *Detroit – I Do Mind Dying: A Study in Urban Revolution* (1975; reprint, Chicago: Haymarket Books, 2012), 10.
59 "Hell in the Factory," *Time,* June 7, 1971, 41–42.
60 Georgakas and Surkin, *Detroit,* 164–65.
61 Harris, *Black Rage,* 93.
62 Thompson, *Whose Detroit?* 176.
63 Ibid., 177.
64 Quoted in ibid.
65 Quoted in ibid., 177–79. These pages in Thompson's book also pointed me toward the reactions of various newspapers to the ruling: "Ruling Favoring Plant Killing Needs Reversal," editorial, *Macomb* [title cut off], March 17, 1973, Box 5, File 23, Detroit Revolutionary Movements Collection, Walter P. Reuther Library of Urban and Labor Affairs, Detroit (hereafter DRMC).
66 "A Ruling against Reason," editorial, *Detroit Free Press,* March 13, 1973, Box 5, File 23, DMRC.
67 "It Harms the State," editorial, *Detroit News,* March 8, 1973, Box 5, File 23, DRMC.
68 Ronald Glotta, "Press Release," Box 5, File 23, DRMC.
69 Thompson, *Whose Detroit?* 180.
70 Ronald Glotta, interview with author, May 14, 2012.
71 Bill Black, "Back to Black," *Michigan Chronicle,* n.d., Box 5, File 23, DRMC.
72 Taylor, "American Petrograd," 311–12.
73 Agis Salpukas, "UAW Tries to Overcome Opposition to Ford Pact," *New York Times,* November 13, 1973.
74 Agis Salpukas, "They Can Wildcat the Union, Too," *New York Times,* November 18, 1973.
75 Ralph Orr, "Rebellion Stuns UAW Leadership," *Detroit Free Press,* November 19, 1973.

76 Ibid.
77 On the United National Caucus, see Thompson, *Whose Detroit?* 108. On earlier inter-UAW struggles over bargaining, see Serrin, *Company and the Union*, 266–88. This chapter discusses tensions within the UAW over the 1970 contract settlement, as well as touching on the worker rebellion at the General Motors Plant in Lordstown, Ohio.
78 Agis Salpukas, "Skilled Trades Reject Pact at Ford – Violence Erupts," *New York Times*, November 14, 1973.
79 Ralph Orr, "Tradesmen Reject Ford Pact" *Detroit Free Press*, November 14, 1973.
80 Quoted in Billy Bowles and Jo Thomas, "Union Aide Arrested in Shooting," *Detroit Free Press*, November 14, 1973.
81 John F. Head, "UAW Aide Hazy on Shooting," *Detroit Free Press*, January 31, 1974.
82 Salpukas, "Skilled Trades Reject Pact." Salpukas was present at the entire confrontation except for the shooting itself.
83 Salpukas, "They Can Wildcat."
84 Orr, "Rebellion Stuns UAW Leadership."
85 "UAW Ought to Heed Lesson of Ford Fiasco," editorial, *Detroit Free Press*, November 15, 1973.
86 Ibid.
87 Salpukas, "They Can Wildcat."
88 Louis Heldman, "UAW Official's Trial Starts," *Detroit Free Press*, January 22, 1974.
89 "Accused UAW Official Faces Trial in Shooting Incident," *Detroit Free Press*, November 24, 1973.
90 John F. Head, "UAW Aide Found Guilty of Assault," *Detroit Free Press*, February 6, 1974.
91 Head, "UAW Aide Hazy."
92 *Michigan v. Mundy*, Wayne County Circuit Court, Criminal Case No. 73–58433, March 20, 1974, Wayne County Clerk's Office, Detroit, Michigan.
93 Georgakas and Surkin, *Detroit*, 168.
94 *Michigan v. Mundy*. For more on STRESS see Thompson, *Whose Detroit?* 90–94, 145–52; and Georgakas and Surkin, *Detroit*, 151–75.
95 "More UAW Violence," *Eldon Spark* 103 (November 29, 1973), Unprocessed Manuscript Box, Walter P. Reuther Library of Labor and Urban Affairs, Detroit.
96 Rudolf A. Helling, *Position of Negroes, Chinese, and Italians in the Social Structure of Windsor, Ontario* (Toronto: Ontario Human Rights Commission, 1965), 8.
97 Ibid., 16.
98 Ibid., 10.
99 Ibid., 79.
100 Ibid., 80–86.
101 Ibid., 79–81.
102 Ibid., 107.
103 Lloyd McLachlan, "Remains of a Dream: The Man Who Shot Charlie Brooks Looks Back at His Tragic Past and His Future Hopes," *Windsor Star*, June 11, 1994.
104 Susan Brown, "Murder Suspect Faces Life in Windsor UAW Shooting," *Detroit Free Press*, January 19, 1977.

105 See also Thomas Claridge, "Wanted Job Back, Man Tells Murder Trial," *Globe and Mail,* n.d., Charles Brooks Biography File, Vertical File Collection, Walter P. Reuther Library of Urban and Labor Affairs, Detroit (hereafter CBB).

106 Roach and Smith both recalled that Talbot believed that his grievance had been dropped. Charles Roach, interview with author, February 29, 2012; Michael Smith, interview with author, March 14, 2012. See Claridge, "Wanted Job Back." However, according to Gary Parent, the grievance had not been dropped. Gary Parent and Rick Laporte, interview with author, October 17, 2012.

107 Claridge, "Wanted Job Back."

108 Ibid.

109 Parent and Laporte, interview.

110 "Here's How Charlie Brooks Is Remembered," *Windsor Star,* n.d., CBB.

111 Don Lajoie, "Brooks' Legacy 'With Us Forever,'" *Windsor Star,* January 17, 2002.

112 Untitled and undated article, CBB.

113 UAW, "Press Release," January 17, 1977, CBB.

114 "Ranks Join in Farewell to Charlie," *Windsor Star,* n.d., CBB.

115 Kathleen Rex, "Black Women Being Deported to Ease Job Market, Group Says," *Globe and Mail,* January 28, 1978.

116 Roach, interview. On the historical relationship between racism and the Canadian legal system, see, for example, Constance Backhouse, *Colour-Coded: A Legal History of Racism in Canada, 1900–1950* (Toronto: University of Toronto Press, 1999); Clayton Mosher, *Discrimination and Denial: Systemic Racism in Ontario's Legal and Criminal Justice Systems, 1892–1961* (Toronto: University of Toronto Press, 1998); and Barrington Walker, *Race on Trial: Black Defendants in Ontario's Criminal Courts, 1858–1958* (Toronto: University of Toronto Press, 2010).

117 Roach, interview.

118 "Records of the Law Society of Upper Canada Discipline Committee," November 28, 1978, in author's possession (hereafter "LSUC").

119 Roach, interview; "LSUC."

120 Canadian Press, "Talbot Trial Is Moved to Toronto," *Globe and Mail,* September 14, 1977.

121 "Man Who Killed Leader of Union Sent to Hospital," *Globe and Mail,* December 17, 1977.

122 Ibid. Psychiatrists testified that the reason Talbot rejected an insanity claim was that he preferred prison to an indefinite stay in a mental facility. "Unionist's Killer Ruled Insane," *Toronto Star,* December 17, 1977.

123 Roach, interview.

124 Claridge, "Wanted Job Back."

125 Royson James, "Law Society Controls with 'Reign of Terror,'" *Contrast,* January 18, 1979, in Personal Papers of Charles Roach, Toronto (hereafter PCR).

126 Roach-Smith Defense Committee, "Organize to Defend Civil Rights Lawyers," PCR.

127 "LSUC."

128 Roach, interview.

129 "LSUC."

130 "Charges of Touting against Two Lawyers Dismissed by Board," *Globe and Mail,* December 21, 1978.
131 Michael Smith to Peter Rosenthal, February 6, 1978, PCR.
132 Lennox Hinds, "Submission of Intervenor," PCR.
133 "Rutgers Professor Fights Disbarment," *Harvard Crimson,* September 20, 1980, http://www.thecrimson.com/article/1980/9/20/rutgers-professor-fights-disbarment-pnew-brunswick.
134 "LSUC."
135 Ibid.
136 Ibid.
137 Ibid.
138 Ibid.
139 "Charges of Touting."
140 Ibid.
141 Ibid.; Peter Rosenthal, interview with author, April 30, 2012.
142 Harris, *Black Rage,* 119.
143 Glotta, interview.

Chapter 6: Out of the Back Streets and into the Workplace

1 John Belbow, Paige St. John, and Said Deep, "'I Just Shot Four People,'" *Detroit Free Press,* September 11, 1994; John Belbow, Paige St. John, and Said Deep, "Suspect, Victims, Called Dedicated Union Advocates," *Detroit Free Press,* September 11, 1994.
2 "Deadly Trail in the Workplace Keeps Growing," *Detroit Free Press,* September 11, 1994; John Lippert, Dennis Niemec, and Amber Arellano, "Union Struggle Led to Slayings," *Detroit Free Press,* September 12, 1994; Mike Hamlin, interview with author, June 13, 2012.
3 The best account and analysis of the workplace massacres of the 1980s and 1990s is Mark Ames, *Going Postal: Rage, Murder, and Rebellion – From Reagan's Workplaces to Clinton's Columbine and Beyond* (New York: Soft Skull, 2005).
4 United States Department of Labor, Bureau of Labor Statistics, "Violence in the Workplace Comes under Closer Scrutiny," August 1994, http://www.bls.gov/iif/oshwc/ossm0006.pdf.
5 David Ballingrud and Carol Gentry, "Stress in Workplace Leading to Employee Violence, Say Experts," *St. Petersburg Times,* January 28, 1993.
6 Reuters News Agency, "Work's Murder: On-the-Job Homicide on the Rise in U.S.," *Globe and Mail,* May 3, 1991.
7 Julia Lawlor, "Homicides at Work on the Rise," *USA Today,* October 18, 1993.
8 Ibid.
9 Frances Barrick, "Ontario Glove Shooting: 20 Years Later," *Waterloo Region Record,* February 2, 2012, http://www.therecord.com/news-story/2598212-ontario-glove-shooting-20-years-later/.
10 The women murdered that day were Geneviève Bergeron, Hélène Colgan, Nathalie Croteau, Barbara Daigneault, Anne-Marie Edward, Maud Haviernick, Maryse Laganière, Maryse Leclair, Anne-Marie Lemay, Sonia Pelletier, Michèle Richard, Annie St-Arneault, Annie Turcotte, and Barbara Klucznik-Widajewicz.

11 Virginia Galt and Lila Sarick, "Breaking the Silence on Assault," *Globe and Mail,* December 7, 1991.
12 Virginia Galt, "Steelworkers Combat Attacks on Women," *Globe and Mail,* May 28, 1992.
13 Mike King, "Labour Federation Starts Campaign to Halt Violence in the Workplace," *Montreal Gazette,* December 6, 1994.
14 Vinay Sharma and Julie White, interview with author, January 11, 2012; Pat Cunningham, interview with author, February 25, 2013.
15 Lawlor, "Homicides at Work"; Jolie Solomon, "Waging War in the Workplace," *Newsweek,* July 19, 1993, http://www.newsweek.com/waging-war-workplace-194734; Sheri South, "Preventing Workplace Violence," *Montreal Gazette,* December 7, 1992.
16 On this proletarianization, see Ames, *Going Postal,* 87–119.
17 Solomon, "Waging War."
18 "Loner in 30s Called Typical Workplace Killer," *New York Times,* December 19, 1993; Solomon, "Waging War"; Ames, *Going Postal,* 119–20.
19 Bill Black, "What Manner of Man Is James Johnson Jr.?" *Michigan Chronicle,* July 25, 1970.
20 "Hail Brother Johnson," *Inner City Voice,* April 1971.
21 "It's Personnel as Well as Personal," *Psychology Today,* January 1994, 20–21.
22 Ames, *Going Postal,* 119–20.
23 Donna Rosato, "New Industry Helps Managers Fight Violence," *USA Today,* August 8, 1995.
24 See Gary Namie and Ruth F. Namie, *The Bully-Free Workplace: Stop Jerks, Weasels, and Snakes from Killing Your Organization* (Hoboken, NJ: Wiley and Sons, 2011); Bob Rosner, "Fired in Real Time: The Perp Walk," *Today's Workplace,* March 22, 2011, http://www.todaysworkplace.org/2011/03/22/fired-in-real-time-the-perp-walk/.
25 Ames, *Going Postal,* 75.
26 Committee on Post Office and Civil Service, *A Post Office Tragedy: The Shooting at Royal Oak* (Washington, DC: Government Printing Office, 1992).
27 Franco Berardi, *Heroes: Mass Murder and Suicide* (London: Verso, 2015), 2.
28 Richard Sennett and Jonathan Cobb, *The Hidden Injuries of Class* (New York: Vintage Books, 1973), 182.
29 Ibid., 98, 171. The quotation from page 98 is cited in Jefferson Cowie, *Stayin' Alive: The 1970s and the Last Days of the Working Class* (New York: New Press, 2010), 217.
30 Sennett and Cobb, *Hidden Injuries of Class,* 173, cited in Cowie, *Stayin' Alive,* 217.
31 Sennett and Cobb, *Hidden Injuries of Class,* 185–86.
32 For the concept of American automakers burning out plants at the end of their useful life, see Richard David Riddle, "The Rise of the Reagan Democrats in Warren, Michigan, 1964–1984" (PhD diss., Wayne State University, 1998), 263.
33 Santanu Sarkar, "Murderous Violence at Work: Conflict and Aggression in Indian Auto Factories," *Work Organisation, Labour and Globalisation* 9, 1 (2015): 38–62.
34 Jessica Wolpaw Reyes, "Environmental Policy as Social Policy? The Impact of Childhood Lead Exposure on Crime," *B.E. Journal of Economic Analysis and Policy* 7, 1 (2007): 1–43.

35 Rick Nevin, "How Lead Exposure Relates to Temporal Changes in IQ, Violent Crime, and Unwed Pregnancy," *Environmental Research* 83, 1 (2000): 18.

36 Kevin Drum, "Lead: America's Real Criminal Element," *Mother Jones,* February 11, 2016, http://www.motherjones.com/environment/2016/02/lead-exposure-gasoline-crime-increase-children-health.

37 Janet L. Lauritsen, Maribeth L. Rezey, and Karen Heimer, "When Choice of Data Matters: Analyses of U.S. Crime Trends, 1973–2012," *Journal of Quantitative Criminology,* December 28, 2015, 1–21.

38 James J. Feigenbaum and Christopher Muller, "Lead Exposure and Violent Crime in the Early Twentieth Century," March 22, 2016, http://scholar.harvard.edu/files/jfeigenbaum/files/feigenbaum_muller_lead_crime.pdf?m=1460569452.

39 Ballingrud and Gentry, "Stress in Workplace."

40 British Columbia Workers' Compensation Appeal Tribunal, Decision No. WCAT-2006-02696, June 29, 2006, 4, http://www.wcat.bc.ca/research/decisions/pdf/2006/06/2006-02696.pdf.

41 Ibid., 2.

42 Sharma and White, interview; Cunningham, interview.

43 "Murder Victim Was Preparing for a New Beginning," *Windsor Star,* November 22, 2005, http://www.canada.com/story.html?id=e9d59b80-713a-4bc0-bc7f-d535472cd04e (item no longer available); Joel Tiller, "Settlement Reached in Case of Slain Windsor Nurse, *Globe and Mail,* January 5, 2010, http://www.theglobeandmail.com/news/national/settlement-reached-in-case-of-slain-windsor-nurse/article4300776.

44 Sara Murray, "Guns in the Parking Lot: A Delicate Workplace Issue," *Wall Street Journal,* October 15, 2013, http://www.wsj.com/news/articles/SB10001424052702303983904579095532026750354. Item no longer available.

45 Dave Holmes, Trudy Rudge, and Amelie Perron, eds., *(Re)Thinking Violence in Health Care Settings* (Farnham, UK: Ashgate, 2012) 7.

46 Ibid., 8–9.

47 Ibid., 7.

48 E.P. Thompson, *The Making of the English Working Class* (New York: Vintage Books, 1963), 9–10.

Bibliography

Archive Collections

Arthur Hughes Collection, Walter P. Reuther Library of Urban and Labor Affairs, Detroit (AHC).

Canadian Auto Workers Fonds, Library and Archives Canada, Ottawa (CAW).

Charles Brooks Biography File, Vertical File Collection, Walter P. Reuther Library of Urban and Labor Affairs, Detroit (CBB).

Detroit Revolutionary Movements Collection, Walter P. Reuther Library of Urban and Labor Affairs, Detroit (DRMC).

Ed Liska Papers, Walter P. Reuther Library of Urban and Labor Affairs, Detroit (ELP).

Personal Papers of Charles Roach, Toronto (PCR).

Unifor Local 444 Private Collection, Unifor Local 444 Offices, Windsor, Ontario (UL444).

United Automobile Workers Chrysler Department Collection, Walter P. Reuther Library of Urban and Labor Affairs, Detroit (CDC).

United Automobile Workers Local 3 Collection, Walter P. Reuther Library of Urban and Labor Affairs, Detroit (UL3C).

United Automobile Workers Local 444 Collection, Walter P. Reuther Library of Urban and Labor Affairs, Detroit.

United Automobile Workers Region 1 Collection, Walter P. Reuther Library of Urban and Labor Affairs, Detroit (UR1C).

United Automobile Workers Region 1B Collection, Walter P. Reuther Library of Urban and Labor Affairs, Detroit (UR1BC).

United Automobile Workers Region 7 Collection, Walter P. Reuther Library of Urban and Labor Affairs, Detroit (UR7C).

Newspapers

Contrast
Criterion
Detroit Free Press
Detroit News
Dodge Workers Speak
DRUM
Eldon Ave. Liberator
Eldon Spark
Eldon Wildcat
Globe and Mail
Guardian
Harvard Crimson
Inner City Voice
Local 444 News
Michigan Chronicle
Montreal Gazette
New York Times
St. Petersburg Times
Toronto Body Politic
Toronto Star
USA Today
Wall Street Journal
Windsor Star

Publications

Abraham, Nabeel. "Detroit's Yemeni Workers." *MERIP Reports* 57 (1977): 3–9, 13.

Adamic, Louis. *Dynamite: The Story of Class Violence in America.* 1931. Reprint, New York: Chelsea House, 1958.

Ahmad, A. Muhammad. *A Study of the League of Revolutionary Black Workers.* Baltimore, MD: Collective Action Notes, 1979.

Ames, Mark. *Going Postal: Rage, Murder, and Rebellion – From Reagan's Workplaces to Clinton's Columbine and Beyond.* New York: Soft Skull, 2005.

Anastakis, Dimitry. *Death in the Peaceable Kingdom: Canadian History since 1867 through Murder, Execution, Assassination, and Suicide.* Toronto: University of Toronto Press, 2015.

Andrews, Thomas G. *Killing for Coal: America's Deadliest Labor War.* Cambridge, UK: Harvard University Press, 2008.

Aretxaga, Begoña. "Before the Law: The Narrative of the Unconscious in Basque Political Violence." In *Violence,* ed. Neil Whitehead, 125–56. Santa Fe, NM: SAR Press, 2004.

Asher, Robert, and Ronald Edsforth, eds. *Autowork.* Albany: State University of New York Press, 1995.

Austin, Curtis J. *Up against the Wall: Violence in the Making and Unmaking of the Black Panther Party.* Fayetteville: University of Arkansas Press, 2008.

Backhouse, Constance. *Colour-Coded: A Legal History of Racism in Canada, 1900–1950*. Toronto: University of Toronto Press, 1999.

Bardacke, Frank. *Trampling out the Vintage: Cesar Chavez and the Two Souls of the United Farm Workers*. New York: Verso, 2014.

Belleseilles, Michael, and Christopher Waldrep, eds. *Documenting American Violence: A Sourcebook*. New York: Oxford University Press, 2006.

Berardi, Franco. *Heroes: Mass Murder and Suicide*. London: Verso, 2015.

"Black Rage on the Auto Lines." *Time,* April 11, 1969, 109.

Boyle, Kevin. "The Kiss: Racial and Gender Conflict in a 1950s Automobile Factory." *Journal of American History* 84, 2 (1997): 496–523. http://dx.doi.org/10.2307/2952568.

–. *The UAW and the Heyday of American Liberalism, 1945–68*. Ithaca, NY: Cornell University Press, 1995.

Brenner, Aaron, Robert Brenner, and Cal Winslow, eds. *Rebel Rank and File: Labor Militancy and Revolt from Below during the Long 1970s*. New York: Verso, 2010.

Brody, David. "Workplace Contractualism in Historical Perspective." In *Industrial Democracy in America: The Ambiguous Promise,* ed. Nelson Lichtenstein and John Howell Harris, 176–205. New York: Woodrow Wilson Center for International Scholars, 1993.

Brown, Ronald D. *Dying on the Job: Murder and Mayhem in the American Workplace*. Lanham, MD: Rowman and Littlefield, 2012.

Brown, Wendy, and Janet Halley, eds. *Left Legalism/Left Critique*. Durham, NC: Duke University Press, 2002. http://dx.doi.org/10.1215/9780822383871.

Bukowczyk, John J. *Permeable Border: The Great Lakes Basin as Transnational Region, 1650–1990*. Pittsburgh: University of Pittsburgh Press, 2005.

Committee on Post Office and Civil Service. *A Post Office Tragedy: The Shooting at Royal Oak*. Washington, DC: Government Printing Office, 1992.

Cowie, Jefferson. *Stayin' Alive: The 1970s and the Last Days of the Working Class*. New York: New Press, 2010.

Davidson, Bill. "If We Can't Solve the Problems of the Ghetto *Here,* God Help Our Country." *Saturday Evening Post,* October 5, 1968.

Denby, Charles. *Indignant Heart: A Black Worker's Journal*. Detroit: Wayne State University Press, 1989.

Drum, Kevin. "Lead: America's Real Criminal Element." *Mother Jones,* February 11, 2016. http://www.motherjones.com/environment/2016/02/lead-exposure-gasoline-crime-increase-children-health.

Edwards, Peter. *Waterfront Warlord: The Life and Violent Times of Hal C. Banks*. Toronto: Key Porter Books, 1987.

Fabian, Katalin. "Introduction: The Politics of Domestic Violence in Postcommunist Europe and Eurasia." In *Domestic Violence in Postcommunist States: Local Activism, National Policies, and Global Forces,* ed. Katalin Fabian, 1–33. Bloomington: Indiana University Press, 2010.

Faue, Elizabeth. *Community of Suffering and Struggle: Women, Men, and the Labor Movement in Minneapolis, 1915–1945*. Chapel Hill: University of North Carolina Press, 1991.

Feigenbaum, James J., and Christopher Muller. "Lead Exposure and Violent Crime in the Early Twentieth Century." March 22, 2016. http://scholar.harvard.edu/files/jfeigenbaum/files/feigenbaum_muller_lead_crime.pdf?m=1460569452.

Fine, Sidney. *Violence in the Model City: The Cavanagh Administration, Race Relations, and the Detroit Riot of 1967.* Ann Arbor: University of Michigan Press, 1989.

Frank, Miriam. *Out in the Union: A Labor History of Queer America.* Philadelphia: Temple University Press, 2014.

Fudge, Judy, and Eric Tucker. *Labour before the Law: The Regulation of Workers' Collective Action in Canada, 1900–1948.* Toronto: University of Toronto Press, 2004.

–, eds. *Work on Trial: Canadian Labour Law Struggles.* Toronto: Irwin Law for the Osgoode Society for Canadian Legal History, 2010.

Gage, Beverly. *The Day Wall Street Exploded: A Story of America in Its First Age of Terror.* New York: Oxford University Press, 2009.

Gavrilovich, Peter, and Bill McGraw, eds. *The Detroit Almanac: 300 Years of Life in the Motor City.* Detroit: Detroit Free Press, 2000.

Georgakas, Dan, and Marvin Surkin. *Detroit – I Do Mind Dying: A Study in Urban Revolution.* 1975. Reprint, Chicago: Haymarket Books, 2012.

Geschwender, James A. *Class, Race, and Worker Insurgency: The League of Revolutionary Black Workers.* Cambridge, UK: Cambridge University Press, 1977.

Goings, Aaron. "Red Harbor: Class, Violence, and Community in Grays Harbor, Washington." PhD diss., Simon Fraser University, 2011.

Goldberg, David. "Community Control of Construction, Independent Unionism, and the 'Short Black Power Movement' in Detroit." In *Black Power at Work: Community Control, Affirmative Action, and the Construction Industry,* ed. David Goldberg and Trevor Griffey, 90–111. Ithaca, NY: Cornell University Press, 2010.

Goldberg, David, and Trevor Griffey, eds. *Black Power at Work: Community Control, Affirmative Action, and the Construction Industry.* Ithaca, NY: Cornell University Press, 2010.

Graeber, David. *The Utopia of Rules: On Technology, Stupidity, and the Secret Joys of Bureaucracy.* Brooklyn, NY: Melville House, 2015.

Griffey, Trevor. "History Declassified: Using U.S. Government Intelligence Documents to Write Left History." *Left History* 16, 1 (2012): 115–28.

Hackworth, Jason. "Why Is There No Detroit in Canada?" *Urban Geography* 37, 2 (2016): 272–95. http://dx.doi.org/10.1080/02723638.2015.1101249.

Harris, Paul. *Black Rage Confronts the Law.* New York: NYU Press, 1997.

Hele, Karl S., ed. *Lines Drawn upon the Water: First Nations and the Great Lakes Borders and Borderlands.* Waterloo, ON: Wilfrid Laurier University Press, 2008.

"Hell in the Factory." *Time,* June 7, 1971, 41–42.

Helling, Rudolf A. *The Position of Negroes, Chinese, and Italians in the Social Structure of Windsor, Ontario.* Toronto: Ontario Human Rights Commission, 1965.

Heuton, Robert. "Urban Sprawl: A Comparative Study of the Detroit-Windsor Region." PhD diss., Wayne State University, 2005.

High, Steven. *Industrial Sunset: The Making of North America's Rust Belt, 1969–84.* Toronto: University of Toronto Press, 2003.

Hill, Rebecca. *Men, Mobs, and Law: Anti-lynching and Labor Defense in U.S. Radical History*. Durham, NC: Duke University Press, 2009. http://dx.doi.org/10.1215/9780822381464.

Hinton, Elizabeth Kai. "The Black Bolsheviks: Detroit Revolutionary Union Movements and Shop-Floor Organizing." In *The New Black History: Revisiting the Second Reconstruction,* ed. Elizabeth Kai Hinton and Manning Marable, 211–28. New York: Palgrave McMillan, 2011. http://dx.doi.org/10.1057/9780230338043_13.

Hofstadter, Richard. "Reflections on Violence in the United States." 1970. Reprinted in *The Baffler,* 28 (2015): n.p. http://www.thebaffler.com/ancestors/reflections-violence-united-states.

Holmes, Dave, Trudy Rudge, and Amelie Perron, eds. *(Re)Thinking Violence in Health Care Settings*. Farnham, UK: Ashgate, 2012.

Honey, Michael. *Black Workers Remember: An Oral History of Segregation, Unionism, and the Freedom Struggle*. Berkeley: University of California Press, 2002.

–. *Going down Jericho Road: The Memphis Strike, Martin Luther King's Last Campaign*. New York: W.W. Norton and Company, 2011.

"It's Personnel as Well as Personal." *Psychology Today,* January 1994, 20–21.

Jefferys, Steve. *Management and Managed: Fifty Years of Crisis at Chrysler*. Cambridge, UK: CUP Archive, 1986.

Johnson, Ashley. "Illegal Detroiters: Undocumented Europeans and Unions in America's Motor City, 1924–42." Paper presented at the North American Labor History Conference, Wayne State University, Detroit, October 2012.

Jones, A.C. "Rank-and-File Opposition in the UAW during the Long 1970s." In *Rebel Rank and File: Labor Militancy and Revolt from Below during the Long 1970s,* ed. Aaron Brenner, Robert Brenner, and Cal Winslow, 281–310. New York: Verso, 2010.

Karibo, Holly. "Detroit's Border Brothel: Sex Tourism in Windsor, Ontario, 1945–1960." *American Review of Canadian Studies* 40, 3 (2010): 362–78. http://dx.doi.org/10.1080/02722011.2010.496905.

Kramer, Reinhold, and Tom Mitchell. *When the State Trembled: How A.J. Andrews and the Citizens' Committee Broke the Winnipeg General Strike*. Toronto: University of Toronto Press, 2010.

La Botz, Dan. "The Tumultuous Teamsters of the 1970s." In *Rebel Rank and File: Labor Militancy and Revolt from Below during the Long 1970s,* ed. Aaron Brenner, Robert Brenner, and Cal Winslow, 199–228. New York: Verso, 2010.

Lauritsen, Janet L., Maribeth L. Rezey, and Karen Heimer. "When Choice of Data Matters: Analyses of U.S. Crime Trends, 1973–2012." *Journal of Quantitative Criminology,* December 28, 2015, 1–21.

Lewchuk, Wayne. "Men and Monotony: Fraternalism as a Managerial Strategy at the Ford Motor Company." *Journal of Economic History* 53, 4 (1993): 824–56. http://dx.doi.org/10.1017/S0022050700051330.

Lewis-Colman, David M. *Race against Liberalism: Black Workers and the UAW in Detroit*. Champaign: University of Illinois Press, 2008.

Lichtenstein, Nelson. *Walter Reuther: The Most Dangerous Man in Detroit*. Champaign: University of Illinois Press, 1995.

Lichtenstein, Nelson, and Steve Meyer, eds. *On the Line: Essays in the History of Auto Work*. Champaign: University of Illinois Press, 1988.

Lipold, Paul F., and Larry Isaac. "'Striking Deaths' at Their Roots: Assaying the Social Determinants of Extreme Labor-Management Violence in US Labor History, 1877–1947." *Social Science History* 38, 3–4 (2014): 541–75. http://dx.doi.org/10.1017/ssh.2015.24.

Lucier, Brandi. "'The Black Man Doesn't Present a Problem until He Presents Himself': The Windsor Council on Group Relations, UAW Canadian Region 7, and the Hiring Policies of Chrysler Canada, 1944–54." Unpublished paper in author's possession. 2015.

Marx, Karl. *Capital: Critique of Political Economy*. Vol. 1. Trans. Ben Fowkes. 1976. Reprint, New York: Penguin Classics, 1990.

–. *The Eighteenth Brumaire of Louis Napoleon*. New York: International Publishers, 1963.

McInnis, Peter S. "'Hothead Troubles': Sixties-Era Wildcat Strikes in Canada." In *Debating Dissent: Canada and the Sixties*, ed. Lara Campbell, Dominique Clément, and Gregory S. Kealey, 155–72. Toronto: University of Toronto Press, 2012.

Meyer, Steve. "Rough Manhood: The Aggressive and Confrontational Shop Culture of U.S. Auto Workers during World War II." *Journal of Social History* 36, 1 (2002): 125–47. http://dx.doi.org/10.1353/jsh.2002.0098.

–. "Work, Play, and Power: Masculine Culture on the Automotive Shop Floor, 1930–60." *Men and Masculinities* 2, 2 (1999): 115–34. http://dx.doi.org/10.1177/1097184X99002002001.

–. "Workplace Predators: Sexuality and Harassment on the U.S. Automotive Shop Floor, 1930–1960." *Labor: Studies in Working-Class History of the Americas* 1, 1 (2004): 77–93. http://dx.doi.org/10.1215/15476715-1-1-77.

Milligan, Ian. *Rebel Youth: 1960s Labour Unrest, Young Workers, and New Leftists in English Canada*. Vancouver: UBC Press, 2014.

Monk, Jim. "Working on an Assembly Line." In *Working in Canada*, ed. Walter Johnson, 49–57. Montreal: Black Rose Books, 1983.

Morton, Desmond. *Working People: An Illustrated History of the Canadian Labour Movement*. Montreal and Kingston: McGill-Queen's University Press, 1999.

Mosher, Clayton. *Discrimination and Denial: Systemic Racism in Ontario's Legal and Criminal Justice Systems, 1892–1961*. Toronto: University of Toronto Press, 1998.

Namie, Gary, and Ruth F. Namie. *The Bully-Free Workplace: Stop Jerks, Weasels, and Snakes from Killing Your Organization*. Hoboken, NJ: Wiley and Sons, 2011.

Neumann, Tracy. *Remaking the Rust Belt: Space, Citizenship, and the Postindustrial Transformation in North America*. Philadelphia: University of Pennsylvania Press, 2015.

Nevin, Rick. "How Lead Exposure Relates to Temporal Changes in IQ, Violent Crime, and Unwed Pregnancy." *Environmental Research* 83, 1 (2000): 1–22.

Norwood, Stephen. *Strikebreaking and Intimidation: Mercenaries and Masculinity in Twentieth-Century America*. Chapel Hill: University of North Carolina Press, 2002.

Palmer, Bryan. *Canada's 1960s: The Ironies of Identity in a Rebellious Era*. Toronto: University of Toronto Press, 2009.

–. *Working-Class Experience: The Rise and Reconstitution of Canadian Labour, 1800–1980*. Toronto: Butterworth, 1983.

Pawel, Miriam. *The Crusades of Cesar Chavez: A Biography*. New York: Bloomsbury, 2014.

Pizzolato, Nicola. *Challenging Global Capitalism: Labor Migration, Radical Struggle, and Urban Change in Detroit and Turin*. London: Palgrave McMillan, 2013. http://dx.doi.org/10.1057/9781137311702.

Portelli, Alessandro. *They Say in Harlan County: An Oral History*. Oxford: Oxford University Press, 2010.

Reyes, Jessica Wolpaw. "Environmental Policy as Social Policy? The Impact of Childhood Lead Exposure on Crime." *B.E. Journal of Economic Analysis and Policy* 7, 1 (2007): 1–43.

Riddle, Richard David. "The Rise of the Reagan Democrats in Warren, Michigan, 1964–1984." PhD diss., Wayne State University, 1998. http://digitalcommons.wayne.edu/cgi/viewcontent.cgi?article=2188&context=oa_dissertations.

Roberts, Chris. "Harnessing Competition? The UAW and Competitiveness in the Canadian Auto Industry, 1945–90." PhD diss., York University, 2002.

Roediger, David. *The Wages of Whiteness: Race and the Making of the American Working Class*. New York: Verso, 2007.

Rogers, Donald Wayne. *Making Capitalism Safe: Work Safety and Health Regulation in America, 1880–1940*. Champaign: University of Illinois Press, 2009.

Rosner, Bob. "Fired in Real Time: The Perp Walk." *Today's Workplace*, March 22, 2011. http://www.todaysworkplace.org/2011/03/22/fired-in-real-time-the-perp-walk/.

Russell, Jason. *Our Union: UAW/CAW Local 27 from 1950 to 1990*. Edmonton: Athabasca University Press, 2011.

Rutherford, Tod D., and John Holmes. "Manufacturing Resiliency: Economic Restructuring and Automotive Manufacturing in the Great Lakes Region." *Cambridge Journal of Regions, Economy and Society* 7, 3 (2014): 359–78. http://dx.doi.org/10.1093/cjres/rsu014.

Sangster, Joan. "Just Horseplay? Masculinity and Workplace Grievances in Fordist Canada, 1947–1970s." Paper presented at the Annual Meeting of the Labor and Working Class History of the Americas, New York City, June 7, 2013.

–. *Transforming Labour: Women and Work in Postwar Canada*. Toronto: University of Toronto Press, 2010.

–. "'We No Longer Respect the Law': The Tilco Strike, Labour Injunctions, and the State." *Labour/Le Travail* 53 (2004): 47–87. http://dx.doi.org/10.2307/25149446.

Sarkar, Santanu. "Murderous Violence at Work: Conflict and Aggression in Indian Auto Factories." *Work Organisation, Labour and Globalisation* 9, 1 (2015): 38–62. http://dx.doi.org/10.13169/workorgalaboglob.9.1.0038.

Schlosser, Eric. *Fast Food Nation: The Dark Side of the All-American Meal*. New York: Perennial, 2002.

Scott, Rachel. *Muscle and Blood*. New York: E.P. Dutton, 1974.

Seaman, Barrett. "In Michigan: Goodbye, Dodge Main." *Time*, February 11, 1980, 10.

Seigel, Micol. "Beyond Compare: Comparative Method after the Transnational Turn." *Radical History Review* 2005, 91 (2005): 62–90. http://dx.doi.org/10.1215/01636545-2005-91-62.

Sennett, Richard, and Jonathan Cobb. *The Hidden Injuries of Class*. New York: Vintage Books, 1973.

Serrin, William. *The Company and the Union: The "Civilized Relationship" of the General Motors Corporation and the United Automobile Workers*. New York: Vintage Books, 1974.

Sinclair, Upton. *The Jungle*. 1905. Reprint, New York: Signet Classics, 1963.

Smith, Robert Michael. *From Blackjacks to Briefcases: A History of Commercialized Strikebreaking and Unionbusting in the United States*. Athens: Ohio University Press, 2003.

Solomon, Jolie. "Waging War in the Workplace." *Newsweek*, July 19, 1993. http://www.newsweek.com/waging-war-workplace-194734.

Statistics Canada. *Publication Crime Statistics 85-205*. Ottawa: Statistics Canada, 1962–76.

Stonebanks, Roger. *Fighting for Dignity: The Ginger Goodwin Story*. Edmonton: Athabasca University Press, 2004.

Sugiman, Pamela. *Labour's Dilemma: The Gender Politics of Auto Workers in Canada, 1937–79*. Toronto: University of Toronto Press, 1994.

–. "Privilege and Oppression: The Configuration of Race, Gender, and Class in Southern Ontario Auto Plants, 1939 to 1949." *Labour/Le Travail* 47 (2001): 83–113. http://dx.doi.org/10.2307/25149114.

Sugrue, Thomas. *The Origins of the Urban Crisis: Race and Inequality in Postwar Detroit*. Princeton, NJ: Princeton University Press, 2005.

Taylor, Kieran. "American Petrograd: Detroit and the League of Revolutionary Black Workers." In *Rebel Rank and File: Labor Militancy and Revolt from Below during the Long 1970s*, ed. Aaron Brenner, Robert Brenner, and Cal Winslow, 311–34. New York: Verso, 2010.

Thompson, E.P. *The Making of the English Working Class*. New York: Vintage Books, 1963.

–. "The Moral Economy of the English Crowd in the Eighteenth Century." *Past and Present* 50, 1 (1971): 76–136. http://dx.doi.org/10.1093/past/50.1.76.

Thompson, Heather Ann. *Whose Detroit? Politics, Labor, and Race in a Modern American City*. Ithaca, NY: Cornell University Press, 2004.

–. "Unmaking the Motor City in the Age of Mass Incarceration." *Journal of Law and Society* 15 (2013): 41–61.

–. "Why Mass Incarceration Matters: Rethinking Crisis, Decline, and Transformation in Postwar American History." *Journal of American History* 97, 3 (2010): 703–34. http://dx.doi.org/10.1093/jahist/97.3.703.

Tyson, Timothy B. *Radio Free Dixie: Robert F. Williams and the Roots of Black Power*. Chapel Hill: University of North Carolina Press, 1999.

United States Department of Labor, Bureau of Labor Statistics. "Violence in the Workplace Comes under Closer Scrutiny." August 1994. http://www.bls.gov/iif/oshwc/ossm0006.pdf.

"Violence in the Factories." *Newsweek,* June 29, 1970, 66–67.

Walker, Barrington. *Race on Trial: Black Defendants in Ontario's Criminal Courts, 1858–1958.* Toronto: University of Toronto Press, 2010.

Whitehead, Neil. "Introduction." In *Violence,* ed. Neil Whitehead, 3–24. Santa Fe, NM: SAR Press, 2004.

–, ed. *Violence.* Santa Fe, NM: SAR Press, 2004.

Williams, Charles. "Reconsidering CIO Political Culture: Briggs Local 212 and the Sources of Militancy in the Early UAW." *Labor* 7, 4 (2010): 17–43. http://dx.doi.org/10.1215/15476715-2010-027.

Wood, Amy Louise. *Lynching and Spectacle: Witnessing Racial Violence in America, 1890–1940.* Chapel Hill: University of North Carolina Press, 2009. http://dx.doi.org/10.5149/9780807878118_wood.

Wright, Richard. *Black Boy (American Hunger): A Record of Childhood and Youth, 1945.* New York: Perennial Classics, 1998.

Yates, Charlotte. *From Plant to Politics: The Autoworkers Union in Postwar Canada.* Philadelphia: Temple University Press, 1993.

Žižek, Slavoj. *Violence.* New York: Picador, 2008.

Films

Bird, Stewart, Rene Lichtman, Peter Gessner, and John Louis Jr., dirs. *Finally Got the News.* Documentary. Produced in association with the League of Revolutionary Black Workers. Detroit: Black Star Productions, 1970. https://www.youtube.com/watch?v=RgJd_MvJVzg.

Gilson, Gary, dir. *Do You Think a Job Is the Answer?* Documentary. 1969.

Index

Note: DRUM stands for Dodge Revolutionary Union Movement; UAW stands for United Auto Workers; "(i)" after a page number indicates an illustration; "(t)" after a page number indicates a table.